P9-ART-245

The Films of Sergio Leone

The Films of Sergio Leone

Robert C. Cumbow

The Scarecrow Press, Inc.
Lanham, Maryland • Toronto • Plymouth, UK
2008

SCARECROW PRESS, INC.

Published in the United States of America
by Scarecrow Press, Inc.
A wholly owned subsidiary of
The Rowman & Littlefield Publishing Group, Inc.
4501 Forbes Boulevard, Suite 200, Lanham, Maryland 20706
www.scarecrowpress.com

Estover Road
Plymouth PL6 7PY
United Kingdom

British Library Cataloguing in Publication Information Available

Library of Congress Cataloging-in-Publication Data
Cumbow, Robert C., 1946–
  The films of Sergio Leone / Robert C. Cumbow.
    p. cm.
  Filmography: p.
  Discography: p.
  Includes bibliographical references and index.
  ISBN-13: 978-0-8108-6041-4 (pbk. : alk. paper)
  ISBN-10: 0-8108-6041-4 (pbk. : alk. paper)
  1. Leone, Sergio, 1929–1989—Criticism and interpretation. I. Title.
  PN1998.3.L463C86 2008
  791.43'75092–dc22   2007030467

Contents

Acknowledgments

So many people have, over the years, made a difference to my experience and vision of the films of Sergio Leone that it is impossible to thank them all properly, and daunting even to try to list them all. But I must make the effort. They earned it.

The story starts one day in 1978, when, after watching *The Good, the Bad and the Ugly* for the umpteenth time, at The Cinema in Olympia, Washington, I remarked to proprietor Nancy Duncan that someone ought to write a book on Sergio Leone. "Why don't you?" she replied.

A couple of articles constituted dry runs at the subject. Then, in the early '80s, I took a shot at a book, to be called *Sergio Leone's West*. The plan had to change when Leone began work on his longtime dream project, *Once Upon a Time in America*. So I revised an already completed manuscript, and in 1987 *Once Upon a Time: The Films of Sergio Leone* saw the light of day as the first full-length book on Leone's work. There had been articles here and there, one monograph in French and one in Italian, and chapter-length discussions in Christopher Frayling's *Spaghetti Westerns* and Laurence Staig and Tony Williams's *Italian Western: The Opera of Violence*. But mine was the first effort at a book-length consideration of Leone's films, what makes them work, and what makes them fascinate us.

It was not without its warts. That first edition was written at a time when information on Leone, his work, and Italian Westerns in general was in short supply and unreliable. Even prints of the films contained misspelled names, characters assigned to the wrong actors, insufficient credit crawls or none at all. For names of characters and lines of dialogue, one had to rely on what one heard—or thought one heard—on an often badly dubbed soundtrack, and scribbled down, barely legibly, in a dark movie house.

As Sergio Leone went from a stylistic oddity of film history, appreciated by a fistful of followers, to a household word and an acclaimed influential cinematic original, I became increasingly painfully aware of—and embarrassed by—the errors and inadequacies of the 1987 edition. But nearly two decades would pass before I got the opportunity to revise the book. During that interim, as the age of the Internet brought fans together and made information more readily available, detailed information on the films and the talent behind them became abundant, and I am pleased and honored at last to present this revised, enhanced, and corrected edition—*The Films of Sergio Leone*.

I repeat here the names of those I thanked in 1987 for their help in making this book happen in the first place: Nancy Duncan, R. C. Dale, Anna White, Bill McCallum, Stephanie Ogle, Douglas Holm, Ernest Callenbach, Stuart Kaminsky, Leonard Maltin, Danny Peary, Richard T. Jameson, Kathleen Murphy, and Steven Buss—all of whom provided help, encouragement, and inspiration. I also acknowledged the generous assistance in locating photographs provided by

Mary Corliss, Museum of Modern Art Film Stills Archive; Val Almendarez, Academy of Motion Picture Arts and Sciences National Film Information Service; Bruce York, Memory Shop West; Forrest Greene, Larry Edmunds Bookshop; Jerry Ohlinger's Movie Materials Store; Jeff Hauser of SRO and Ad Agency West; John Teegarden of Seven Gables Theatres; Gary Tucker of Seattle International Film Festival and the world-famous Egyptian Theatre; Jim Emerson; Kathie Arnold; and John Hartl of the *Seattle Times*. Almost none of them still work for those organizations, and some of the organizations don't even exist anymore.

In addition, I renew my thanks to the University of California Press for permission to quote from Donald Richie's *Films of Akira Kurosawa*; Routledge & Kegan Paul for permission to cite Christopher Frayling's *Spaghetti Westerns*; Alfred A. Knopf for the passages from Bruno Bettelheim's *The Uses of Enchantment*; Farrar, Straus & Giroux, Inc. for the citation from William Golding's essay "Custodians of the Real," anthologized in *A Moving Target*; and *Variety* for permission to reprint in full two items from the 1975 volume.

And today, in 2007, I have a whole new generation of friends and supporters to thank—many of whom I would never have met had it not been for the first edition of this book. Those cherished companions, whose help, encouragement, advice, and just good conversation have enhanced my life and my writing, include Tony Williams, Cenk Kiral, Dominique Guigneau, Austin Vince, Jean-Jacques Malo, Tom Betts, Tom Weisser, Simon Rogers, Bill Boehlke, Don Trunick, David Chapman, Christopher Butler, Sally Craley, Albert Sbragia, Iole Alessandrini, Mark Rahner, Robert Horton, Jeff Shannon, Tom Keogh, Bruce Reid, Clarke Fletcher, Kathy Fennessy, E. Steven Fried, Keith Simanton, Matthew Rovner, Ann Hockens, David Lowery, Peet Gelderblom and James Moran of 24 Lies a Second, Col at MovieGrooves.com, the late Peter Tevis and his wife Noi, John Bender, Sean Axmaker, and others I may soon be ashamed to have forgotten. I am especially indebted to Stephen Ryan and Sally Craley of Scarecrow Press for getting the project jump-started, and to Sandy Jenne for making it so much easier.

Part 1
INTRODUCTION

1

"The Key to Your Clock"

David "Noodles" Aaronson, age about sixty, with thirty-five years of anonymity behind him, and nine years of notoriety behind those, stumps into the bar-deli run by the brother of his childhood sweetheart. His greeting is simple: "I brought back the key to your clock." Fat Moe takes the key and restarts the long-silent pendulum. His doing that is not just an inroad to Noodles's memories and to the film—it's an announcement: Sergio Leone is making movies again.

Twenty years earlier, Leone's first film had been an overnight success, making household words of its title and the name of its star. But Leone himself remained an unknown quantity: He had masked himself behind the name "Bob Robertson"—not, as many might assume, to conceal the Italian origin of *A Fistful of Dollars* from its American audience, but to conceal it from Italian viewers, who liked their Westerns imported, not homegrown.

All that's changed now. For one thing, we couldn't have known at the opening of *Once Upon a Time in America* that the film that celebrated Leone's return to the screen after too long an absence would also be his last. For another, even then Leone was not yet a recognized master. His fame, success, and critical and popular acceptance have been largely a posthumous phenomenon. Long after the first edition of this book appeared, mention of Leone's name was often answered by "Who?" and sometimes by a vague reference to Clint Eastwood or "Spaghetti Westerns," but rarely with much of a fix on what was unique and important about the man's films.

Leone did not invent the Italian Western, of course. He was not the first, the only, nor the most prolific creator of the genre. But the success of his films was the key factor in establishing credibility for European directors in this most American of genres. After the name "Sergio Leone" was unveiled in the opening credits to *For a Few Dollars More*, it became a drawing card in Europe. And once the late-coming American critical establishment discovered Leone, through the more overtly artful *Once Upon a Time in America* and *Duck, You Sucker!*, even an "idea" or "presented by" credit for Leone was enough to make a film worthy of attention.

The name "Bob Robertson" was a tribute to Leone's deepest roots in cinema: "Roberto Roberti" was the pseudonym under which his father, Vincenzo Leone, became an early and important force in Italian film, directing more than a hundred films from 1905 on. Sergio Leone was born January 3, 1929, in Rome. With an actress mother and a director father, his career in film was virtually predetermined. He entered the Italian film industry in 1947 and played a bit part in De Sica's *Bicycle Thief.*

But his destiny lay on the other side of the camera. Leone served his apprenticeship assisting Italian directors, as well as advising Americans who came to Italy in the '50s to work at Cinecittà on then-popular, ancient-world epics. These included William Wyler, Raoul Walsh, Robert Wise, Fred Zinneman, and Robert Aldrich, on whose *Sodom and Gomorrah* (1963) Leone was an assistant director.

From under the shadow of the big-budget, American, biblical spectaculars crawled the modest domestic peplum—the "sword and sandal" epics with which a new generation of Italian filmmakers began to make their names. Based on the world of classical mythology and ancient Italian history, these films came to the fore following Joseph E. Levine's successful international promotion of Pietro Francisci's *Hercules* (1957), starring Steve Reeves. The trend led in two directions: to the so-called "peplum" films, in which muscular superheroes competed with one another in increasingly bizarre combinations (*Ulysses Against Hercules, Maciste Against the Vampires, Samson and the Treasure of the Incas, Maciste Against the Men in the Moon*), and to the more conventional revisions of classical antiquity imitative of the internationally successful American spectacles. In this latter subgenre, Leone began to emerge as an individual talent, contributing to the screenplay of *Sign of the Gladiator* (1958), stepping in to finish *The Last Days of Pompeii* (1959) when illness struck credited director Mario Bonnard, and directing, himself, *The Colossus of Rhodes* (1961).

He came into his own, of course, with the three Clint Eastwood Westerns he directed from 1964 to 1967. By then he had begun to feel he'd exhausted the possibilities of the Western, and he was already laying plans for an expansive American gangster film, to be called *Once Upon a Time in America*. But when Paramount brought him to the United States it was for another Western. *Once Upon a Time in the West* failed at the box office, yet refused to die, capturing critical attention over the years as a definitive statement on—and in—the Western genre.

Leone turned his attention again to preparing *Once Upon a Time in America*. He began producing for his own company, Rafran Cinematografica, to raise money and support for the project. But he ended up directing another Western—well, semi-Western—*Duck, You Sucker!* (1972) when a planned collaboration with Peter Bogdanovich fell through. Leone then served in a supervisory capacity on *My Name Is Nobody* (1973), reportedly directing a number of scenes of the Leone-based script himself, while looking over the shoulder of signatory director Tonino Valerii. He was a producing creative supervisor on *A Genius* (1975), a sequel to *My Name Is Nobody*, directed by Damiano Damiani.

By the late '70s the "Spaghetti Western" vogue had faded. Leone's name appeared less frequently in the trade journals. And though several laudatory critical articles appeared, as appreciation of his Westerns grew, it began to look as if—as a working creative talent—Sergio Leone had become a memory.

But beginning in 1978, reports began to surface now and again that Leone was about to start shooting *Once Upon a Time in America*. The reports were true, but filming was postponed again and again. For a time, Leone tried to lure James Cagney out of retirement to appear in the film, but without success. At last, in 1982, principal photography began. The appearance, in 1984, of three different cuts of *Once Upon a Time in America* heralded a renewal of interest in Leone's work, even as it presaged a dark and disappointing debut for the film. A full European cut, a shorter cut for U.S. festival play, and the Ladd Company's drastically shortened and rearranged version left audiences and critics puzzled and concerned about whether the real *Once Upon a Time in America* existed at all. But a limited theatrical tour of the 225-minute U.S. festival version enthralled audiences, and went on to become a popular and successful video cassette. Indeed, the enthusiasm prompted Paramount at last to release, after seventeen years, a fully restored American version of *Once Upon a Time in the West*.

Leone was back, at last getting the recognition he deserved. In 1987, he went to work on a long-planned film about the Russians' desperate defense of Leningrad against Hitler's *Winterschlacht im Osten*. He had two or three other projects in development as well. And then, suddenly, it was over. On April 30, 1989, the news hit that Sergio Leone was dead of a heart attack at age sixty. What we had was all we were going to get; there would be no more Sergio Leone films.

The foregoing is the briefest synopsis of Leone's too-short career, and I'll attempt no more, since Leone has already been more thoroughly biographed by Sir Christopher Frayling than anyone else could hope to equal. Readers interested in the details of Sergio Leone's life and career will wish to seek out Sir Christopher's book.

This book, by contrast, includes little biography, no behind-the-camera "making of" research, no cinematic archaeology, no theory of film in general or Leone in particular. I assay nothing more than an appreciative critical response to the sights and sounds of the handful of films upon which Leone's reputation rests. The discussions, catalogues, and occasional essays that make up this book are intended as a tribute to an important film stylist and master mythmaker. If longtime Leone enthusiasts find here something to illuminate their viewings of his films, and if newcomers find there is more to the world of Sergio Leone than they had perhaps expected, I'll have succeeded in my task.

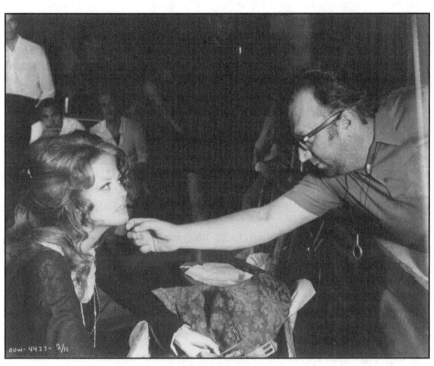

Sergio Leone
(directing Claudia Cardinale on the set of *Once Upon a Time in the West*)

Part 2
THE FILMS

2

"A Sergio Leone Film"

From Sandals to Six-Shooters

On May 21, 1975, *Variety* reported that

> Fida distrib *Edmondo Amati* is entering the disaster film cycle with ingenious economy. He has taken "The Last Days of Pompeii," directed by *Mario Bonnard* and *Sergio Leone* (his first) for re-issue with added scenes of earthquakes and other natural catastrophes.

Soon afterward, this letter appeared in *Variety*, under the headline "Leone on His Past":

> Rome.
>
> Editor, *Variety*:
>
> With reference to the news item published in Variety on May 21st, 1975, I should like to specify that before becoming a full-fledged director, I have worked as an assistant director in 58 films. In many of these (including "The Last Days of Pompeii"), I have also directed the second unit.
>
> Clever distributors digging up these old pictures and exhibiting my name in block letters are obviously trying to make a few pretty pennies by misleading the spectator into believing that they are Sergio Leone films.
>
> Sergio Leone

By the time he wrote this letter, Sergio Leone had clearly developed a notion of what constituted "a Sergio Leone film," and wanted the film world to understand that notion in no uncertain terms. In the first edition of this book, I expressly deferred to Leone's self-definition, and limited myself to the "true" Leone films by beginning my examination of the director's work with *A Fistful of Dollars*. But today, with the perspective of two additional decades, there is value in taking at least a brief look at the "sword and sandal" films that formed the context of Leone's apprenticeship—especially since those films offer early manifestations of the kind of narrative form that Leone ultimately refined and made his own.

The "peplum" films—so named for the Roman-style sandal worn by the characters in them—were a result of the fusion of a traditional interest of Italian cinema and the incursion of American filmmakers into Italy in the mid- to late '50s to get the advantage of inexpensive labor and Mediterranean landscapes for the biblical spectaculars that were in particular demand at the time. A generation of young Italian filmmakers, raised on American films, inspired by postwar neorealism, and eager for new modes of expression for their hungry talent, found their tools in the detritus of American production companies' Roman holiday—not only sets, props, and costumes, but cameras, cranes, raw film, and stock footage. Serving as assistant directors and in other capacities on American productions afforded these young men the opportunity to grab what they could and make films of their own on the fly. This was the beginning of the careers of many writers and directors who would make names for themselves in the years ahead: not only Leone but Sergio Corbucci, Sergio Sollima, Mario Bava, Antonio Margheriti, Gianfranco Parolini, Pietro Francisci, Mario Caiano.

The peplum formula presents a narrative model that these young writers and directors would later adapt to the nineteenth-century American Southwest, both affronting and revitalizing the ailing Western genre. There are many peplum films, the genre is rich and varied, and one may do it a disservice by generalizing. But it is important to recognize that the genre that came to be known by the flippant title "Spaghetti Westerns" did not emerge through spontaneous combustion. Most of the narrative and character elements of the Italian Western were already present in the peplum films, which got them in turn from mixing and matching Greek, Roman, and early Christian history and myth.

The typical peplum story centers on an outsider, a man from another land or country, whose wanderings bring him to a new land, rich, decadent, and oppressed. This land is customarily ruled by either a powerful tyrant or a good but weak king who is about to be overthrown by a would-be tyrant. The outsider is either welcome or unwelcome at court, and sometimes both; but his fate becomes intertwined with that of an attractive woman of noble birth, who is caught up in the political turmoil (on one side or the other). The outsider makes it his business to strike a blow for freedom and right, and to rid the country of the oppressor. In doing so, the outsider often also gets his revenge on the very forces that destroyed his family or village, and caused him to become a rootless wanderer in the first place. To put it another way, the typical peplum hero has a private mission and a public mission—to gain revenge for a personal wrong done to him, and to free others from a similar wrong—and in the purest iterations of the formula, the two missions merge when the oppressor turns out to be the same villain.

Leone worked on American-produced biblical epics as well as writing and co-directing Italian-produced peplums of the mythic world. The two films in which he played the most important role were *Gli ultimi giorni di Pompei* (*The Last Days of Pompeii*, a 1959 widescreen and color remake of an ever-popular Bulwer-Lytton potboiler that had already been filmed many times before), which Leone co-directed with an ill and aging Mario Bonnard; and *Il colosso di Rodi* (*The Colossus of Rhodes*, 1961), which gave Leone his first solo director credit. Leone's peplum films do not exhibit much of what would later come to be recognized as the Leone style. But they do exemplify the mythic and narrative patterns that interested him as a writer, an inventor of stories, characters, and plot structures. Both involve a visitor or outsider who comes to a city especially noted for beauty and spectacle on the one hand, corruption and treachery on the other. Both films' protagonists are at odds with—and briefly suffer at the hands of—oppressive regimes. And in both films the protagonist escapes an apocalyptic disaster that destroys the city and the evil within it.

If films such as *Gli ultimi giorni di Pompei* and *Il Colosso di Rodi* are similar to Leone's later work more in their dialogue, structure, and character relationships than in their visual style and technique, it is partly because Leone was still learning his craft, developing the tools and fine-tuning the techniques that he would later make uniquely his own, and partly because of the severely limited budgets and shooting schedules faced by the young Italian filmmakers working in the peplum genre. There is little in *Il Colosso di Rodi* to suggest the stylist that Leone would become just a few years later—though the film does contain one clever and prophetic trompe l'oeil shot involving eyeballs filling the widescreen frame.

It was the shift in filmmakers' and audiences' interest from the peplum to the Western that made Leone's growth to artistic maturity take the path it did. The peplum experience laid the basis for Leone's mythic vision and his episodic approach to narrative and character. When, in 1961, some of the peplum makers had got the idea of plowing fresher ground by using the landscapes of Spain to make Westerns set in the American Southwest, the process was already set in motion by which Leone would emerge as a cinematic giant of unique vision.

As already noted, Leone was not the first of the peplum directors to attempt a Western; even today too many moviegoers who know Leone's name and what it came to stand for fail to appreciate the impact the Italian Western had, or the masterpieces it produced, during the slightly less than two decades the genre held sway in Europe. A mere fraction of the more than five hundred "Euro-Westerns" produced between 1961 and 1978 ever reached the United States, notwithstanding the enthusiasm Leone's films met with American audiences (who seemed to understand and appreciate what the genre was doing far faster than most critics did).

Sergio Corbucci, whose *Romolo e Remo* (*Duel of the Titans*, 1961) is one of the best peplum films, and who remarked more than once that the Italian Western grew directly from the peplum genre, is also responsible for two of the greatest "Spaghetti Westerns": *Django* (1966) and *The Great Silence* (1969). Sergio Sollima's *La Resa dei Conti* (*The Big Gundown*, 1966) and *Faccia a faccia* (*Face to Face*, 1967) are little-seen masterpieces. Giulio Petroni's brilliant *Da uomo a uomo* (*Death Rides a Horse*, 1968) was allowed to fall into the public domain and is thus the subject of many inferior DVD transfers, not one of which preserves the proper widescreen ratio of the original film. Giulio Questi's bizarre *Se sei vivo, spara* (*Django Kill*, 1967) brought European existential expressionism to the Western well before *El Topo* (1970). But the films of Sergio Leone remain the principal exemplars of the Italian Western.

The degree to which Leone's films became the benchmark for all later assays of the Western genre was apparent in 2006, when John Hillcoat's film of Nick Cave's *The Proposition* hit U.S. screens, to be widely and enthusiastically compared with the films of Sergio Leone. And, true enough, the Australian film employed many of the techniques associated with Leone's Westerns: realistic emphasis on dirty hair, mud- and blood-caked skin, unshaven faces; uncompromising depictions of violence and cruelty; stunning landscapes of natural beauty contrasted with an ugliness of both character and event; shock cuts from wide to extreme closeup; self-referential use of the frame as a boundary of reality; the yearning struggle to find redemption for the most unredeemable of people and acts.

But there is, it seems to me, a key difference in vision between the Australian film and the films of Leone and his American models, and identifying it will serve as an introduction to the patterns of the Western genre in which Leone's genius ultimately matured. The myth of the American Western (not necessarily of the historical American West) is, at its simplest, that strong men tamed a frontier, making it safe for a civilized society that then had no room for them. The myth of Australia, by contrast—at least as represented in *The Proposition*, various screen versions of the Ned Kelly story, and a handful of other Australian "Westerns"—is that strong men, both good and bad, were not builders of civilization but obstacles to its advancement. In both myths, civilization is the relentless, inevitable force that drives out the strong; but in the Australian myth, civilization opposes the strong men, and comes about in spite of them, not because of them.

Analyses, both deep and shallow, of the American Western abound with references to "the wild West" and "the lawless land." But the myth of the American Western is not that of civilization bringing law into a lawless place; it is the giving way of natural law to civil law—or, since the myth is modeled on the New Testament, the emergence of a New Law as a fulfillment of the Old. The strong men—again, both good and bad—are not men who have no need of law, or who flout the law, but rather men who are law unto themselves. The Old Law characterizes men who live by unwritten, internalized codes. Often these are individualized, personal codes—a sense of what a man has to do or ought to do. But they can also be communally shared codes. Bands of outlaws live according to a shared code of values; so do the aboriginal native tribes who play an important role in the Western myth; and so do the "good guys," who ultimately stand for human dignity and the protection of the weak against strong men who would work them harm. Indeed, the "good guys" (sometimes, though rarely appropriately, called "cowboys") consistently find themselves set off against one or both of the other two groups: The traditional model is "cowboys and Indians"; but the conflict in the American Western is more often "good guys and bad guys"—the bad guys being sometimes outlaws, sometimes land-grabbers (railroads, banks, mining companies, or big cattle ranchers), sometimes hired guns in the service of the land-grabbers. Popular perception to the contrary, the Indians—though usually a presence and often a threat—are rarely the bad guys in American Westerns. By at least as early as 1948, the bad guys were those who sold guns or whiskey to the Indians, or lied to them, or otherwise exploited them; and when the bad guys were Indians, they were usually renegades who went against the interests of their own people, the will of their tribal government, or the wisdom of their elders. John Ford's *Fort Apache* and *She Wore a Yellow Ribbon* were hardly ground-breaking in this respect. And while sometimes the good guy finds himself in alliance with the tribes against the bad guys, more often there is an uneasy, shifting balance of power among all three. (We'll see later how Leone adapted this three-way model—which we might call "the Good, the Bad, and the Other"—to the structure of character relationships in his Western films.)

The American Western is about the tensions among these codes: The good man paves the way for civilized society because his sense of natural law—his moral sense, if your will—wins out over the codes of both outlaws and aboriginals, both of which, in very different ways, emphasize insularity and the protection and betterment of one's own group over the good guys' outgoing sense of acceptance and protection of others. It is on the good guys' essentially Christian code that civil law is built, written law that ultimately replaces the natural law written in the hearts of stronger, pre-civilized men.

The Western may depict this tension at any of several phases in its development, giving writers and directors of Western films a varied palette from which to choose. John Wayne, in his most memorable performances, exemplifies the Old Law, a man struggling within himself over issues of right and wrong, constantly weighing passion against reason, often making wrong choices and having to redeem himself by righting them in the end. This is certainly true of Tom Dunson in *Red River* and Ethan Edwards in *The Searchers*. It's also true of most of the characters portrayed by Randolph Scott in the films he made with director Budd Boetticher—the films that, of all American Westerns, had the most direct influence on the Italian Western, given their crisp, spare dialogue; their sparsely populated landscapes; and their tight, quasi-mythic storylines, often iterating the same private/public mission that characterizes the peplum hero.

James Stewart, by contrast, is often the New Law, a man living by codes written by others, by civilization, and charged with enforcing those codes, often against exemplars of the Old Law. John Ford's iconic landmark *The Man Who Shot Liberty Valance* is a key film in placing the man of the New Law in the context of strong men of the Old Law, one bad, one good, but both committed to a very different, pre-civilized kind of morality.

Henry Fonda, in Ford's earlier *My Darling Clementine* (like Gary Cooper in *High Noon*), may seem to be a representative of the New Law, but is really a man of the Old Law, uneasy with the badge he wears, out of step with the society he serves, more bound by what a man's heart tells him he must do than what the political order demands. Indeed, this iconography of Fonda is what enabled Leone to get away with casting this American movie archetype of nice-guy idealism as the mercenary and amoral titan Frank in *Once Upon a Time in the West*.

Two things are apparent from this brief and admittedly simplistic analysis of the narrative and moral structure of the American Western myth. First: the American Western was uniquely suited to the visions and temperaments of fledgling Italian directors, coming of age while working in the peplum genre, rich as it was with mythic visions and narrative structures set nominally in the antiquity of their own culture but more fundamentally in a past of elemental, pre-civilized conflict among titans. Second: underlying both the peplum and the Western is the notion that civilized society and the people who live within its strictures are essentially weak (Leone called it "a world without balls"), and have need of civil law to control, protect, and comfort them. The strong, whose protection of the weak in the pre-civilized frontier ultimately facilitates the displacement of the strong by the weak, have no need of civil law and its limitations, have no use for it, and when it prevails, they must move on.

This Nietzschean idea, uneasily merged with the Christian values of the good-guy protector of the innocent, is the stuff of which Sergio Leone's Westerns are made.

3

"Me Right in the Middle"

A Fistful of Dollars

Because a mere fraction of the more than five hundred "Spaghetti Westerns" released between 1961 and 1978 were distributed outside of Italy, fewer still in the United States, and none enjoyed as much attention and exhibition as the five directed by Sergio Leone, there is a double disadvantage. It means that—for good or ill—Leone's films carry virtually the whole burden of representing the genre to its international audiences, and that critics and viewers tend to make little distinction between Leone's films and the genre as a whole. Leone is judged in a vacuum rather than in the generic context in which he worked. For this reason, people often praise as innovative in his work what is merely genre convention.

The Italian Western is an extension of the Hollywood Western layered over a reaction against it. The films are lush with references to the Hollywood classics and the directors to whom the Italians acknowledge a debt: John Ford, Howard Hawks, John Sturges, Budd Boetticher, Anthony Mann, Nicholas Ray, Henry King, Henry Hathaway, Robert Aldrich, and Samuel Fuller, as well as such popular institutions as *Shane* and *High Noon* more honored for their narrative form than for their directorial style. Even the most outrageous turns of plot, character, and ethic in Italian Westerns are basically variations on—or inversions of—Hollywood Western conventions. The Italians, like their Hollywood paragons, were working in an established mythos, their differences in approach attributable to dissimilar individual visions and sociohistorical contexts. Leone is to Ford as Euripides is to Aeschylus; and they are all of them beholden to Homer.

The Italian overhaul of American myth is characterized by a more cynical view of people, of their motivations, and of their capabilities. Violence and cruelty are emphasized—particularly the abuse of innocents. Often, an impossibly fast mercenary gunman is the antihero.

The proliferation of constructions like "My Name Is" or "They Call Me" in the titles of Italian Westerns signals an existential approach to the B-Western cliché of the anonymous loner. Identity is not inherent in the name but in the style and in the act. "Nobody," "Trinity," "The Man with No Name," and others are what they do, not what they're called. The mythic subtext of the Hollywood Western has become the main text of the Italian Western—more abstract, at times almost allegorical.

The unstated allegorical pretensions of the Italian Western are nowhere more evident than in the films' emphasis on currency, whether in titles (*One Silver Dollar, A Fistful of Dollars, For a Few Dollars More, For a Dollar between the Teeth, One Hundred Thousand Dollars for Ringo*), as image, or as "Macguffin"-like motive—something whose acquisition justifies the most amoral behavior, but which never seems to matter much to the plot, the audience, or even the characters who vie for its possession. The word "dollar" is a handy compression of everything Europeans think of when they think of America: the Wild West, capitalism, profit-motivation, ostentatious wealth.

This tradition and vision is readily apparent in *A Fistful of Dollars*, the remarkable film in which Sergio Leone exhibits, for the first time, the thematic concerns and stylistic traits that recur throughout his work: the mercenary bounty killer haunted by unspecified ghosts from his past; the uneasy partnerships created by the gunman for his own profit; double- and triple-crosses; pervasive death imagery; breathtaking, rule-breaking uses of widescreen; a near-fetishist devotion to the closeup; cryptic dialogue and quirky plotting that have nothing to do with motivation or logic; an unprecedented marriage of music and image; and, the relentless pace of mythic storytelling.

A Fistful of Dollars remains a special case in film history, being a sometimes shot-for-shot remake of Akira Kurosawa's *Yojimbo* (1961). Of course the story's roots go deeper than that: *Yojimbo* is reputedly based upon the Budd Boetticher-Randolph Scott film *Buchanan Rides Alone* (1958), from Jonas Ward's novel *The Name's Buchanan* (again the magic and mystique of names), in which the hero takes advantage of an interfamilial conflict in a small town. The structure, theme, and amoral-comic tone owe a debt to Dashiell Hammett's *Red Harvest* (1929), in which a private cop wipes out nearly an entire town while working alternately for two equally corrupt opposing factions. Sergio Leone saw the *Fistful* story as a reworking of eighteenth-century comic dramatist Carlo Goldoni's *Arlecchino servo di due padroni* (*The Servant of Two Masters*), which rendered the same idea in commedia dell'arte.

If this genealogy of *A Fistful of Dollars* is more or less correct, the cross-cultural roots of the film are so complex as to distract from its distinctive stylistic character, making it all the more remarkable that so much that is uniquely Leone's still shines through. An Italian plot idea, American history and myth, Japanese history and myth, and the tradition of the European Western all make up the matrix of imagery and theme from which Leone fashioned *A Fistful of Dollars* in 1964.

The similarities between *Yojimbo* and *A Fistful of Dollars* are too numerous to mention in much detail. Besides, the differences, not the similarities, will serve us best in a consideration of the genius of Sergio Leone. Nevertheless, acknowledgment of the essential points of agreement of the two films is important: an unattached warrior wanders into a town torn by corruption and violence. He learns that the depressed condition of the town is due to the unrelenting rivalry of two criminally inclined mercantile families who divide the town's loyalty between them and whose virtual civil war has taken its toll of innocents as well as partisans. Offering his paid services first to one family and then to the other, the wanderer pads his purse well and brings about—by accident or design—the total destruction of both families. Along the way, he manages to rescue a peasant family who has been abused by one of the mercantile families. He also protects the welfare and interests of a food-and-drink purveyor, a public servant, and a coffinmaker. Captured and savagely beaten by the family that gains the upper hand, the warrior escapes, nurses himself back to health, and "rises again" to exterminate the last of the corrupt villains; then he moves on before the impending government intervention, leaving the town's few surviving citizens to begin anew.

Most of the incidental details of *Yojimbo* remain intact in *A Fistful of Dollars*.[1] Though *Yojimbo*, unlike *A Fistful of Dollars*, carefully distinguishes between the patriarchs who run the business and the henchmen who handle the dirty work in each family, Leone retains the basic power structure of the families of *Yojimbo*: One is headed by a trio of brothers, the other by a domineering woman whose husband is weak and whose son is cowardly. The silk merchants become gunrunners; the saké dealers liquor smugglers. The saké seller becomes a cantina proprietor, the town crier a bellringer; the coffinmaker remains a coffinmaker. The saké family in *Yojimbo* rests its strength not on its patriarch but on his henchman's younger brother, whose pistol gives him an advantage over the swordsmen and wrestlers who make up the rest of the town's warriors. In *A Fistful of Dollars*, where everyone has a pistol, the sliding scale gives younger brother Ramón Rojo a Winchester. In *Yojimbo*, the pistol-vs.-sword challenge is a confrontation of the new and the old, which Kurosawa ultimately resolves in favor of the old. (Another pistol-vs.-blade battle was similarly resolved in John Sturges's *The Magnificent Seven*, a remake of Kurosawa's own *Seven Samurai*.) In Leone's film, too, the weapon presumed to be the weaker prevails, an affirmation of skill and honor over raw power.

From start to finish, dust is a key image in both films. It gives emphasis to geographic realism and becomes an emblem of the cruel realities of peasant life. But there is an important difference in one key image: In *Yojimbo*, early in the film, the pistol-carrying younger brother emerges from a cloud of blowing dust ("Even the winds welcome you"), while in *A Fistful of Dollars* this dramatic effect appears just before the climax of the film, and it is the Man with No Name, the "good guy," who enters from a cloud. The cloud, in this case, is not wind-borne dust but the smoke from a series of dynamite explosions that No Name has engineered to announce his resurrection.

"Both sides are composed of the brand-marked," says Donald Richie of the rivals in *Yojimbo*, "the tattooed, of dwarfs and giants. Evil—finally—becomes grotesque. This horrid assortment, then, is the world." Physical deformity is a motif equally visible in Leone's work, though it is more important in later films than in *A Fistful of Dollars*, which does not feature the interest in the grotesque that Kurosawa displays in *Yojimbo*.

At the end of each film, the café owner, the watchman, and the coffinmaker survive. As in *Seven Samurai*, the humble, who do not make war, prevail. Nevertheless, in *A Fistful of Dollars* Silvanito, the cantina proprietor, takes a more active role than his counterpart in *Yojimbo* does. Twice he takes up arms against the oppressive families, gunning down the last Rojo at the end of the film. The coffinmaker, too, is somewhat changed in Leone's film. In *Yojimbo*, he complains there is too little killing; he says he doesn't have enough business. Then later he complains there is so much killing no one bothers with coffins. In *A Fistful of Dollars*, the coffinmaker never lacks business. The town of San Miguel is already "a graveyard" when the Man with No Name rides in; by the time he rides out, the coffinmaker is running from body to body, measuring the corpses with a length of rope.

Death is more pervasive in Leone's film than in Kurosawa's, though neither director spares the carnage. It is likely that Leone substituted simple death imagery for the complex of grotesque and deformity images that inform Kurosawa's film. This notion seems to be reinforced by comparison of two key scenes: As the wanderer enters the town in *Yojimbo*, he sees a dog carrying a human hand in its mouth; later, in his first armed combat in the film, he visibly severs limbs from his opponents. In *A Fistful of Dollars*, the Man with No Name rides into town and passes a mounted corpse, on whose back is a crudely lettered sign: "Adios, Amigo." During the brief shootout in which he "auditions" for Don Miguel Rojo, No Name casually shoots four men dead.

The two episodes in *A Fistful of Dollars* that have no analogues in *Yojimbo* also are death-oriented. The first is the massacre of the soldiers, from whom Ramón Rojo and his men, without turning over the guns they were supposed to deliver, wrest the gold they are escorting. The second, a plot extension of the first, is the sequence in the cemetery, during which No Name arranges two corpses from the massacre as if they are still alive. Then he tricks the Rojos into tipping their hand by telling both families that two soldiers "survived" the massacre.

Besides adding two episodes that intensify the atmosphere of death (and the number of bodies) in the film, Leone deleted one segment that was crucial to the plot of *Yojimbo*. The episode had nothing to do with slaughter; in fact, the scene threatened to put an end to it. In Kurosawa's film, agents investigate the events occurring in the town, momentarily suspending both the war between the families and the double-dealing activities of the hero. In *A Fistful of Dollars*, such an investigation is anticipated by Ramón Rojo. He proposes a truce with the Baxter family in order to keep San Miguel relatively clean for the time being. But, though the Man with No Name effectively sabotages that truce and keeps the families fiercely at war, the investigation conveniently never occurs. By the end of the film, when No Name decides to move on because it would be "too dangerous" to stay "in the middle" between the U.S. Cavalry and the Mexican army, no government official has appeared. It is as if Leone were scrupulously avoiding the introduction of any credible authority figure. Indeed, throughout his films the only law-and-order figures who appear are weak men whose badges are bought by corrupt bosses.

A stylistic difference between Kurosawa and Leone is seen in the timing and placement of the hero's liberation of the café owner, who has been tied up for torturous interrogation by the surviving villains. Kurosawa's Sanjuro dispatches the villains, then slashes his sword at the old man (and character and context make us think he might really mean the man harm); the man screams; the ropes, cut, fall loose; and Sanjuro turns and walks away to music and an end title. It's a punch ending, stylish, placing all of the emphasis on the caprice of the hero's final gesture. Leone's Man with No Name, by contrast, disposes of the bothersome business of freeing Silvanito before he faces Ramón Rojo: Leone wants to allow himself room to draw out the moment of reckoning and to end on a slow, dying chord as the camera pulls up and No Name rides away.

In some prints of *A Fistful of Dollars*, there is another sequence with no analogue in *Yojimbo*, and with no apparent purpose: In a prologue, in prison, we are introduced to the Man with No Name by means of a series of details that conceal his face. He's led from his cell and told by the prison warden that he will be granted a full pardon if he can clean up the town of San Miguel in sixty days. There's no motivation for this challenge, no further mention of it in the film, and no one ever seems to be checking up on whether No Name is actually doing the job. No theatrical release print I have seen contains the scene, but I have seen it twice in television prints. The effort to provide an explanation for the Man's actions in San Miguel is something Kurosawa never needed to do with his Sanjuro. The scene is easily excised from the film, since it is separated from the film proper by the arrestingly bizarre title sequence, after which *A Fistful of Dollars* actually begins, with a series of shots much like those that open *Yojimbo*. Perhaps the careful concealment of No Name's face is meant to preserve the revelation of his countenance until after the Kurosawan opening shot of his back; more likely it was necessitated because the sequence was shot without Clint Eastwood. The film's better without it, of course, and most of the prints in circulation show that somebody else thought so, too.

The anonymity of the central figure, his peripatetic nature, and his relationship to society are all stressed in *Yojimbo*'s opening shot of the back of Sanjuro's head, moving away from us. Leone wisely retained the concept (and, in fact, used it to introduce the Eastwood character in his next two films as well). The second shot of *Yojimbo* shows Sanjuro's feet, walking in the dusty, gravelly road. He arrives at a fork in the road, stops, finds a stick in the grass, tosses it into the air, and chooses the trail it points to when it lands. His attention is quickly distracted by the appearance of a headstrong boy who, against his family's wishes, wants to leave home to become a warrior. The wanderer advises against it: "A life eating gruel is best."

A rather different sort of family image opens *A Fistful of Dollars*: For the shot of No Name's back, Leone tilts up from the hooves of a mule plodding along the dry, rocky trail; he shows us the mounted figure and the now-familiar but then startling poncho. A new angle reveals the Man's face. He stops for water. A child whom we at first take to be playing, gains entrance to a small house and is quickly thrown out, howling. A brutish gunman kicks at the child and fires his pistol at the boy's feet as the boy cries for his mother. A man appears. He collects the crying child. Then he is told by the gunman to keep the boy away from the small house. The Man with No Name watches all this, then rides on into San Miguel. A bell tolls as he passes under a hangman's noose, and he encounters the mounted corpse with the cryptic message on its back.

In both openings, the basic terms of the hero's relationship with his environment are established. But, without our really knowing it, Leone has already begun his story by introducing us to several important characters. In contrast Kurosawa uses the opening to lay the groundwork for the young-vs.-old, glory-vs.-grit thematic subtext of *Yojimbo*; he does not set his plot in motion until several shots later. Whereas Kurosawa emphasizes character and theme, Leone concerns himself first with event, if not plot, and only later with the interaction of characters.

"Myself, I've always wanted to somehow or other stop these senseless battles of bad against bad," Kurosawa has said.[2] "But we're all more or less weak—I've never been able to. And that is why the hero of this picture is different from us. He is able to stand squarely in the middle and stop the fight." Very well. But in *A Fistful of Dollars* the man in the middle is less a peacemaker than an avenging angel, a protector of the innocent who "stops the fight" only by demolishing the combatants.

Taking his cue from Kurosawa's highly personal "peacemaker" analysis of Sanjuro, Donald Richie sees the character as a specific emblem of the film director: "What [he] likes best is to arrange something and then sit back and watch it." This is evident throughout both *Yojimbo* and *A Fistful of Dollars*, and nowhere more so than in the scene in which the lone warrior slaughters his own employer's henchmen, then "arranges" the scene to look as if a gang from the other family was responsible (though in *A Fistful of Dollars* it is timing and circumstance more than arrangement of the scene that create this impression). Richie soon comes to relate Sanjuro explicitly to Kurosawa:

> [*Yojimbo*'s] cheerfully anarchistic philosophy is presented with a kind of stylistic unity which (far from realistic) is the product of that rare kind of art that hides itself. [Sanjuro] beats the world by seeing through it, and he beats it on its own terms. Kurosawa shows us a seen-through world, one where "reality" as such has ceased to count just as for [Sanjuro] the world's idea of "reality" is unimportant. It is because [Sanjuro] sees through and reorders the moral world that we feel delight. It is because Kurosawa has seen through and reordered the "actual" visible world in terms of dance, spectacle, movement, composition that we feel beauty.

All this talk of "reality" pertains to the central theme of *Yojimbo*, which is grounded in the peasant boy's dreams of the romance and glory of a warrior's life, as it contrasts with the old swordsman's vision of a nasty, corrupt world that offers nothing but grotesque evils to be destroyed but never defeated. Though the good-vs.-bad atmosphere works in *A Fistful of Dollars*, the notion of differing visions of reality and value does not. Leone's film is more elemental, more procedural, less philosophical. It is, finally, more Dashiell Hammett than Carlo Goldoni.

But the characterization of the middleman serves Leone's purpose as well as it served Kurosawa's. "*Yojimbo* is a thrashing administered to the world using its own weapons," Richie writes, and later:

Disinterest, selfishness, suspicion—these are weapons used by the bad world. Very well. Then Kurosawa will make a hero in which just these three unattractive characteristics are outstanding. ... Let us have a hero whose only virtue is a negative one: he is not actively concerned in being bad. ... He, in fact, behaves as though his human generosity is a weakness.

And there we have the Man with No Name. He does not "clean up" San Miguel out of any high-minded notions of right and wrong, or because he honors the law or any other absolute authority. What gripes him about the powers that be in the town is evident from the opening scene: the victimization of the innocent. It is for the victims' sakes that he extends his activities in San Miguel long after the profit has gone out of his venture. Also, he recognizes that he is different from the likes of the Baxters and the Rojos; the people in these families cannot long tolerate one another's existence—(a definitive Leone motif that becomes explicit in *The Good, the Bad and the Ugly* and *Once Upon a Time in the West*).

In both *Yojimbo* and *Sanjuro*, Kurosawa's 1962 sequel, the protagonist identifies himself as Sanjuro, which means "thirty-year-old," choosing as surname whatever happens to be handy: In *Yojimbo* it's "mulberry field"; in *Sanjuro*, camellias. The Man with No Name in *A Fistful of Dollars* doesn't go even that far. Silvanito and the coffinmaker call him Joe and he lets the name stand. No one else ventures to call him anything. The suppression of identity is final and unquestioned. But if the Man doesn't want to be famous, neither does he want to be rich. Despite Sanjuro's "How about giving me some money?" and No Name's palm-upward salute, the money motivation is never a satisfying one. Of Sanjuro, Richie notes, "In order to avert suspicion he pretends in both pictures to a greed he does not feel." The studied anonymity, the obvious pretense of the profit motivation, the utmost superhuman wit and endurance, and the mysterious arrival and departure of the hero imply that the Man is the instrument of a higher form of justice, that implacably he serves a power even he does not understand.

During the years immediately preceding the advent of the Italian Western, an important change had begun to occur in the American Western. The protagonist—especially as personified by John Wayne and Randolph Scott—had, throughout the '50s, been a man who carries with him his code of moral rightness, and who, simply by doing what he individually knows is right, serves the greater cause of producing and protecting civilized society. But beginning with *Rio Bravo* and bursting into full bloom in *The Magnificent Seven*, Western protagonists began to be valued more for being cool than for being right. To be sure, the deputies of *Rio Bravo*, who were "good" in a Hawksian sense, and the hired guns of *The Magnificent Seven*, who took a pay cut to strike a blow for the downtrodden, were still emphatically concerned with doing the right thing. But it was their personal style more than their moral rectitude that attracted audiences to them. It thus became less important what they did for a living and more important how they did it.

The next step in this tradition (a result of the first rock'n'roll generation's growing cynicism about society and its deification of individual cool) was the wandering bounty killer of the Italian Western. Leone's Man with No Name is hardly a peacemaker—at least not in the near-angelic terms in which Kurosawa describes Sanjuro. In fact, when Ramón Rojo proposes a truce with the Baxters, it is No Name who deliberately disrupts the peace. His contempt for the truce is clear even when it is proposed:

> Ramón: Life can be so precious; it makes no sense to risk losing it all
> the time. ...
> Miguel: I think Ramón has the right idea. I, too, am getting tired of all
> this killing.
> No Name: This is all very touching.
> Ramón: Don't you admire peace?
> No Name: It's very hard to like something you know nothing about.

Besides providing one of several cryptic clues to the Man's past and personality, this exchange emphasizes his sneering contempt for the Rojos' hypocrisy. He knows that Ramón's truce idea has nothing to do with being sick of killing and everything to do with wanting to keep San Miguel quiet for awhile, so as not to attract undue attention from the government authorities who are, by now, wondering what happened to a certain gold shipment.

No Name's motivation for sabotaging the peace may be the desire to continue putting money in his purse, or a growing interest in saving the victimized Marisol, or a compulsion to work as an instrument of fate toward the apocalyptic destruction that climaxes the film. In any case, by engineering the ruse in the graveyard (a significant departure from the Kurosawa model), he single-handedly forestalls peace.

In spite of himself, perhaps—and more than Kurosawa ever did—Leone makes an effort to motivate the Man's liberation of the victimized family. For example, No Name explains to Marisol his reason for helping her and her husband and child to escape—"I knew someone like you once, and there was no one there to help." The statement is more an effort to justify his good deed to himself than to answer Marisol's question. This, the most explicit reference in the film to the central character's past, serves the same purpose that Leone's haunting flashbacks serve in *For a Few Dollars More*, *Once Upon a Time in the West*, and *Duck, You Sucker!*

Another veiled reference to the Man's past comes early in the film when Don Miguel welcomes No Name into the fold:

> Don Miguel: This is Chico. He will bring you to your room. I trust you will
> feel at home.
> No Name: Well, I never found home all that great.

He refuses the quarters offered by the Rojos, preferring to sleep—fully clothed—in the humbler bed at Silvanito's. By choice, he remains emphatically an outsider, even when a cash payment allies him with one side or the other. "Baxters there ... Rojos there ... and me right in the middle. Crazy bellringer was right. There's money to be made in a place like this."

Leone's visual style adds emphasis to the Man as mysterious outsider, whose presence is central to the film and about whom all events turn. As a shot begins, No Name, usually, already occupies the frame. Or he enters the shot from the background or foreground near the center; rarely does he come in from the sides. Whether by moving or by standing still, the camera tends to discover or reveal his presence, rather than forcing him to walk into the frame. (This stylistic approach is, of course, destroyed by the "scanned" prints shown on television.)

The importance of the Man's centrality as a third party, tipping to one side then another the delicate balance of the two-family rivalry already established in San Miguel before his coming, is strengthened by Leone's insistence upon trios in the film's character groupings.

First, there is a trio of forces at work in the film: the combatants, the neutrals, and the victims. Second, each of these forces is a trio: the combatants—the Baxters, the Rojos, and the Man with No Name; the neutrals—Silvanito, Juan de Dios, and the coffinmaker; and the victims—Marisol, Julián, and their son Jesus.

Further, each of the warring families is headed by a trio: the Baxters by John, his wife Consuelo, and their son Antonio; the Rojos by three brothers, Don Miguel the patriarch, Ramón the policymaker, and Estéban the sadistic hardhead. (If No Name is, as some have suggested, a perverse Christ-figure, then, in the Catholic imagery of the Trinity, he, too, might be a "trio" unto himself.)

Each of the three trios—combatants, neutrals, and victims—consists of two extremes and a middle. No Name is obviously "right in the middle" between the two warring families. The Rojos are liquor smugglers; the Baxters are gunrunners; and the Man in between is associated with money—thus covering the three great roots of evil.

Similarly, Silvanito, a cantina owner, is associated with liquor; the coffinmaker's inevitable association with death echoes the death image of the Baxters' association with guns; and in between Silvanito and the coffinmaker stands the bellringer, Juan de Dios, both a mediator in human affairs and, as head of the town's only system of public communication, a representative of "the media" (though he is never as important or as interesting as the analogous character in *Yojimbo*). The family of the victims has as its two extremes the husband and wife, Julián and Marisol—kept physically separate by the Rojos, but also separated by their contrasting characters: Julián is relatively weak and unassertive; Marisol is strong and fierce. Between them is their son, Jesus, who moves physically from one to the other, both in the opening scene and in the prisoner exchange scene that is one of the film's stylistic and thematic high points.

Into this world of studied trichotomy, the Man with No Name brings the force of unity. "Every town has a boss," he says to Silvanito, but has to agree when the innkeeper replies, "When there are two around, I'd say there's one too many." People who have noted the Christian imagery associated with the Man— his mule, his good works, his torture at the hands of the Rojos, his days in the "tomb," and his triumphant resurrection—may easily see him as a proponent of monotheism in a town (world) where loyalty is divided between two gods, arms

The Man with No Name (Clint Eastwood) in the graveyard: a composition that reinforces the "me in the middle" imagery of *A Fistful of Dollars*.

The Rojos	THE COMBATANTS	The Baxters
	The Man with No Name	
(Liquor)	(Money)	(Guns)
Don Miguel		John
Ramón		Consuelo
Estéban		Antonio
	THE NEUTRALS	
Silvanito	Juan de Dios	The Coffinmaker
(Liquor)	(Bellringer)	(Coffins)
(Cantina)	(Mediator)	(Graveyard)
(Life)		(Death)
	THE VICTIMS	
Marisol	Jesus	Julián
(Mother)	(Child)	(Father)
(Wife)	(Innocence)	(Husband)
(Strength)	(Tears)	(Weakness)

and liquor, both in the service of Mammon. Nor is it inappropriate to note that the town itself bears the name of the avenging archangel.

Julián, Marisol, and Jesus are, of course, a Holy Family type, a "JMJ" who stand outside the evils of the world and who escape the slaughter by fleeing into the desert and hightailing it for another land. The separation of Julián and Marisol is emblematic of the way in which the Baxters and the Rojos have split the town between them; and, in this analogy, the town itself is a kind of archetypal victim—a Jesus.

This "Holy Family" is the emotional center of the film. Their plight causes the Man to do good—perhaps in spite of himself—and even rouses the neutrals to action. At two key points in the film, Silvanito finds he cannot remain neutral: first, when Rubio threatens to kill Julián who, during the prisoner exchange, fails to keep Jesus from disrupting the proceedings by running to his mother; and second, in the end, when Estéban, the last surviving Rojo, positions himself at a window and, holding a shotgun, draws a bead on No Name.

No one calls Silvanito's challenge in the first instance, for reasons that are unclear (why shouldn't Rubio simply shoot down both Julián and Silvanito?); in the second, Silvanito personally kills the last nemesis of the town's harmony, an indication that the "little people," though clearly reduced in number, will now be capable of defending themselves against future Baxters and Rojos.

Though Silvanito endures because he chooses not to remain neutral, the coffinmaker's survival is a statement of neutrality of the most awesome kind. The Man is able to force the coffinmaker into helping him escape and survive his days of hiding, but the significantly anonymous merchant of death remains the most impartial element in San Miguel—and the only one who still works and makes a profit.

Death the Leveler is the presiding justice of the greater portion of the film. The swinging noose, the tolling bell, the mounted corpse, and the dialogue references to "a dead town" and "a cemetery" in the opening scenes have prepared his way. He has his orgy when the Rojos, swept into a frenzy, massacre the unarmed Baxters as they flee their burning home. A sort of death's head laugh is evoked by the hypocrisy and cosmic irrelevance of Consuelo Baxter's accusatory "Murderers!" shouted at them just before Estéban shoots her down, completing the Rojos' collection of Baxter corpses. Nowhere is the Man with No Name more solidly a "man in the middle" than in this scene. Half-dead from the Rojos' savage beating, he is a quick man in a coffin, peering out to watch the Rojos mercilessly slaughtering the Baxters.

Undeniably, there is a sexual quality to the relish the Rojos take in slaughter. Ramón is associated with an assortment of weaponry, most notably his Winchester (and one recalls the pride with which Inosuke, his prototype in *Yojimbo*, produces his own pistol from beneath the folds of his kimono): "When you want to kill a man, shoot for his heart—and a Winchester is the best weapon." After No Name and Silvanito stealthily observe Ramón's treacherous double-cross and massacre (with a machine gun) of the detachment of *federales* accompanying the gold, Silvanito identifies Ramón not from his appearance but from his sharpshooting, when he uses his Winchester to pick off a lone survivor who is escaping on horseback across the river.

A homosexual subtext dovetails with the sadomasochism characterizing the Rojos, particularly in the person of Estéban. When he finds the Man packing to move into Silvanito's cantina (No Name has overheard the Rojos plotting to kill him in his sleep), Estéban tries to stop him: "All our men sleep here with us," he says, to which No Name replies, "That's all very cozy," and provocatively blows Estéban a faceful of cigar smoke, "but I don't find you men all that appealing." Much later, when No Name returns from setting the "Holy Family" free, he finds Ramón, Estéban, and henchmen waiting in his darkened bedroom. As Rubio savagely beats No Name, Estéban lies by the fireplace laughing, his hands between his legs.

The Man with No Name, despite the absence of any explicit heterosexual behavior on his part, stands firm against this homosexual sadism—admittedly a simplistic form of characterization, but one that is familiar in Italian Westerns (probably the most extreme example being Giulio Questi's *Django, Kill*) and, indeed, in much Italian literature (one recalls Alberto Moravia's novel, as well as Bertolucci's film, *The Conformist*). In fact, No Name's key encounters with the two women in the film are handled almost as semicomic reflections of Rojo behavior: He sneaks up on Consuelo Baxter in her boudoir, as if for a tryst or a rape, covering her mouth to stifle the scream—but all he wants to do is tell her a bedtime story. Later, the first time he gets close to Marisol, whom he has admired from a distance, he punches her in the face and knocks her unconscious, mistaking her for a Rojo guard.

The overtones of sexual sadism, both serious and comic, serve to emphasize the inversion and subversion of the family unit that occur in the film. The one Man with No Name, the mock "family" of the neutrals, the unscrupulous criminal family of the Baxters, and the all-male family of the Rojos are all set against the normal family of Julián, Marisol, and Jesus. Family ties, of course, provide central motif and motivation in the Western myth as extended by Hollywood; they are even more crucial, however, in the Italian Western where they echo the family-centered worldview of Italian Catholicism. The perverse images of the "anti-families" in *A Fistful of Dollars* establish an important theme that Leone has made uniquely his own and has treated with more sophistication in *For a Few Dollars More* and *Once Upon a Time in the West*: the defenders (or avengers) of family versus the violators of family.

The family motif is, of course, present in the Kurosawa prototype as well: a victimized family is saved by the anonymous hero; one of the town's two ruling families is dominated by a shrewd but shrewish wife; and, emphasis is placed upon another family not appearing in the Leone film, the family of the peasant boy who dreams of becoming a warrior. Kurosawa's sustained drawing of contrasts among these families serves quite a different purpose from Leone's, who calls attention in the dialogue to the theme of family and mock-family ("That's all very cozy"), and who goes for a more direct approach to contrast.

In the prisoner exchange sequence, for example, we see side-by-side two distinct mother-and-son reunions. All is tension; Leone cuts from face to face, angle to angle, as Marisol—delivered by the Man to the Baxters—walks back toward the Rojos, in trade for Antonio Baxter, who has been captured by the Rojos in the gunfight at the cemetery. Suddenly little Jesus breaks away from Julián's grasp and runs toward his mother. In high-angle long shot we see Marisol, too, break and run toward the boy. Leone cuts from the long shot to a fast zoom-in from midshot to close on their tearful embrace. Julián breaks. Rubio starts to draw on him, and Silvanito restores calm by getting the drop on Rubio with his shotgun. After a moment, Jesus is returned to his father, and the prisoner exchange continues. Antonio Baxter rejoins his family, giving his mother a respectful kiss. She hugs him warmly, then slaps him sharply in the face—the sign of shame for his having got himself captured in the first place. The contrast between the two mother-son relationships is intentional, and Leone takes care to reverse his approach: the cut from long shot to zoom-in to close on Marisol and Jesus is a progress from distance to intimacy, while the succession of gestures between Consuelo and Antonio moves from intimacy to distance.

A similar economy is employed earlier in the film, when Leone introduces us—and the Man with No Name—to the patriarchs of the two warring families. We have not yet had time to learn that the Rojos are really run by Ramón and that the Baxters are really run by Consuelo, so No Name's first encounter with the two ostensible patriarchs, Don Miguel Rojo and John Baxter, characterizes the two men for us and establishes the visual and thematic motif of No Name as man-in-the-middle. No Name stands in front of the Rojo house and speaks in a normal voice to an unseen Don Miguel. The Man doesn't turn to see if Miguel will appear or acknowledge him; for him, confidence is all. And Leone doesn't cut or pan away from the Man to show us the Rojo reaction, if indeed there is one. Instead he keeps the camera on the Man, who, having said his piece, starts down the street to perform his "audition" for Don Miguel. Leone's camera tracks backward in front of the man. Only when the camera is far enough away from the Rojo house that the shot is wide enough to include the balcony do we see Don Miguel come out and stand there, watching. No Name never turns; he knows the Don is there. What follows is the business with the coffinmaker, and the seriocomic "mule" speech that the Man uses to incite the Baxters' henchmen to draw on him. Don Miguel remains visible on his balcony in the background, silent, stolid. But watching the Man shoot down four of his men, for no better reason than to prove himself to the Rojos, the Don is taken with No Name's style. John Baxter, the nominal sheriff of San Miguel, outraged by the killing and visibly unnerved, comes up and haltingly challenges the Man, fumbling in his inside pocket for the long-unused sheriff's badge. Authority vested in a badge is a bad joke in San Miguel. It is Don Miguel, silent, firm, and distant—viewed from a respectfully low angle—who holds the real authority in the scene, and No Name who has the power.

Space and spatial relationships are beautifully established in this scene, as they are in the prisoner exchange and in a few other scenes. But in the film as a whole we remain hazy about the geographical relationships of key locations. Which way is the border? Where is the small house in relation to the Baxters', the Rojos', and Silvanito's homes? Where are the cemetery, the hideout where

No Name recovers, the pass through which he rides to head off the Rojos in those confusing day-for-night riding-around scenes? We could not sit down and draw a map of San Miguel as, for example, we could of the village where Kurosawa's *Seven Samurai* takes place. The cavalier attitude Leone takes toward the establishment of spatial relationships in *A Fistful of Dollars* prefigures the peculiar mastery over space that his characters enjoy in later films; in this movie, it is probably more legitimate to view his casualness as one of the weaknesses of his apprenticeship.

Apprenticeship or not, *A Fistful of Dollars* announces, one way or another, all the hallmarks of the Leone style. In at least seminal form we have here the fascination with (and reliance on) closeups for structural rather than emotional effect; the occasional respectful subservience of the image to the remarkable music; emphasis on images of intrusion and penetration (the Man attempts to peep into the *federales'* wagon and comes up with a gun in his face); a preponderance of floor-level or ground-level shots, particularly of boots and spurs in huge, almost fetishistic closeups that stress if not celebrate the earthiness, the lowness of this particular world; the elliptical dialogue, cryptic, aphoristic, playful, echoing the fairy tale: "There was once a wagonload of gold that the soldiers were taking to the border ..." is the Man's unique way of telling Consuelo Baxter about Ramón Rojo's secret.

Leone's geometric approach to composition is, to some extent, dictated by function, as in the "audition" scene, with Baxter men in the foreground, Don Miguel watching from the background, and "me right in the middle." But Leone emphasizes the interplay of trinity and unity in the incidental compositions as well. During the rendezvous with the gold wagon at the river that culminates in Ramón's bloody massacre of the *federales*, three wagons roll across the river to meet with a single one. Gratuitously or otherwise, the film is filled with such three-and-one or three-in-one shot compositions.

There may be a debt to Kurosawa here. Certainly the clean-cut, sharply structured compositions of the director of *Yojimbo* had a profound effect on the look of *A Fistful of Dollars*, and on the still-forming cinematic vision of Leone. "Mostly," writes Richie of Kurosawa's *Rashomon*, "he insists on the triangle through composition." Both *Rashomon* and *Yojimbo* are based on triangles—the former on the interaction among the lord, his lady, and the bandit, as well as on the three framers of the story, the beggar, the woodcutter, and the priest; the latter on the tension between the two warring families, which is upset by the intrusion of the freelance bodyguard who sways the balance first one way, then the other. This careful structuring of character groups and relationships—and the way the structuring is reflected in shot composition—looks ahead to the celebrated triangular showdowns of Leone's next two films. (Richie uses the phrase "uniform geometry" to describe the balanced frame composition and the emphasis on right angles that characterize *Rashomon* and *Yojimbo*. Significantly, both films were shot by the brilliant cinematographer Kazuo Miyagawa.)

Typically the omniscient, omniopic narrative stylist, Leone avoids the specifically subjective shot—that is, unless it carries special meaning or at least offers the irresistible opportunity to do something flashy at a climactic moment.

Thus when the arch-nemesis of the film, Ramón Rojo, finally dies, we get—illogically but importantly—his reeling, blurring, staggering point-of-view of the triumphant Man with No Name, and then the calm sky above as he falls.

In later films, Leone finds death itself less interesting than the moments that precede it (recalling Bergman's Squire in *The Seventh Seal*: "the immense triumph of this last minute when you can still roll your eyes and move your toes"). In this approach, too, he may have taken a cue from Kurosawa, though this time from *Sanjuro*, whose remarkable climax—a swordfight choreographed as a gunfight—Richie describes thus:

> There is no bluffing offensive, no strategic retreat, no slashing. Swords still in scabbards they confront each other and there is a long wait—a very long one, fifteen whole seconds, an enormous amount of time at the climax of a film. Then, in a single movement, both draw and (at the same time) strike.

For Leone, that wait *became* the climax, and in his later films he so protracts the time before the moment of reckoning that Kurosawa's fifteen seconds seem laughably short. To be fair, though, Leone extends the time through montage, rather than by stressing the duration of the moment in a single static shot, as Kurosawa does in the *Sanjuro* showdown. The intense and rhythmic montage of closeup details preceding a big gundown has become a Leone trademark, as often imitated as satirized. The assembly of detail shots to create a serial depiction of a single event from many views is reminiscent of the woodcutter's walk through the forest in *Rashomon*, one of Kurosawa's great tours-de-force, a virtual encyclopedia of ways to shoot a man walking (in a film that is, of course, *about* varying points of view). The idea becomes, in Leone's films, a lexicon of ways to shoot a man getting ready to shoot a man—and the self-referential cinematic pun cannot be unintended.

In *A Fistful of Dollars*, there is little use of this rhythmic kind of montage, rhythm being established mostly within the shot rather than in the cutting. Ennio Morricone's score establishes the pace at which the characters move through space in a given shot or scene. There are occasional exceptions to the rule, however; the best of these is a semicomic effect that is a veritable satire on montage theory. While the Baxters and the Rojos are exchanging gunfire at the cemetery, the Man is prowling around the guarded house where Ramón Rojo is hiding (among other things) Marisol. He taps on liquor kegs with his pistol butt, looking for one empty enough to suit his purpose. Four taps, and Leone cuts to four quick shots of men firing their pistols, bang-bang-bang-bang, at the cemetery; he moves back to the Man, who taps twice, tap-tap; he cuts to the cemetery and two shots of men firing, bang-bang; the Man gives one tap; Leone cuts to one final rifle shot at the cemetery. It's an astounding little sequence that not only conveys information but advances the action of the story and creates a great deal of fun at the same time—and that's what Leone always does at his best.

Notes

1   A detailed plot-synopsis of each of the films discussed in these opening chapters will be found, with cast and credit listings, in the appended filmography.

2   In Donald Richie's *Films of Akira Kurosawa* (Berkeley: University of California Press, 1965).

4

"I Can See That It Means a Lot to You"

For a Few Dollars More

One of the most frequent and misguided criticisms of Leone's Westerns is that the characters are thin and clichéd. *For a Few Dollars More* provides one of the best arguments against that criticism. Its plot is both looser and more complex than that of *A Fistful of Dollars*, taking more than half an hour of screen time to get under way and never satisfactorily justifying its opaque, illogical storyline. But that doesn't matter a bit, because the film is all character.

A lone horseman rides lazily from the background into the center of a spacious desertscape. A low, tuneless whistling is heard (provided by Leone himself), followed by the striking of a match and a short inhale-exhale. Unseen, the "Man with No Name" is back, and his presence quickly makes itself known: A single shot is heard, and the rider topples off the horse—a neat reversal of the expectations built up by Leone's wry quotation of the time-honored convention (*Shane, The Searchers*) of the hero who rides out of landscape into center-frame and goes on to dominate the film.

While the unhorsed rider continues to lie there, dead center, additional shots scare off the horse and bring up the main titles. The titles float in and out like moving targets on a wire, the gunshots that punctuate the music knocking them cockeyed now and again. When the director's credit appears, the letters of Leone's name are shot away a few at a time, until only this remains: 0 0—a pair of bullet holes, of circles, of zeros. One of them drops away, and the other blurs and spreads as the screen fades to black for this legend:

> Where life had no value, death, sometimes, had its price. That is why the bounty killers appeared.

Life was never so cheap, nor body counts so high—certainly not in the American West or the American Western—as in the Italian Western. It's tempting to see this epigraph as self-referential. The epigraph is replaced by the opening shot of the film-proper, a closeup of the cover of the Bible (and if you don't feel even at this early point that you're watching something very special, you may never be a Leone convert). Behind the Bible is, improbably, the face of that archetype of B-Western villainy, Lee Van Cleef; yet there's an even bigger reversal in store for us, for if the association of that face with the Bible seems iconoclastically to assign a tone of righteousness and moral order to Van Cleef's character (Colonel Douglas Mortimer), that is, in fact, how he finally turns out, no matter what happens along the way.

Mortimer wants to get off in Tucumcari. Told that the train doesn't stop there, he pulls the emergency brake. As he leads his horse out of a stock car, an agitated conductor appears on the scene to upbraid him for abusing the emergency system. Mortimer stares the man down, withering him into deference; and, when the conductor finally stammers that the railway is, of course, happy to accommodate him if, after all, he wants to get off, Mortimer replies, "I did get off, thank you."

The imposing figure of Mortimer, in dark duster and cape, enters Tucumcari like Death himself, looking with interest at a "Wanted" poster for an outlaw named Guy Calloway, to whose $1,000 price two additional 0s have been added in crayon. The station man tells Mortimer that the extra zeros were added by Calloway himself, who contends he's worth more than a thousand. But the reward will go uncollected, says the station man, because "there isn't anyone got the guts to face that killer, eh?" Again the Van Cleef glare whips a menial into submission: "Er ... at least it's been that way 'til now." Mortimer takes the poster off the wall.

In the saloon below the town's hotel, Mortimer shows the poster to the bartender. While verbally denying any knowledge of Calloway's whereabouts, the bartender rolls his eyes upward. Mortimer nods. He climbs the stairs to a room above the bar and slides the poster under the door. Then he knocks and steps aside. Four bullets rip through the door (more zeros!). When the shooting stops, Mortimer opens the door and crosses to the window, ignoring a woman lying in bed. Seeing Calloway trip across the roof and drop to the ground, he turns and leaves the room, pausing to say, "Pardon me, ma'am," then paces evenly, unhurriedly, back down through the saloon. Exiting, he finds Calloway tearing off on horseback.

Mortimer steps to his own horse and pops two snaps on the saddle bag, unrolling a leather panel to which are affixed weapons, stocks, and barrels of assorted sizes. He selects a short rifle and shoots Calloway off his horse. Only now does Leone give us a look at Calloway. A close shot reveals him to be a snaggletoothed kid who looks like a dissipated Ronny Howard. Calloway fires four times but can't hit Mortimer, who, still unhurried, snaps a rifle stock onto a high-powered cannon of a pistol and finishes his mark with one shot.

While collecting the money for finishing off Calloway, the bounty killer (who is not actually identified as "Mortimer" until well into the film) spots another poster: this one offers a reward for one Baby Red Cavanaugh. Expressing an interest, Mortimer is told, "Somebody else is after him, too," and when Mortimer asks who, the informant replies, "I never seen him before. His name's Manco." In many early English-language release prints, the line was truncated to exclude the last three lines—probably to preserve the "Man with No Name" mystique (although a later line in the film remained unchanged in all prints: Indio's query to his henchman Niño, "How long have you known that Manco is a bounty killer?").

The name "Manco" could as easily be "Monco"—"the Monk"—a name in fact used for an itinerant antiheroic gunfighter in another Italian Western. But in both Spanish and Italian, the word "manco" has the sense of "one-handed"—an apt epithet, considering that the Eastwood character eats, smokes, drinks, and does everything except shoot, left-handed—presumably to keep his gun hand free. He even fistfights left-handed during his first scene in the film, which briefly imparts a kind of martial arts tone to the proceedings. Frequently Leone introduces him using a close shot, both of his hand and of its emblematic leather wrist protector. The bilingual pun is almost certainly intended in this Italian-Spanish co-production. The one-handed "Manco" is also a type of "Il Monco," a man of quiet style in a cowl-like poncho, firmly in the "Spaghetti Western" tradition of killer-priests (*Django, A Bullet for the General, God's Gun*) and gunmen with religious-sounding names (Trinity, Providence, Requiescant).

It's possible that the use of the punning name "Manco" was intended to give No Name a name; but it's also possible that the Eastwood character in *For a Few Dollars More* was conceived as a different person from the Man in *A Fistful of Dollars*. Certainly he is less sentimental and drops no hints about his past life. No doer of good deeds, this time he is purely a middleman.

Like No Name in *A Fistful of Dollars*, however, he is first seen from the back, just after the lawman gives (or does not give, depending on the print you're watching) Mortimer his name. Our first look at "Manco" is in close shot, lighting—left-handed—his cigarillo in the rain. He then enters a saloon and asks the sheriff about someone named Cavanaugh. The sheriff points out the mark, who is seated at a nearby card table. Before leaving the bar, the lawman adds: "His back is to you."

Manco sits down at Cavanaugh's table and deals—with his left hand—a hand of poker to himself and to Cavanaugh. In the meantime, the sheriff signals to a man who is sitting in a barber chair, getting a shave. This man brusquely stays the barber's hand, wipes off the lather, and gratuitously throws the cloth over the barber's head and he leaves the shop. Back at the poker game, Cavanaugh and Manco have preposterously good hands. Cavanaugh's draw fails to improve his three kings, while Manco's draw of an ace matches the pair he already holds, proving that either luck is on his side or that he cheats better than his opponent. "I didn't hear what the bet was," says Cavanaugh, as the hands are shown. "Your life," whispers Manco.

A scuffle follows. Cavanaugh gets the worst of it until the man from the barbershop and two other men intervene. Manco draws and kills them with three shots. But the interruption gives Cavanaugh time to go for his own gun, and Manco must whirl and shoot him, too.

Leaving the saloon, Manco pauses to ask the sheriff a question: "Isn't a sheriff supposed to be courageous, loyal, and, above all, honest?" "That he is," says the sheriff, whereupon Manco takes the tin star off the sheriff's vest and walks away. Outside, he tells two townsfolk, "I think you people need a new sheriff," and he drops the badge in the dirt—a gesture that will echo resoundingly in later personifications of the Clint Eastwood icon.

The film's third sequence begins with a shot of someone snoozing under a wide hat in a prison cell. Percussive bells chime as a handful of men creep spectrally about the prison's battlements, knocking off guards. (The bell tune will become increasingly important in what is Leone's most complex and satisfac-

tory union of music and film.) The snoozer's cell mate gets more and more nervous. An eye appears under the hat. The hat is then lifted off, and we have our
first look at the film's third major character, Indio.

The attackers—they are Indio's men—break into the cell to free their comrade. Before leaving his cell Indio gives just cause to his cell mate's agitation.
He shoots the man dead and takes with him, from among the man's things, a
small model of a cabinet. The gang shoots its way out of the jail. Indio has a
little fun with the last guard. He shoves the barrel of his pistol against the man's
face while he fingers a locket-watch in his other hand. Indio squeezes the trig-
ger. The gun clicks. "I am not going to kill you," Indio tells the fainting guard.
"I'll let you live so you can tell everyone what takes place here." And he laughs.
Howls of mad laughter overlap the cut from this scene into a shot of a "Wanted"
poster being nailed up with a pistol butt: "El Indio. $10,000 Reward."

Here, Leone does an extraordinary thing. From the poster, he cuts to
Manco, then back to the poster, Manco's gun hand and wrist protector at screen-
left still signaling his presence. Immediately, there's a cut to Mortimer, which
begins a staccato montage that intercuts increasingly closer shots of Mortimer's
and Indio's eyes—all of this punctuated by gunshots (heard, not seem) that unify
these two characters in a way we won't fully understand until the end of the film
(if even then). The three major figures in the film are thus brought together stylistically long before they ever meet spatially. Manco, who sees the poster first,
is the "medium" by which Mortimer and Indio come together. The divisive
shock-cutting from one man's face to the other's signals collision between them,
while the "zoom-in" effect of mounting closer-and-closer shots draws the viewer
into that collision. The story hasn't started yet (well, just barely: the little cabinet
does have something to do with it); the men haven't met; but *For a Few Dollars
More* has established its characters and their relationships.

That montage puts a period—more like an exclamation point—to Leone's
unprecedentedly long introduction. It also stresses the similarities that already
have been established among the three characters through the use of parallelism
during the three introductory sequences. Each man is hidden the first time we
see him: Mortimer, by a Bible; Manco, by having his back turned; and, Indio, by
his hat. Our first good look at each character comes in succeeding shots when he
looks out from under a wide-brim hat. In each sequence there is a betrayal: The
bartender gives away Calloway's hiding place; the sheriff points out Cavanaugh;
Indio kills his cell mate. A killing occurs in each sequence, and each ends with a
brief conversation between the key character and an officer of the law.

This study in parallel structure—already more studied and baroque than
the emphasis on triangles in *A Fistful of Dollars*—prepares us for an approach to
character relationships that we already anticipate from having seen the obsessive
trisections of the earlier film. But notions of good and bad are less clearly defined in *For a Few Dollars More*, and the characters who form the other two
points of the triangle—against Manco—are less classifiable than are the Baxters
and the Rojos. They're more alive, too, and capable of anything.

After that remarkable poster montage, Leone returns unexpectedly to
Indio. Indio and his gang have come back to the abandoned church outside El

Paso where they make their hideout. There, Indio confronts the man he believes betrayed him and got him sent to prison. This man has a wife and child, in whom Indio shows great interest:

Indio: How old is the boy?
Reply: Eighteen months.
Indio: Just the time I was in jail. You used the reward money to start raising a family—and that's why I feel your family is partly mine. I'll take my part now—outside.

At Indio's instructions, the man's wife and son are taken out and summarily shot. Typical of his inclination to overdo things, Indio has them killed partly for revenge but chiefly to bait the betrayer into facing him in a showdown. He gives the man a pistol and opens the locket-watch, which begins playing the little chime tune that underscored the raid on the prison. "When you hear the music finish, begin," Indio says; and after Leone's first great moment-of-truth montage, shown as we hear Ennio Morricone's fatalistic organ and trumpet tune—known variously as "La Resa dei Conti" ("the rendering of accounts"), "Sixty Seconds to What?," and, in a song version not used in the American release of the film, "An Eye for an Eye"—the hapless family man draws and is shot dead.

"Now ..." says Indio, impatiently, holding out a hand and gesturing. One of his men hands him a joint of marijuana; Indio takes a deep pull on it. To say that Indio is unattractive is to give him the benefit of the doubt. Loathsome comes closer to the truth; yet—thanks partly to the splendid acting of Gian Maria Volontè—by the end of the film we will see this tortured, unredeemed soul as Leone's most developed and *understood* villain (even including Henry Fonda's Frank in *Once Upon a Time in the West*).

Indio *is* the villain, of course. If we didn't know it before, we do once he's killed a child. Leone's bad guys are always destroyers of the innocent. But Indio is a lot harder to get a fix on than Ramón Rojo. Late in the film he has one of his men, Niño, steal the knife of another gang member, Cucillo, and with it kill yet another henchman, Slim, who is guarding the prisoners, Manco and Mortimer. This, without his taking responsibility for it, is all part of a plan to allow the two bounty killers to escape. Once the deed is done, Cucillo is brought before the dead body of Slim and the glowering Indio.

Cucillo: Who did it?
Indio: Look at the knife.
Cucillo: It's mine!
Indio: And it shouldn't be there, should it?

Without another word, Indio flicks open the locket-watch. Cucillo knows what this means. Stammeringly, he denies killing Slim, though he speaks only halfheartedly because, in any case, he is guilty of allowing his weapon to be taken from him. Indio, though treacherous, is a stern military leader, and Cucillo has committed an unpardonable offense; besides, once the locket is open, there's no recourse. "One of the horses is outside," Indio tells Cucillo. "Let's see if you can make it." He doesn't.

Although Indio is a hard taskmaster, he is also a leader without a plan. Throughout the second half of the film he kaleidoscopically changes his strategy—and with it, all plot logic—depending on whom he's talking to; his increasingly oblivious reveries make it finally apparent that he has no plan at all, except to hurtle himself toward his own destruction. (In a sense, Indio's fatalism and his murderous obsession are reflected on a grand scale by Leone's whole approach to filmmaking.)

Indio is not only a violator of family but a sadist in the mold of Estéban Rojo. He takes delight in the one-sided gun "duels" he sets up with hopelessly outmatched opponents, and also in the ritual beating he has his men administer to Manco and Mortimer when they are caught trying to flee Agua Caliente. Another particularly sadistic pastime of Indio's is killing bugs—an activity a lot of Leone characters participate in. (When Manco comes to spring Indio's man Sancho Perez from prison, using this act as the peace offering which will allow him to join Indio's gang, there is a beetle of some sort on the dozing Perez's face. Sancho picks it off and squashes it with relish as Manco appears at his cell window to plant a dynamite stick; Perez's eyes widen as Manco lights the stick with his cheroot.) Indio toys with a cockroach as he and his last loyal man, Groggy, wait out the gunfight in Agua Caliente. Indio hopes the fight will wipe out the bounty killers and the gang with whom he was to split the loot from the El Paso bank robbery. A few shots later, the cockroach tries to walk with half its body mashed. Indio watches the process intently—perhaps even empathetically. And he takes out the watch.

"That watch—" says Groggy. "It's been a long time that I wanted to ask. I can see that it means a lot to you, Indio. Why?" Why, indeed? It is at this point that the film goes into its last flashback—and it is Indio who is haunted by the flashbacks; a shot of him precedes each one. This reversal sets *For a Few Dollars More* apart from the other "flashback films" (*Once Upon a Time in the West* and *Duck, You Sucker!*), in which it is the *good* (well, more or less good) guys who are tormented by memories.

A little at a time, the flashbacks in *For a Few Dollars More* establish Indio's background. A younger Indio had come upon a young woman and man in bed together. Indio killed the man and proceeded to rape the woman when, in the midst of the act, she had taken Indio's pistol and killed herself. The locket-watch Indio took from her obsesses him, though it's never clear why this episode should have affected him so strongly. A thousand equally ugly things must have happened during his vicious life. Yet this event was, apparently, a significant defeat for Indio. Certainly, for a rapist, the suicide of his victim must constitute a particularly deflating humiliation—the ultimate sexual rejection, one might say. But the young woman's suicide is as much a response to the killing of her lover as it is an embrace of death rather than face rape. In this, it is emblematic of a kind of love that Indio can never feel.

Following this incident, killing becomes the central sexual act of Indio's life. He is, metaphorically if not literally, impotent, and compensates for his impotence in the obsessive way he kills people when the chimes of the dead woman's locket stop playing. Indio's guilt and humiliation are worked out violently, in a symbolic repetition of the traumatic event.

Given Leone's penchant for triads, it's hard not to relate Indio to Calloway and Cavanaugh, the other two marks of bounty killers Mortimer and Manco. Both of these targets are presented in terms of juvenilia: Calloway's crude zeros marked onto the "Wanted" poster; his gawky, adolescent appearance, which Leone takes the trouble to impress on us in closeup; and, Cavanaugh's nickname, "Baby," as well as his petulance at losing a game of cards (albeit admittedly a crucial one). All this cues us to regard Indio, even before we meet him, as third in a series of juveniles. And, as the film progresses, we recognize Indio as a case of arrested emotional development—his fixation on sexual failure pressing most of his personality into torpor and leaving violent action as his only form of personal expression.

It is possible that Indio genuinely loved the woman he attacked during the locket incident, or believed he could. The encounter with her could have taken place before Indio became a crazed criminal, could even have been the cause of it. Did Indio love the woman, find her with another man, in a rage kill the man, and then force himself on the woman, only to have her kill herself from the agony of the encounter? The flashbacks don't want to tell us this much, but a little speculation is not a bad thing if it sheds any light at all on our perception of the film and its characters.

Indio is certainly the villainous sadist of the film; for him people and bugs are all one. In *For a Few Dollars More*, however, there is cruelty throughout—much more so than in *A Fistful of Dollars*, which seems restrained by comparison. Manco doesn't hesitate to wipe out three of Indio's men in order to save himself a little time getting back to El Paso from the decoy bank job Indio's sent them out on—he even seems to relish the act. And even Colonel Mortimer, who is an unknown quantity for much of the film, acts in a gratuitously cruel way when he baits Wild, the hunchback—the most memorable member of Indio's gang, played in a hissingly alive performance by Klaus Kinski.

Wild is the fourth most important character in the film, if only because of his visibility and his pivotal importance in turning the plot. Wild's first encounter with Mortimer tips the two bounty killers to the fact that Indio's men are up to something, and his second encounter precipitates Indio's fate-filled query to Mortimer: "Who are you?"

Wild's physical deformity in a sense balances Indio's spiritual one, and it is no accident that Mortimer should choose Wild as the temporary victim of his wrath until the time is right for him to face his real nemesis. There's a haunting kind of black humor in the relationship between Mortimer and Wild that captures in miniature some of the key motifs of the film—sadism, hatred, revenge, justice, deformity, smoke, guns, and, as always, death.

The two encounters between Mortimer and Wild are explicit and well developed. They are examples of an extensive pattern that show Leone gunfighters insulting menials and minor functionaries—a tradition, by the way, that is observable in many films of the oddly class-conscious "Spaghetti Western" genre.

In *For a Few Dollars More*, the pattern is clearly established in the introductory sequences: Mortimer gets the better of the train conductor, the station man, and the bartender; Manco humiliates the town's corrupt sheriff; Indio torments and ridicules the prison guard.

In the scene with Wild, four of Indio's men are in the saloon. Manco is there, too, having been told by Fernando, his hired boy, that some strangers have come into the bar. Mortimer comes downstairs from his hotel room and surveys the gathering. He walks to the bar, takes out his pipe, and ostentatiously strikes a match across Wild's hump. The hunchback whirls as Mortimer calmly sets the match to his pipe. Wild blows it out. The room is hushed. Mortimer takes the cigar out of Wild's mouth and uses it to light his pipe. Wild's hand creeps toward his pistol, but is stayed by another member of Indio's gang. The humpback's cheek twitches spasmodically with barely controlled rage—an archetypal Klaus Kinski moment. Mortimer, his pipe lit, offers the cigar to Wild, who turns and leaves the saloon. Undaunted, Mortimer offers the cigar to another of Indio's men.

"You're a lucky man, mister," the bartender tells Mortimer, to which Mortimer asks, "Why should a man walk around with a pistol on his belt and let himself be insulted?" Here is the code of Leone's movie West in its simplest form—the gun as arbiter and equalizer, insurance against humiliation, adjudicator of the simplest dispute. Arising from the American Western myth, first in dime novels, later in movies and television, this gun-centered ethic is elemental to the Italian Western genre, and is the "given" framework in which Leone plots his more detailed and ambiguous system of honor.

"If the hunchback didn't shoot you," replies the barman, "he had a very, very important reason." Mortimer replies, satisfied, "That's what I was thinking." And it is from this episode that both Manco and Mortimer cotton to Indio's plan. The barman's emphatic use of "very, very" is repeated much later during Mortimer's next encounter with Wild in a dingy little cantina in Agua Caliente. Mortimer sits eating from a bowl, while Wild and others stand at the bar, their backs to him. But when Mortimer says something, Wild's eyes widen, he turns to look at the bounty killer (one of the many little illogicalities in Leone's plotting, for as far as we know, Wild has never heard Mortimer's voice before and so would not be able to recognize it). "Wellll ..." says Wild, sounding like Bugs Bunny with bronchial asthma, "if it isn't the smoker." He saunters over. "Remember me?" Mortimer, with only a cursory glance, says "No." Wild prods his memory: "El Paso." Mortimer looks again. "It's a small world." Wild hisses a key line: "Yes—and very, very bad." He proffers his hump: "Now you light another match."

The fun isn't over. Mortimer coolly replies, "I generally smoke just after I eat. Why don't you come back in ten minutes?" Bested again, Wild straightens and steps back. "In ten minutes you'll be smoking in hell! Get up!" Mortimer rises; Indio prevents his men from intervening. Wild draws, and Mortimer shoots him dead. Indio looks at the bounty killer, and the little chime theme is heard. "Who are you?" he asks.

Who, indeed? From the old man called "Prophet," who lives in torment amid the noise, steam, smoke, and quaking of the nearby railroad, Manco learns: "He's Mortimer. Colonel Douglas Mortimer. He was known as the best shot in the Carolinas—a great soldier. Now he's reduced to being a bounty killer, same as you." This capsule biography tells everything and nothing. From having seen Leone's emphatic intercutting of Indio's face on the poster with Mortimer's eyes, we're tempted to imagine there's something more to their relationship than hunter and hunted.

Mortimer tracks Indio just as a bounty killer would. He knows his quarry well, and presents himself at a bank as a prospective depositor in order to find out the safest place to secure a large amount of money. "In your case, I would suggest the Bank of El Paso," the banker tells him. "Not even Indio would attempt that one." This information persuades Mortimer that the Bank of El Paso is precisely the one Indio will strike (another plot flaw, since it is not the bank's fabled impregnability that attracts Indio to it, but the fact that he had been imprisoned with the man who know the bank's secret). Another bank officer assures Mortimer of the security at the bank. "Only a complete fool would attempt it," the banker says, and Mortimer replies, "Yeah—or a complete madman."

Mortimer's interest in Indio has begun to look like more than a business venture. It's become something like an obsession, in fact, and we wonder how Mortimer comes by so much knowledge of Indio's character. When the Man in Black proposes a partnership to "the Man with No Name," the former says he has three reasons for doing so: "First reason—there's fourteen of them, no small number even for the two of us. Second reason—you could make it fifteen to one. Don't forget I want to play this game too." The Man in Black never lists his third reason, but by the end of the film we learn he has one—the most important of all in the cosmos of the Italian Western (and indeed, perhaps the Italian literary tradition altogether): revenge.

Mortimer proposes a deal. He'll keep the reward money for killing Indio and let Manco take the bounties on all the others. Much later, in Agua Caliente, before they begin their gundown with Indio's gang, Mortimer pointedly says, "Leave Indio to me." Manco, too, has come to understand that there is more to Mortimer's quest than bounty, and he says, "All right."

Another link between Mortimer and Indio: they both have a past, which Manco—unlike No Name in *A Fistful of Dollars*—does not. "Were you ever young?" Manco asks Mortimer as they seal their partnership with a drink. "Yes," says Mortimer, "but then something happened that made life very precious to me." "What was that?" asks Manco, "—or is the question indiscreet?" "The question isn't," allows Mortimer, "but the answer could be." He looks at his watch. The chime theme has entered during this exchange, though not from the unopened watch Mortimer holds. The music swells and bridges a cut to Indio with his joint. Then, as layer upon layer of chimes in different keys create an eerie, discordant sound, we drift into the first flashback. The flashback is Indio's. But through this use of cutting and music, it is strangely "shared" by both men and presages the revelation that comes at the end of the film.

Mortimer lays out his arsenal in preparation for the day when Indio will rob the Bank of El Paso. He checks the clock against his locket-watch. Here we become aware that not only Indio and Mortimer are united with the image of the watch (time past as memory, time future as destiny)—the two men's lockets are linked, too: they are identical. We recognize them as the lockets of the flashback, and assume that the woman whose picture is in the cameo is the suicide beneath Indio.

Despite Clint Eastwood's top billing, Manco—or the "Man with No Name"—is the least important of the three principals in *For a Few Dollars More*. Both Mortimer and Indio appear to be in pursuit of something that transcends the mere monetary recompense of the successful thief and bounty killer, but Manco never seems interested in anything but the game and the money. At one point an odd motivation is ascribed to him: "When I get my hands on Indio and that ten thousand dollars, I'm gonna buy myself a little place—possibly retire." The No Name mythos that has been built up through *A Fistful of Dollars*, and the ad campaign built around it and this sequel, make No Name's line grate on the ears the way fingernails on the blackboard will do. Who does he think he's kidding?

The Man with No Name becomes something of an attendant lord in *For a Few Dollars More*, like those television lead characters who, after two or three outings, are fated to become observers and minor participants in their weekly episodes, never the heroes or the center of focus. Clint Eastwood is back to playing Rowdy Yates here, with Van Cleef and Volontè as guest hero and guest villain.

As in *A Fistful of Dollars*, a sexual subtext is established that associates the Man with "normal," heterosexual machismo. Like all of Leone's wandering loners, though, he never has the opportunity or the inclination to perform. Here, the focus of his heterosexuality lies in the reaction of Mary, the hotel landlady, and not in anything Manco does himself. She is introduced when the boy Fernando directs Manco to one of the town's two hotels, adding the information, "This one has a landlady!" "Married?" asks Manco. "Yes—but she doesn't care!" sings the boy.

At the desk, Manco is told the hotel is full. Unfazed, he paces evenly upstairs to the front upper room he wants and persuades its occupant that he was just leaving. Manco's quiet confidence and strength attract Mary, an overheated, fleshy, working-class woman whose fantasy is only fueled by her foppish husband's insistence that men like Manco are animals. To Mary's apparent delight, Manco appears on the stairs and tosses the departing Senor Martinez a pair of long-johns. "I don't wear 'em," he says. The landlady is beside herself though her husband scolds, "You're just dirty!"

This comic sequence is echoed by a reversal later on. Having freed Sancho Perez from prison and brought him to Indio as a sign of good faith, Manco is ready to infiltrate Indio's gang. He learns of the planned decoy robbery, but he doesn't know the details of the attack on the Bank of El Paso. Indio assigns Manco to participate in the decoy job at Santa Cruz. Manco abruptly walks out of the abandoned church where Indio's gang is still holed up. "Where are you going?" asks Indio. Manco replies, "If there's going to be any shooting, I have to get my rest." He goes outside with his saddlebags. As in *A Fistful of Dollars*, he doesn't find it all that appealing to sleep in a room full of men.

Manco's character takes on meaning only in interaction with others. His uneasy partnership with Mortimer is more a nominal recapitulation of the "servant of two masters" idea from *A Fistful of Dollars* than a relationship that has value to him. In fact, contrary to the expectations built up by the introductory sequences, Mortimer is a man of honor, while Manco is one purely of opportunity. Manco persists in working alone, and it is he who, several times, tries to double-cross Mortimer; never does Mortimer try to do the same to him. Mortimer recognizes Manco's lack of integrity and cautions him: "When two hunters go after the same prey, they usually end up shooting each other in the back, and we don't want to shoot each other in the back." (Delightfully for the viewer, Mortimer doesn't recognize the physical impossibility of such an occurrence.)

The semicomic rivalry between Manco and Mortimer provides some of the film's most stylish sequences. Checked into hotels that face each other across the main street of El Paso, they follow the movements of Indio's men as they map out their timing for the bank job. Mortimer has an elegant spyglass, Manco a homey pair of binoculars. Mortimer sweeps the hotel across the street with his glass, stopping suddenly at center-screen, looking right into the camera. Cut to Manco, opposite, in a telescope's mask, also looking straight center. This telescopic meeting of their eyes recalls the symbolic meeting of eyes between Mortimer and Indio-on-the-poster. The shot also signals the impending collision between the two. But all the while the comic tone assures us that things aren't as serious between these two men as they are between Mortimer and Indio.

The Chinese bellhop enters Mortimer's room and silently packs the man's satchel for him, then goes out with it. Mortimer, curious, follows the bellhop downstairs and finds Manco in the street. Manco tells the bellhop to take Mortimer's bag to the station. Mortimer tells the bellhop to put the bag back in the hotel room. "The station," says Manco. "The hotel," says Mortimer. The only victim of this psychological warfare is the bellhop himself, who—in an instance of ethnic humor rare in Leone—becomes the stereotypical subservient Chinaman, throwing his hands in the air, dropping the bag, and running back into the hotel, moaning.

Manco steps on Mortimer's shiny boot. Mortimer reciprocates. Manco boldly punches Mortimer, knocking him down. Mortimer gets up and reaches for his hat, but, as he does, Manco shoots it away from his grasp. Mortimer goes for the hat again; Manco shoots it again. This incident is repeated until Manco has to reload. Mortimer then gets his hat back on and stands spread-legged in the street. Manco fires several shots that pit the dirt between Mortimer's feet. Finally, Mortimer draws his cannon-like pistol and shoots Manco's hat off his head. He shoots it again and again in midair, each time changing its trajectory, finally letting it fall to earth with a long, dying whistle and a distant thud. Cut to the hats side-by-side in Mortimer's hotel room as a drink is poured and a partnership is offered.

The hat-shooting sequence establishes a mutual respect between the two bounty killers; but it also establishes several other things. A difference of style separates Mortimer from Manco. The man from Carolina is elegant and tasteful as well as witty, while the Man with No Name is blunt, direct, and physical. Of equal importance is the fact that Mortimer is a better shot than Manco and that he kills only outlaws. Presumably that is true of Manco, as well, for neither of them ever attempts to kill the other. Even when Mortimer shoots Manco a grazing wound in the neck (so it won't seem suspicious that Manco alone survived the Santa Cruz decoy bank job unscathed) Manco doesn't instinctively return his fire. And, considering the context in which the shooting occurred, the viewer might have expected that. Manco tells Mortimer that the partnership is dissolved, and Mortimer says, "In that case ..." and draws, shooting Manco's neck. Manco, far from feeling threatened or outraged at this, is only puzzled. "That's not bad," says Mortimer, and then he explains himself.

The rivalry between the two marksmen is again taken up—and again to Manco's disadvantage—in Agua Caliente. Indio tests Manco by having him ride alone into the ill-famed hole of a village. Threatened by the appearance of armed locals at the end of the street, Manco avoids a shootout by demonstrating his skill: A boy is trying to knock apples off a tree. Manco fires his pistol to knock first one and then another apple off the tree. Apples fall all around the delighted boy. The sound of a new pistol enters, and more apples fall. On the veranda behind Manco stands Mortimer, whom Manco thought he'd double-crossed and sent off in the wrong direction. Mortimer's sharpshooting display puts the threatening villagers to flight and fills the little boy's serape with windfall. "Bravo," mutters Manco, quietly, unenthusiastically. He'll say "Bravo" again at the end of the film when Mortimer puts an amen to his life's mission by killing Indio.

Manco's relationship with Indio is attended by a sense of destiny and by a lack of logic. In the old church, when Manco brings the rescued Sancho Perez to Indio as a peace offering, Indio asks Sancho, "Why did he help you out?" Sancho, puzzled, as if he'd just thought of the matter for the first time, asks Manco, "Why did you help me?" The bounty killer replies, "Since there's such a big reward being offered on all you gentlemen, I thought I'd tag along on the next robbery—might just turn you in to the law." There is a stunned silence, broken by a gun report when Blackie shoots the tip off Manco's lighted cheroot. Manco coolly relights the stub, Indio signals Blackie not to shoot again, then tells Manco, "That is the one answer that would have proved you all right." Laughter.

Much later, when Manco attempts to escape from Agua Caliente with the loot from the bank robbery hidden in his saddlebags, he is caught. As he climbs off the roof, his foot hits Indio's shoulder, and he has just enough time, as Indio and Niño pull him down, to toss the saddlebags into a tree. Indio tells Manco, "You should never have shot the apples off that tree." (It's a clever line at this point, since it contrasts shooting something off a tree with adding something to a tree, which Manco has just surreptitiously done.) Indio produces Manco's wrist protector, saying, "Put it on." Presumably the apple-shooting incident and the familiar leather strap are the means by which Manco's cover has been blown.

Indeed, the "put it on" implies an equation between the strap and Manco's identity, which the bounty killer acknowledges and reassumes by putting his fist through the strap. Leone cuts to a fist beating Manco. A few moments later, Indio asks Niño, "How long have you known that Manco is a bounty killer?" Niño, puzzled, says, "I found out tonight, why?" "I knew it," says Indio smugly, "from the first moment he arrived." This adds to the sense of commingled destiny that ties Indio to both bounty killers. In retrospect, Indio's failure to expose and kill Manco earlier gives even more weight to the notion that he is essentially self-destructive, half in love with the idea of his own deliverance from life at the hands of such as Manco and Mortimer.

The money, unnoticed, stays in the tree until the end of the film, when Manco hauls it out and rides on his way. Money is considerably mere important in *For a Few Dollars More* than it was in *A Fistful of Dollars*, where it served only a nominal motivation, never a real greed. Here, Manco seems genuinely interested in the money and in how much he can get. When Mortimer offers to split the bounty with him—Indio's for Mortimer and everyone else's for Manco—Manco still questions the deal; he adds it all up before he agrees. "Death, sometimes, had its price," we recall. In a world where bullet holes are compared with the zeros that make the difference between hundreds and tens of thousands, men's lives are measured in dollars.

When Manco and Mortimer transfer the bank money from the strongbox to the saddlebags that end up in the tree, Mortimer indulges himself in a sardonic witticism. He places Indio's "Wanted" poster in the cashbox (Indio, to the bounty killers, is the equivalent of money). Later, after Indio has engineered the escape of the two bounty killers and sent his gang after them, confident that everyone will be killed, Groggy returns. Groggy kills Niño and makes Indio open the cashbox (unlike Indio, Groggy has a plan). The poster laughs at Indio—his *own* laugh. And then, so does Groggy. But Indio doesn't take offense; he's too concerned about the money. Together Groggy and Indio search for it, and this sequence is intercut with Manco's and Mortimer's methodic tracking down and shooting down of Indio's men in the streets of Agua Caliente. Lives and money are equated—and nowhere more so than in the denouement when Manco is counting up the collected bodies in terms of dollars. "Ten thousand," he says, "twelve thousand, fifteen, seventeen, twenty-two ... twenty-two ..." He hesitates, looking around. Groggy, not quite dead, rises up from his hiding place and aims his pistol at Manco. Manco fires, Groggy drops, and Manco says, "Twenty-seven!" Mortimer hears the shot and calls, "Any trouble, boy?" Manco replies, "No, old man; thought I was havin' trouble with my adding. It's all right now." (One recalls Donald Richie's reference to the satirical tone of Sanjuro's "matter-of-fact accounting" and No Name's "My mistake—four coffins" in *A Fistful of Dollars*.) Manco, of course, is counting money and bodies simultaneously, and, as he rides out of town in the final sequence, that is what his cargo is: money (the saddlebags he retrieves from the tree) and bodies (which are worth more money).

Like *Sanjuro*, *For a Few Dollars More* is a "sequel" that is showier and more baroque than its predecessor. People tend to twirl their guns a lot before putting them back in their holsters. Also like *Sanjuro*, *For a Few Dollars More* is process-oriented, in a sense a merger of the Spaghetti Western with the caper film. *Sanjuro* replaces the dust and desolation of *Yojimbo*'s tatty village with the lush vegetation of a wealthy fortress city, and the criminal families' rivalry with palace intrigue. *For a Few Dollars More* doesn't go that far—in fact, Agua Caliente is at least as godforsaken a place as San Miguel—but there is less emphasis on dust and the earth, and more on architectural structures and spatial relationships. Consistent, even ornate, patterns of imagery establish themselves. The film, for example, is filled with scenes shot through barred windows and doors: Indio's prison; Mortimer's visit to the vaults of two different banks; Manco's raid on Alamogordo Prison to rescue Sancho Perez; the bank guard's munching a sandwich behind protective bars while Indio blows a hole in the wall of the Bank of El Paso; the bars in the storehouse in Agua Caliente where Indio hides the strongbox. "Me on the outside, you on the inside," Mortimer says of the way in which he and Manco will crack Indio's gang; the film is filled with this inside-outside imagery, the structural opposite of *A Fistful of Dollars*'s "me right in the middle." Manco and Mortimer take the outside ends, leaving Indio the man in the middle. The frequent imagery of bars makes a prison out of the inside—makes a prison, in fact, of the world, the prison that each man's obsession creates for him.

Even more ornamental is the incidental imagery of smoking: Manco's cheroots, Mortimer's Meerschaum, Indio's marijuana—what and how a man smokes characterizes him in the film. Even the hapless Wild affected a small but narratively crucial cigar.

The death imagery from *A Fistful of Dollars* is also restated: With remarkable prescience, Indio says of Agua Caliente, "It looks just like a morgue ... and it could be one so easily." But the most obvious image pattern in the film is its use of the trappings of Christianity. Mortimer's Bible, Indio's empty church and his "little parable," and the Man with No Name's punning soubriquet "Manco" all recall the Italian Western tradition of the gunfighter-cleric.

This imagery is strongest in the sermon sequence. At the beginning of the film, when Colonel Mortimer stops the train to disembark at Tucumcari a gratuitous shot of the engine's bell established an image that is echoed in the beginning of the church scene: Groggy rides up, and his men announce their arrival by taking potshots at the bell of the old church that is Indio's headquarters. The image recurs when Leone cuts to the interior: one man is shooting the points off another man's spurs. Indio calms the mob. He explains his plan by relating that he doesn't like wasted time, that the presence of a safe doesn't mean there is money inside it. "To help you understand what I mean," he says, "I would like to relate a nice little parable." Indio mounts the pulpit and begins his parable in fairy-tale style: "Once upon a time, there was a carpenter." Indio reveals that the carpenter had been hired by the bank to make a cabinet that would house a safe, disguising the safe to look like an innocent piece of furniture. One day the man happened, by accident, to see the cabinet he had designed sitting against the wall in the Bank of El Paso. "From that day on, he couldn't work anymore; there was something he had to do—this crazy idea ..." Indio presses his fingers to his temple to illustrate the notion of an idea that won't go away—an obsession (something Indio understands at least as well as the carpenter). "Later, in prison, he told me the story, and I tell it to you now." Indio's sermon, besides establishing the basis for the "caper" portion of the plot, emphatically enhances the characteristically Leonean tone of parable and the quasi-scriptural use of language.

The abandoned church, the Bible supplanted by Van Cleef's iconically villainous visage, Mortimer's rejection of the train conductor's evocation of "the rules," Manco's tossing the sheriff's badge into the dirt—all are images of the absence of law and order, or moral authority, in Leone's West. The sheriff whom Manco exposes is reminiscent of John Baxter in *A Fistful of Dollars*. The scene looks ahead to the sheriff in *Once Upon a Time in the West*: the first sheriff is one of the bad guys; the second just can't do anything about the bad guys. The ineffectuality, and the displacement, of law and order in Leone's West is what gives rise to his illusion-shattering antiheroes, who, for better or worse, impose some kind of order on the chaos around them. Again, Kurosawa provides a useful referent: Richie describes Sanjuro as "a man who cares nothing for codes"; indeed, both *Yojimbo* and *Sanjuro* present a studied contrast of the chivalric code with Kurosawa's "life as it is."

Little in *For a Few Dollars More* gives us a sense of life as it is really lived, of a normal quotidian reality. But that is because Leone is a cinematic primitive who is not concerned with placing events in a "real" context—social, historical, or otherwise. His stories are like fairy tales or parables, and the more divorced they are from a recognizable context, the more effectively they support the myth-making.

As in *A Fistful of Dollars*, Leone's myth-making approach to shot and montage deliberately eschews the establishment of any clear geographical context. Spatial relationships remain within the scene and rarely extend from one sequence to another. The contempt for geographic realism is reflected in the ruse that Mortimer pulls on Manco—the first bold demonstration by Leone of his utter disregard for the restrictions of movement in space, as well as for logic.

Manco wonders how Mortimer managed to turn up in Agua Caliente ahead of him and Indio's gang. "Easy," says Mortimer: "When I told you to tell Indio to go north, I knew you'd tell him just the opposite, and he, being suspicious, would go a different direction altogether. Since back to El Paso was out of the question, here I am." Leone's characters here begin to demonstrate that almost supernatural power over space that attends their comings and goings in his later films.

Geometry begins to play an important part in Leone's work in *For a Few Dollars More*. The movie becomes an extension of the crisscrossings of character, movements, and relationships in *A Fistful of Dollars*. Just as No Name bypassed the Rojos on his way back into San Miguel after setting up the fake scene in the graveyard, so, in this film, Manco bypasses the posse roaring out of El Paso to answer the call for help from Santa Cruz—the message that Manco has managed to send without actually having pulled off the decoy bank robbery as planned. Later, when Manco gets into El Paso and watches the operation with Mortimer, there are two stressed shots that reveal their dismay and bewilderment

upon seeing Indio blow the back wall out of the bank. The reason for these ex-
pressions is their realization that, in watching the plotting-out of the job by Indio's gang, they have been consistently watching the wrong side of the bank!
(This is unclear in "scanned" prints of the film.)

So space retains a certain amount of controlling power—but only when
Leone wants it to. More often, incidental geometric detail is used to define and
extend character relationships. Nowhere is this approach more apparent than
during the shot of the stone circle at the climax of the film. (The structure must
have been there all along, in terms of the geography of Agua Caliente, but it is
seen only when Leone needs it to be seen.) It's an amplification of the circular
locket-watch, in addition to its being an arena in which the final ritual combat
must occur. Also, the stone circle is a neat geometric shape in which to inscribe
the triangle of principal characters.

Once the circle is reached, once the minor matters of supporting players
and plot contrivances are out of the way, mythic order holds sway. Mortimer
calls Indio out, and for the first time identifies himself by his real name. Indio
gets the drop on Mortimer by sending Groggy out first; Mortimer shoots
Groggy, and Indio shoots the gun out of Mortimer's hand. Indio takes out his
locket-watch and snaps it open: "When the chimes end, pick up your gun. Try
and shoot me, Colonel—just try." The chimes, almost inaudible, are suddenly
interrupted by a second, faster chiming. Manco appears. He sits on the circumference of the circle, holding an identical locket. Mortimer checks his pocket
and finds a broken watch-chain. "Very careless of you, old man," says Manco,
reveling in his brief moment of importance as the mediator who will rebalance
the odds in this uneven gundown. Leaving Mortimer's gun on the ground, he
says, "Try this." He gives Mortimer his own gunbelt, the act reminding the
viewer that the two bounty killers had compared weapons systems earlier and
that Manco had wondered at the odd way Mortimer wore his pistol tucked inside
his pants.

"Now we start," says Manco, and he opens the locket for the final count-
down. Indio and Mortimer finally face each other on even terms. After an extended pre-gunfight montage in the best Leone-Morricone manner comes the
draw, and Indio is downed with one shot. He raises his pistol to shoot Mortimer
(who waits, more the gentleman duelist than the amoral bounty killer), but rolls
over dead instead. Manco delivers a mirthless "Bravo." Mortimer steps on the
dead Indio's wrist and pulls the watch from his hand.

"There seems to be a family resemblance," says Manco, looking at the picture in the locket. He's already surmised the truth. "Between brother and sister,"
says Mortimer: "Of course." And we finally have Mortimer's motivation and his
story. The revenge motive anticipates the even more elaborate flashback fabric
to be woven around the Man with the Harmonica in *Once Upon a Time in the
West*; indeed, tapping the B-Western, the Italian Western, and operatic conventions, revenge is a primary motivation in all of Leone's films, whether it be
treated with cosmic importance—as with Mortimer and the Man with the Harmonica—or simply in terms of "getting even"—as with No Name's shifting

Manco (Clint Eastwood, above and below center) officiates over the final reckoning between Col. Mortimer (Lee Van Cleef, left) and Indio (Gian Maria Volontè) in the climax of *For a Few Dollars More.*

loyalties in *A Fistful of Dollars* and with the deadly games of one-upmanship that thread through *The Good, the Bad and the Ugly*.

But this revenge impulse is sharply distinguished from the sadism that characterizes Indio and, in a lighter way, Tuco in *The Good, the Bad and the Ugly*. Mortimer's revenge has no truck with torture. There is no slow, unequal, cruel death for the avenger to delight in. For Mortimer, revenge in a quick-draw showdown brings with it not the thrill of seeing the nemesis laid low but the loftier satisfaction of demonstrating superiority to him, meting out justice. It's the highest act of faith in the Law of the Gun: Moral superiority will mean physical superiority in the draw and the aim. God will be on the side of the just. That Bible wasn't just part of the disguise.

For a Few Dollars More is a meditation on revenge: If Mortimer spends the film trying to get even with Indio (and passing up several chances, waiting for the time to be right), it's also true that Indio spends the film trying to get even with *himself*. He compulsively gives each of his victims a chance—however slim—as if he is waiting, perhaps even hoping, for the one who will be good enough to kill him.

For a Few Dollars More is also a film about obsession: Indio's with death, Mortimer's with revenge, and Manco's with money. Each of them ends up getting what he lusts for. In the end, Mortimer gives Manco all the money, though they'd earlier bargained for a split. "You deserve it," says the Colonel—after all, Manco's intervention as referee has saved his life. "But what about our partnership?" asks the naive Manco—a little ironically, since he several times tried to break that partnership. Mortimer fingers his ear in a gesture that spookily recalls Indio's fingers-to-his-temple move in the "parable" scene. "Maybe next time," says Mortimer (leaving open the possibility of a sequel to the film, of course—though the characters played by Eastwood and Van Cleef turn out quite differently in *The Good, the Bad and the Ugly*).

Mortimer rides off—a slow, limping ride like Ethan Edwards's walk away from the camera at the end of *The Searchers*. He now has both locket-watches and is accompanied by the "gundown" musical theme associated with Indio throughout the film. Mortimer—whose very name connotes death in Leone's language and our own—seems almost to have inherited Indio's burden of guilt. By accepting the use of Manco's pistol in obtaining his revenge, he's also made a change in his approach.

What has he actually received from each man? What has he gained? And where does he go now?

"Two Kinds of People in the World"

The Good, the Bad and the Ugly

The Good, the Bad and the Ugly opens on a landscape. No matter that the film was shot in Spain—it's the American Southwest, on the film's terms, and the scene is breathtaking, the kind of landscape into which the great wanderers of the cinematic West always ride. But not this time.

No distant rider appears. Instead, a derelict gunfighter takes over the screen in extreme closeup. The grotesque face acts like a wipe, sweeping away the landscape with a drunken movement from lower screen-left; the gunfighter stands looking, slightly swaying, trying to focus his eyes. With no recourse to the middle ground, what we took to be a long shot has abruptly turned into a closeup. (There's a reason for Leone's emphasis on that face that wipes out a whole environment, but it won't be discovered for nearly two hours of screen time.)

A coyote howls, its yip-yip-yip recalling the five-note human howl of the just-finished main title music. A reverse angle shows us a new landscape, one quite different from the one that opened the film—a windswept nothing of a ghost town, a broken wagon, a pile of junk, a few claptrap sheds and one run-down building. A coyote—or perhaps just a scroungy dog—emerges from the rubble at screen right and passes all the way across the shot to snuffle into the desolate cluster of dustblown frontier architecture at the left. Then—and only then—as it continues to be held, do we begin to realize what the shot is all about: Two riders, at the far end of the "town," move toward the camera and toward the bleary-eyed, scar-faced, pockmarked watcher in the wind.

Leone intercuts the watcher's face with the arrival of the horsemen—indulging himself in one of his characteristic illogical cuts from long shot to extreme closeup to show us the newcomers' faces, which are less battered, but just as sinister, as the face of the man who waits for them. The riders dismount. They begin to walk toward the watcher, stealing an occasional pregnant glance at each other. The man now begins to walk toward them.

Leone intercuts midshots with long shots to establish the characters' lines of movements and their relentless approach to one another. By starting the film with a gunfight, he's committing another iconoclastic violation of the language of the Western. This kind of suspense and pacing belongs at the end, when it's been earned. You don't throw this stuff at your audience right off the bat—unless you're Sergio Leone.

The solitary man meets the duo in the middle, just in front of the rattrap of a building that dominates the desolation. He looks at them, they look at him. He opens his coat and pulls it back, gaining quick access to his pistol. Hands are ready—open. Eyes are sharp. Muscles are poised. Then, in one movement, the men draw their pistols and all three dive, *together*, into the ramshackle building.

Shots blast out in fast succession. Cries are heard—and the crash of shattering glass. As we hear what's going on inside the building, Leone pulls back to show us the outside. Through the window comes a sight even scroungier than the one of the three men we just left—a sneering, putty-faced troll, wearing a bib and holding a smoking pistol and a half-eaten joint of meat. The frame freezes on him, and a hand-scripted logo scrawls itself onto the screen: "the ugly." Dropping neither gun nor meat, the figure leaps onto a horse and gallops off.

Leone tracks into the doorway of the building as the scar-faced man, holding a wounded arm, comes forward and aims his pistol at the retreating horseman. Another shot. The scar-faced man cries out, staggers back into the building, and falls beside the dead bodies of the other two men.

This cluster of tricks and reversed expectations is a uniquely appropriate opening to a film whose central element is the joke and whose whole plot is built upon tricks: tricks the characters play on one another, tricks fate plays on the characters, tricks Leone plays on the characters, on us, and on the Western genre.

The mood darkens with the next sequence. Leone cuts to a quite different landscape. This one, too, is desolate but at least moderately agrarian. There's a large stone circle on the ground (a threshing floor, perhaps), and there's a water wheel that turns in the vertical plane while a donkey, ridden by a small boy, turns its gears in a circle through the horizontal plane. Again, there is a reason for the emphasis on circles, but we won't discover what it is until near the end of the film.

The boy rides the donkey through two complete revolutions, the camera backing and adjusting to keep the movement centered. Seeing something, the boy stops and looks again. Where no one was visible before, a lone rider approaches the little isolated compound. An elegiac guitar melody is heard, but it sours into discord as the stranger nears: he wears the face of Lee Van Cleef, still cinematic shorthand for the menace of villainy (despite the semiheroic Mortimer of *For a Few Dollars More*).

The boy runs into the adobe structure (more cave than house) where his mother is setting out a bowl of stew. The woman takes the boy away as the stranger enters the hut and approaches the table. The father, a sunburnt, bearded man, sits there. The stranger joins him, in silence, and doles out a substantial serving for himself. Then he eats, eyeing the farmer.

He knows well the value of silence, this tall, narrow-eyed rider on the wind. The farmer speaks first, and in the ensuing dialogue the stranger learns rather more than he came for, getting the gimmick of the film's plot well established. The farmer blurts out something about a cashbox containing two hundred thousand dollars in gold that never got where it was going. He says he knows the stranger has come from a man named Baker, to which the stranger replies his job is to find out the name under which a man named Jackson is now hiding.

"How much does he pay you for murdering me?" asks the farmer. The stranger cagily replies, "Five hundred dollars—to get the name." With a bitten-back, confessional reluctance that we will encounter in another character much later in the film, the farmer blurts out, "Bill Carson." He goes to a drawer and brings back a pouch of money. "One thousand dollars—it's all I've got," he says—another line that will resonate later in the movie. "A tidy sum—and some in gold," observes the stranger. "But the thing is, once I've been paid, I always see the job through." The farmer goes for the pistol he has taken from the drawer along with the money, but the stranger is ahead of him—he's already drawn his gun under the table, and he shoots the farmer through the tabletop and the bowl of stew.

In an evocative bit of economy, Leone cuts, as the shot rings out, to a hand springing open and dropping a water gourd. Music redolent of crisis sounds in high strings as the camera pulls back to show us the frightened face of the farmer's wife. She turns and runs toward the house.

The stranger collects the farmer's thousand dollars even though it hasn't bought the man his life, and he starts to walk out. An older boy, unseen until now, darts from a hallway with a shotgun, and the stranger shoots him down. As the stranger leaves, the woman looks around the house at her dead husband and son. As the younger boy hurries to her, she whirls toward a faint, Leone's camera taking up her point of view as her vision darts, reels, then fades.

In a candlelit bedroom, an aging man dozes. The stranger enters, and the man wakes. This must be Baker. The stranger tells Baker that Jackson is hiding under the name Bill Carson. He also lets Baker know that he's more than a little interested in the information about the cashbox that the farmer—a man named Stevens—let slip before he was killed. "He gave me a thousand dollars," says the stranger. "I think he had in mind that I kill you." They enjoy a nervous laugh together, until the stranger adds, "But you know me. Once I'm paid, I always see the job through." And he presses a pillow over the sniveling face of Baker and shoots him through it. Smoke rises from the hole in the pillow. The stranger turns to the candle and lifts it to his lips. He smiles, and the frame freezes as the words "the bad" are scribbled next to his face; then he blows out the candle, and the screen goes black.

We come up on "the ugly," who is still galloping away. A shot is fired, and "ugly's" horse throws him to the ground. Three men appear from the foreground. One of them holds a "Wanted" poster just in front of the camera and tells the downed man how much money he is worth. The even, unmistakable voice of Clint Eastwood interrupts: "Yes, but you don't look like the ones who'll be collecting it." Eastwood enters, the familiar nameless bounty killer from *A Fistful of Dollars* and *For a Few Dollars More*, now clad more sophisticatedly in a white jacket and hat. The three bounty hunters back away and spread out to face the newcomer. There's a quick face-off montage in the now-familiar Leone manner—eyes, hands, weapons—and the man in white draws and kills all three. "The ugly," impressed, thanks his rescuer profusely, but his gratitude turns to invective as Leone cuts to a new shot of him, hogtied across the back of his horse as the bounty killer leads him into a town.

The wanted man is pulled off the horse and thrown on the board sidewalk in a heap. There he lies screaming about betrayal and begins insulting everyone in sight. With lawmen and bystanders looking on, he lowers his voice and calls the bounty killer near, saying he wants to tell him something—then he spits in his rescuer's face.

All this, however, is only half the joke. The man in white, rescuer turned Judas, becomes the savior again. The wanted man is strung up, his head placed in a noose as he listens to a list of the crimes he's been found guilty of. We learn his name—Tuco—though it hardly seems important at this point to have a name for him since he is standing at death's door. Something seems odd, though: The bounty killer sits just inside the upper window of an adjacent livery barn, taking aim through a rifle's sharpshooter's sight. As the signal is given and the rope tightens, he fires, neatly cutting the noose. Tuco falls to the ground. The rifleman methodically shoots the hats off several of the astounded townsfolk, then jumps onto a wagon, whips up the team, and charges down the main street of the town, Tuco jumping aboard.

In the hills, Tuco and the bounty killer, whom Tuco calls "Blondie," are splitting up the reward money collected for Tuco's capture. And that's the topper to the joke. Apparently Tuco and Blondie have been running this scam for some time, for now Tuco is insisting on a bigger cut. "There are two kinds of people in the world, my friend," he tells Blondie: "Those with a rope around their neck, and the people who have the job of doing the cutting." Because his risk is greater in the extreme, Tuco argues, his share should be proportionately larger as well. Blondie replies, with persuasive logic, that if his own share is diminished, "it's liable to interfere with my aim." Tuco acquiesces, but not before admonishing Blondie that "if you miss, you had better miss very well. Whoever double-crosses me and leaves me alive, he understands nothing of Tuco—nothing!"

In the next town, the paths of the film's three eponymous characters cross for the first time. The tall "bad" stranger talks with a legless man he calls "half soldier" and learns that Jackson, a.k.a. "Bill Carson," has joined up with a Confederate cavalry unit but has a girlfriend in a nearby town who will know his whereabouts. A coin loosens the temporarily snagged memory of the "half soldier," and he gives the name of the town to the tall gunman, whom he calls "Angeleyes." As the shot ends, Angeleyes strides away saying, "So long, half soldier," and the legless Johnny Reb hand-walks himself under the swinging doors of a saloon, from whence we hear his voice calling, "Hand me down a whiskey!"

All the while, Tuco has been standing with his head in a noose, and the familiar litany of his crimes is being read to the townsfolk. These people—an even primmer lot than the last group—are visibly appalled at Tuco's deeds, which include crimes of sexuality as well as of theft and of violence. Tuco enjoys himself, hissing at one impressionable matron. As Angeleyes boards a stagecoach, one of the lady passengers remarks how awful it is that someone could do all the horrible things Tuco's done. Angeleyes agrees, tentatively, but adds that "even a worthless beggar like that has a protecting angel." His eyes search the area, and, readying his rifle, he picks out Blondie in the background. Angeleyes smiles to himself and adds, "A golden-haired angel watches over that boy." An unseen celestial chorus strikes one high dulcet chord. (It never seems to matter much to anyone that Clint Eastwood is neither blond nor golden-haired.)

The hanging proceeds, and Blondie, as if to add emphasis to his earlier remarks to Tuco, misses his first shot. Tuco dances at rope's end for an agonizing instant, before a second shot severs the rope. Tuco hits the ground running; Blondie shoots the hats off, then follows Tuco on horseback, pulling the crook up behind him without ever breaking stride.

Once again in the hills, Blondie has a heart-to-heart talk with his "partner." Blondie is concerned about his future, and he admits he doesn't think Tuco will ever be worth more than two thousand dollars. He lowers Tuco from the horse, saying, "Our partnership is untied." Tuco extends his hands, still tied from the hanging. "Not you," says Blondie: "You remain tied. The nearest town is about sixty miles. If you save your breath, I think a man like you just might make it." Tuco whimpers, pleads, then blusters with invective, but Blondie rides off, leaving Tuco in the desert; he shakes his head sadly: "Such ingratitude, after all the times I've saved your life." Theme music sounds as the words "the good" finally label Blondie for us, and thus, at last, ends what must be the longest introductory passage in film history.

I have gone into some detail about this opening because of the parallels that exist among the three introductory sequences (they match up as nicely as the character introductions of *For a Few Dollars More*), and because most of the film's premises and motives, as well as its intricate pattern of tricks and double-crosses, are firmly established in this lengthy prologue. We are introduced to three main characters, each of whom shoots three people in his opening sequence. We learn the titular epithets of these characters, as well as the names by which they are commonly known. We see their paths cross and learn that Angeleyes is already aware of the existence of Tuco and Blondie and of the con game they run. Most importantly, we become aware of the film's central object, the missing cashbox, which three men—the farmer Stevens, the bedridden Baker, and the missing Jackson (who, as "Bill Carson," is the only one of the three men still alive)—were questing for.

This pattern of threes is established at the outset and is obsessively maintained throughout the film. Even in the opening credits sequence, three animated horsemen are blown away by a cannon that shoots out the three phrases of the film's title; and a single horseman is similarly eliminated, one section at a time, by a cannon that fires three shots: "Directed by," "Sergio," and "Leone." When Tuco emerges from the desert, he makes a pistol by assembling parts of several different pistols he examines in a general store. When he steps out back to test his gun on the target range, there are three man-shaped targets standing there. With three shots he knocks the targets sidewise, then fires three more shots. Two of the targets, drilled sideways by Tuco's impossible sharpshooting, topple in halves; the third remains standing. The storekeeper shakes his head and gives Tuco a tut-tut. Tuco smiles, takes the whiskey bottle, pulls the cork with his teeth, takes a long pull, and then, instead of firing another shot, stamps his feet. The top half of the third target falls off. Tuco laughs. He knew that three shots had been enough. The world of *The Good, the Bad and the Ugly* is a closed set of threes.

Indeed, one can map the film's three archetypal characters onto the three exemplars of the Old Law in the myth of the American Western, as discussed earlier. All are the strong, titanic elements of pre-civilized society. The Good, perhaps in spite of his cynicism, exemplifies a growing tendency toward kindness to others (most notably the dying Union officer and the dying Confederate soldier). The Bad exhibits an unredeemed cynicism, a commitment to self-interest unmodified by human values. And the Ugly analogizes to the third group of primordial titans, the aboriginal tribal people, living with their own codes of insularity, internal loyalty, and distrust of outsiders, neutral third group neither Good nor Bad but something apart, something other. This aspect of Tuco's character is reflected in his habitual but shallow commitment to quasi-superstitious religious ritual, and in a sense of family and ethnicity that contrast sharply with those of his brother, the priest. Tuco is not simply Mexican but *Indio*. This trisection of the titanic archetypes of the myth of the American Western—good guys, bad guys, and Indians—is emphatically underscored by Leone's insistent imagery of threes in *The Good, the Bad and the Ugly*.

As in *A Fistful of Dollars*, there is a tendency for the triangular opposition to resolve itself into two-and-one. Most often, of course, Blondie and Tuco are the two and Angeleyes is the one. This division prevails for most of the film, except for the brief time when Blondie is forcibly partnered with Angeleyes and for the equally short time that he and Tuco are separated early in the film, after Blondie "unties" their partnership. It seems that each time Blondie tries to assert his free-agency by severing his relationship with Tuco, something restores the bond. Once, it is the miraculous appearance of a carriage full of corpses (among whom is the still living "Bill Carson," ready to give half his secret to Tuco and half to Blondie in an effort to save himself). Another time, it is the less miraculous, more ominous, interruption of Angeleyes, who tosses a second shovel into the grave marked "Arch Stanton" and tells Blondie and the already-digging Tuco, "Two can dig a lot quicker than one."

In the battle for the bridge, Blondie and Tuco are also two-and-one with the alcoholic captain of the Union regiment. Leone's composition reaffirms the threeness and the two-and-one grouping by frequently placing the captain between the two adventurers. There is also a sense that the presence of the war transforms the duo of Blondie and Tuco into a single unit. When Tuco makes his second bid for revenge against Blondie by leading him on a waterless trek through the desert, he says, "Sibley's army is retreating over there; Canby's army is advancing there; but no one will go through this hell except you and me." It's the "in the middle" notion from *A Fistful of Dollars* once again. As a team, Blondie and Tuco are the middleman. Like No Name in the earlier film, their "teamship" presents a third alternative to the indistinguishable motives of two warring factions. Nowhere is this intent clearer than in the battle for the bridge (more about this later).

The resolution of threes into two-and-one implies that twos are imagistically as important to the film as threes—and indeed they are. This is made especially clear by Leone's use of a number of deliberately parallel images and events. When the storekeeper tells Tuco "It's all I've got" as the bandit robs the store with his newly assembled pistol, we recall Stevens's ill-fated bid to shift Angeleyes' loyalty earlier in the film: "One thousand dollars—it's all I've got." Stevens's telling-too-much confession to Angeleyes is balanced, moments later, by Angeleyes' equally detailed confession to the about-to-die Baker. The dying "Carson" tells Tuco the name of the graveyard where the cashbox is buried, and, moments later, he gives the name on the grave to Blondie. Tuco's revelation of his half of the secret—under duress—to Angeleyes is echoed by his reluctant blurting out of his half of the secret to Blondie just before they blow up the bridge. His assembly of his "superpistol" at the general store compares with Blondie's hasty assembly of his own pistol, which he has been cleaning as Tuco's hired assassins creep down the hall toward his room. Early in the film, an abandoned Tuco hollers across the desert to Blondie who is riding away after severing their partnership; Blondie rides away at the very end of the film, too. The stone circle of the Stevens compound is analogous to the circle in the middle of the graveyard at the film's climax.

This parallelism suggests the "one for me, one for you" sharing that characterizes Tuco's and Blondie's uneasy partnership. A compulsion to divide the world in half recurs throughout their relationship—not only in the way they split up the take and doggedly try to even the score for each double-cross but also in the bizarre, aphoristic way they talk to each other. We recall Tuco's division of the world: There are people with ropes around their necks and people whose job it is to cut those ropes. If this division holds true, Blondie and Tuco each get their share of both roles. Blondie plays rope-cutter for Tuco and another short-lived partner named "Shorty." But he finds his own head in the noose when Tuco catches up with him after surviving his abandonment in the desert. Tuco spends plenty of time with his head in a noose. But he is a cutter at least once when, with the help of nothing subtler than an entire railway train, he cuts the chain that binds him to the dead Corporal Wallace.

Later Tuco revises his maxim in order to distinguish himself from the trashy goons (three of them, of course) he has hired to kill Blondie. They have just paid for their failure with their lives (their spurs jingled in the hallway and warned Blondie of their approach). Blondie, having wiped them out (emptying his gun in the process), turns to find a grinning Tuco seated on the windowsill; Tuco has the drop on him: "There are two kinds of spurs, my friend—those that come in by the door and these that come in by the window." Tuco tells Blondie to throw down his gun, and Blondie does so, but remarks, "It's empty." Tuco replies, smugly, "Mine isn't."

This situation is reversed during the graveyard scene: After the climactic gunfight, during which Blondie kills Angeleyes and Tuco discovers that his gun is empty (having been unloaded by Blondie the night before), Blondie turns

Tuco's aphoristic dualism against him: "You see, in this world there are two kinds of people, my friend: Those with loaded guns and those who dig. *You dig.*" Tuco, as always, is odd-man-out.

And that is, perhaps, as it should be. If there are "two kinds of people in the world," they must be "good" and "bad" (the odd term "ugly" qualifying as an aesthetic rather than as a moral judgment). Blondie and Angeleyes are defined in terms of moral codes. Neither code is conventional, but Angeleyes' is grounded in a conscienceless exploitation of the innocent or the weak; Blondie's springs from his opposition to the forces of evil and from the sensitivity he often reveals, especially during the bridge battle and at the death of the young Confederate soldier. Tuco, by contrast, is always treated in terms of pure style.

Blondie and Angeleyes are "two kinds" who cannot long abide each other's existence. Leone's West is literally not big enough for both of them. With an unloaded gun and a half-loaded mind, Tuco is ill-equipped to compete with Blondie and Angeleyes but can comfort himself with the knowledge that his inferiority signals his survival. Once one of "those with loaded guns," Tuco is redefined by Blondie as one of "those who dig." Blondie and Angeleyes remain men with loaded guns, and must seek to destroy each other. Blondie emphatically does not dig, even when Angeleyes orders him at gunpoint to do so.

A variation on the separation of the world into gunmen and diggers is suggested by the conversation that takes place between Tuco and his brother, Father Ramirez, who is in charge of the mission where Tuco takes Blondie to recover from the ordeal in the desert. (Discovering that the filthy, amoral Tuco has a priest for a brother is reminiscent of the old joke about Catholic neighborhoods where all the boys grow up to be either killers or priests.) When Tuco speaks to Blondie in his sickbed, he verbally disowns his family: "Not even a mother! You're all alone—like me, Blondie." Moments later, Tuco's brother—very much alive—tells Tuco of the deaths of their parents, and the bandit's lie about being an orphan becomes truth. The priest upbraids Tuco for having abandoned the family to pursue a life of crime, whereupon Tuco reminds the priest that he had to do more than his share because his brother was away at seminary. The prodigal son offers no apology. Tuco tells his brother, "You became a priest because you were too much of a coward to do what I do." This remark brings them to blows. The conversation ends with Father Ramirez begging Tuco's forgiveness as the crusty bandit walks out. The entire Mission San Antonio sequence, which began with Tuco consigning Blondie to the monks and saying, "He's like a brother to me," ends with Tuco and Blondie driving away on the wagon, and Tuco telling Blondie, "My brother—he's crazy about me."

There's no denying that the matter of family divides Leone's world into two parts—loners and family men, perhaps—calling to mind the centrality of family to a Catholic society and worldview. The crucial role of family, reflected here in a Mexican context, is as important to the world of Italian Catholic Sergio Leone as it is to the world of Irish Catholic John Ford. But in Leone's films, people associated with family tend to be victims, while those who willingly disassociate themselves from family are either the family's nemeses or its saviors.

In *A Fistful of Dollars*, Ramón Rojo—despite the fact that he is the strongest member of a ruling family—sets himself up in opposition to the notion of family. He usurps his brother's patriarchal position and rends the family unit of Julián, Marisol, and Jesus. Indio, in *For a Few Dollars More*, is even more contemptuous of family, summarily executing the wife and child of the man who sent him to jail. The central psychological event of the film is Indio's responsibility for the death of Mortimer's sister. His heir, in *The Good, the Bad and the Ugly*, is Angeleyes, who, before he kills family-man Stevens, notes a photograph on the wall: "Your family?" he asks; and, when Stevens nods, he smiles mirthlessly: "Nice family."

The Man with No Name in *A Fistful of Dollars* and Mortimer in *For a Few Dollars More* are, by contrast, defenders—or avengers—of family. The confrontation between Tuco and Father Ramirez in *The Good, the Bad and the Ugly* seems designed specifically to emphasize the issue of family in a film that otherwise has little reference to that theme—a theme that is crucial in Leone's other four films. Yet Blondie—like No Name and Manco—has no association with family whatever. He becomes a defender of family only by default, insofar as he is set in opposition to both Tuco and Angeleyes. In different ways, both men—by means of their crimes—are violators of the sanctity of family. Tuco, in fact, is a kind of Indio without guilt.

There are other, more pertinent, ways of classifying the film's characters into two kinds. When Angeleyes offers Blondie a partnership, after having Tuco beaten into revealing his half of the secret, Blondie is surprised not to receive the same treatment. "Would you talk?" asks Angeleyes. "Probably not," replies Blondie. "Not that you're any tougher than he is," says Angeleyes. "But you're smart enough to know that talking won't save you." It is possible to take a cue from this and divide the people of *The Good, the Bad and the Ugly* into talkers and silents. Blondie is as characterized by his soft-spoken manner and silence as Tuco is by his boisterousness and garrulousness.

The talkers invariably get hurt. Because Angeleyes knows that Tuco will talk, he has Wallace beat Tuco into doing so. Stevens, Baker, and "Bill Carson" all tell too much, and die. It is not talk but at least noise that gives away Blondie's would-be killers in the hotel corridor—a momentary halt in the troop movements outside creates a silence that allows Blondie to hear the spurs of the men stalking him.

Talking is always associated with injury and sometimes is associated with death. The talker from whom Angeleyes gets some of his best information is the legless "half soldier." When the scar-faced man (whose face opens the film) shows up in Tuco's hotel room eight months (and nearly two hours of screen-time) later, he is minus an arm—the result, implicitly, of Tuco's having shot him on the run in the opening scene. Instead of killing Tuco outright, the man makes a speech about his suffering and the time he's spent searching for Tuco. He's obviously savoring the moment of vengeance, confident that he has the drop on Tuco, who, seated in a sudsy bath, seems caught with his pants down. But a shot rings out. Tuco has concealed a pistol in his bathwater. Through the suds, he shoots the scar-faced avenger and admonishes the dying man: "If you have to shoot, shoot! Don't talk!"

Tuco, of course, is the one remarkable exception to the film's message about silent men and talkers; he's a mile-a-minute talker (he's even defined in terms of a love for noise, when he tells Corporal Wallace, "I like big, fat men like you—when they fall, they make more noise"). Tuco gets hurt but, repeatedly, he escapes death by virtue of his wit and toughness. This may be why he earns Blondie's rough mercy by the end of the film.

Silence is the social correlate to that other great Leone motif, anonymity. The two qualities come together in the film's climax, when Blondie tells Tuco and Angeleyes he has written his half of the secret —the name on the grave in which the gold is buried—on the bottom of a rock, which may be claimed by the survivor of a three-way gunfight. After the shootout, Blondie shows Tuco the burial place, a grave marked "Unknown." The illiterate Tuco tries haltingly to pronounce the word. Then he blusters, "There's no name on the grave." Showing Tuco the rock, Blondie says, "There's no name here either." Anonymity is linked with the virtue of silence and the reward of profit. But it is linked ironically with that other "reward," as well—the silence of the grave.

This ambivalent vision underlies the film's odd antiwar stance, a moral view that has nothing whatever to do with non-violence. En route to the cemetery where the gold is buried (an image in itself rich in allegorical implication), Blondie and Tuco find their way blocked by a bridge over which Union and Confederate regiments battle incessantly. "Both sides want it intact," says the Union commander, who drinks heavily to numb his sense of purposelessness, while hurling attack after attack at the bridge ("I never saw so many men wasted so badly," murmurs Blondie). The bridge becomes a multiple symbol: It stands for war in general; the Civil War in particular (blue on one side, gray on the other, and Blondie's ministering to a dying soldier on each bank of the river); and, the character relationships within the film itself (Tuco, a bogus Confederate NCO, and Angeleyes, a bogus Union NCO—both wanting the neutral Blondie intact because his secret is crucial to their purpose).

The irony here is that once the bridge is destroyed, Tuco and Blondie can wade across the river with ease. The absurdity of a river that cannot be crossed until the bridge is *destroyed* is redoubled with the recognition that the bridge was scarcely necessary in the first place! (In another of those quirky parallels with which Leone fills the film, we recall Tuco's emergence from the desert. He crosses a bridge that spans a river long since gone dry—an economic image that stresses his exhaustion, his thirst, and the change that will come with completion of his journey, while pointing forward to the "strategically important" bridge of the battle scene.) This absurdity, of course, is the alcoholic captain's vision all along. He dies with a smile as the bridge blows up, knowing that many lives will be saved. Tuco is more cynical. To him, the destruction of the bridge means only that "these idiots will go someplace else to fight."

Destroying the bridge is, of course, not just a sentimental favor Tuco and Blondie do for the captain—and far less an anti-war protest gesture. The gesture is chiefly utilitarian and has a profit motive. Tuco and Blondie can't get to the gold until an entire battle is moved out of their way. "For three men," reads the promotion tag line for the American release of the film, "the Civil War wasn't hell—it was *practice!*" Actually, for Angeleyes, Blondie, and Tuco the war is more an obstruction than it is an opportunity. Angeleyes is able to use the war to advantage; he improves his position in the search for the gold. Blondie and Tuco, however, see the hostilities as a nuisance to be avoided. It's a carelessly cruel effort, indiscriminately and wastefully taking the lives of thousands of "idiots" who are willingly led.

Tuco wants to avoid being "caught up in the war," but when he and Blondie are overtaken by it, they are quite capable of using the war's devices for their own purposes. As the film progresses, war gets closer and life gets cheaper. More and more people are shot down for fewer and fewer good reasons. The corpses become faceless (contrast, for example, the handful of unmemorable men from Angeleyes' gang that Blondie and Tuco shoot down in the town with the earlier, emphatic closeups of the six would-be bounty collectors who are shot down during the first twenty minutes of the film). They become hideously numerous (the wounded in the hospital, the battle on the bridge, the bodies on the battlefield). Leone is purposely using war—a bloody undertaking blessed by society—to fly in the face of critics offended by the violence in his films. He's saying: How can you oppose the one and endorse the other?

The cannonade unleashed on the town where Tuco first catches up with Blondie, after being abandoned by him in the desert, is the first close contact the men have with the war (though "half soldier" is the film's earliest clear image of its proximity and ravaging effects). As the war closes in on Blondie and Tuco, the cannon becomes more of a symbol: Tuco expects to shoot off the legs of a stool and hang Blondie in his hotel room. But his pistol shot becomes a cannonball that reduces the building to rubble, allowing Blondie to escape (the war is his salvation more than once). After Blondie's and Tuco's destruction of the bridge, both armies protest with volleys of cannonfire that continue into the night. Leone presents a fast-cut montage of cannon firing. He climaxes with a shot of the top of Blondie's head—his wide-brim, round-crown hat looking for all the world like another cannon mouth; then the smoke clears, and we realize we are seeing a human being. By this time, the distinction has become harder to draw. Even as men have become weapons, so are weapons (cannons) being converted to private use. Blondie fires a cannon to check Tuco's double-crossing flight from him on horseback. The blast unhorses the bandit and knocks him right into the graveyard he's seeking.

When Tuco forces Blondie to march through the desert, he points out that the armies are bypassing the desolation. But the war is fated to catch up with them. This intent is signaled in the appearance of the "carriage of the spirits," the wagon full of dead and dying Confederate soldiers that comes from nowhere and once again prevents Tuco from finishing Blondie off. But the first truly intimate intrusion of the war into the two men's lives—and into the world of the film—is the panning shot of the casualties inside Mission San Antonio, which has been converted into a field hospital. There are so many men—so horribly hurt—and they have nothing to show for their sufferings, nothing compared to

"Caught up in the war." Above, Tuco (Eli Wallach, center) and Blondie (Clint Eastwood, right) in the Union camp with the alcoholic captain (Aldo Giuffrè, left) and his "weapon." Below, preparing to blow the bridge.

what Blondie and Tuco hope to have. Leone pulls off a heartrending, elegiac scene of the wounded soldiers being nursed by the monks. The scene is sand-wiched between shots and lines that emphasize Tuco's comic side as he pretends to save Blondie's life. There is a deliberate evocation of the Atlanta railroad station in *Gone with the Wind*, accompanied by the first use in the film of "Story of a Soldier," a morose antiwar ballad that will be sung later by prisoners at the Union camp, while Wallace beats Tuco. The lyrics, in part, run:

> There in the distance, a flag I can see,
> Scorched into ribbons—but whose can it be?
> How ends the story? Whose is the glory?
> Ask, if we dare, our comrades out there to say.

Leone uses grim, absurd scenes to depict the pointlessness of war. The al-coholic captain surprises us because he is inconsistent with the traditional movie image of the Civil War officer, not because he conflicts with known facts about officers and men in nineteenth-century warfare. He does not; it's just that he drinks. But who would not turn to drink when confronted with the mad confu-sion of battle as portrayed in the eerie long-lens shot of the skirmish on the bridge?

The bridge is blown, but Blondie, the human "bridge," keeps himself "in-tact" by keeping his secret until the last possible moment. And when he does reveal the secret, it is nothing—one of those absurd nothings that so fascinate Leone: a grave with no name, the tomb of an unknown soldier as the bridge it-self was for hundreds; at the bottom of this grave is no dead soldier but a fortune in gold. Contrasted thus with the wasteful madness of war, Blondie's life of vio-lence for personal profit comes off rather well. The moral basis of the film's anti-war tone is not one of killing-vs.-not-killing, but of killing-for-one's-own-gain-vs.-killing-for-someone-else's. Tuco, being led out of the prison camp chained to Wallace, stops to tell a one-armed soldier about the price on his head: "Three thousand dollars, friend—that's a lot of money for a head. I'll bet they didn't pay you a penny for your arm." The film's scoffing toward the ideals that motivate war, as well as its alternative celebration of risk and violence for per-sonal profit, is echoed, interestingly, in Brian Hutton's semicomic war film *Kelly's Heroes* (1970), which stars Clint Eastwood and which parodies both Leone and Morricone in a showdown between three American soldiers and a German tank over occupation of a bank full of German gold. Both films, each more than welcome during the Vietnam era, reaffirm a man's right to take what risks he will for personal gain. At the same time, the films attack the right of society to send men off to die for political causes.

The grim implacability of military justice provides the perfect absurdist metaphor for the war mentality, as films like *Paths of Glory* and *King and Coun-try* have demonstrated. Leone gives his nod to the metaphor in a neat little de-vice used to link two scenes and establish a time framework: Tuco, having given his share of the secret to Angeleyes, is marched out of the prison camp in the custody of Corporal Wallace and bound for points unknown. At that moment, another soldier is seen being marched out. He wears a sign on his back, a slab of wood crudely labeled "THIEF"; smaller, illegible print is written there, too. After Tuco escapes from the train, kills Wallace (fulfilling the prophecy implicit in his earlier remark about fat men making more noise when they fall), and uses an entire lumbering train to sever the chain that unhandily binds him to the fat corpse, he hikes into a nearby town to freshen up and resume his quest. As he arrives, the same hapless soldier, now carrying an empty coffin, is marched up to a clearing alongside a passing column of men; he is summarily shot as the Union forces drag past, unmoved.

The same kind of linking device, though on a more expansive scale, occurs right after—during Tuco's bath scene. In this segment, we finally learn why the face we saw in the opening shot was so emphasized, for here is the same man again, now minus an arm, once more aiming a pistol at Tuco—who perfunctorily shoots the man dead. Why did Leone keep that man alive at the end of the opening sequence and later have him interrupt Tuco's bath, only to be killed after making his little speech? To provide us with a time reference ("I've been looking for you for eight months")—and because Leone also wanted Blondie (who was encamped on the other end of town as a nominal "partner" in Angeleyes' new assay for the gold) to hear the gunshot, smile to himself, and say, "Every gun sings its own tune. Perfect timing." The device paves the way for the re-alliance of Tuco and Blondie against Angeleyes, and it moves the story ahead another jump.

The genius of this audacious approach to storyline continuity is somewhat diminished when the viewer realizes that Tuco had no pistol when he left the prison under guard, and that he must have acquired the gun after arriving in town; hence, Blondie could not have heard the gun before to recognize its "song." But every Leone film contains this kind of hole, which demonstrates that plot logic goes only as far as Leone wants it to go. The story, interesting as it might be, is distinctly not the thing; plot has been given a second spot to flamboyance. If there is any literary analogue to Leone's film style, it is the fairy tale, where it is not the resolution but the getting there that is the important thing.

Like any fable or fairy tale, *The Good, the Bad and the Ugly* takes place in a simple, sparsely populated world. It doesn't even seem coincidental that Blondie and Tuco cross paths with the dying Carson in the middle of a hell where no one would have the madness to set foot. Nor does it matter that each is blessed with exactly half of the information necessary to acquiring a fortune in gold, nor that the men are captured and sent to exactly the same prison camp where Angeleyes has set himself up as a trafficker in the confiscated property of prisoners, nor that after leaving the prison they hole up in the same town. Yet these coincidences are crucial to the plot and to the wit that characterizes the film. It is the divinely timed chance encounter with the carriage of spirits in the desert, in fact, that makes the two stories become one—already an hour into the film!

Another fairy-tale motif—the series of tests or trials—has became a recognizably Leonean theme. In *For a Few Dollars More*, Indio said, "When the chimes stop, pick up your gun"; but when the chimes almost stopped, Manco entered with another set of chimes and, after equalizing the adversaries, started the trial over again. Similarly, *The Good, the Bad and the Ugly* is characterized by a false trial and a true one. While Tuco digs up one coffin, Blondie, prompted by the arrival of Angeleyes, tells Tuco that the treasure isn't in that grave. After the final gundown, the Mexican bandit has to repeat his labors when Blondie points out the right grave.

The question, "What would they have done if things had happened differently?" doesn't arise in watching a Leone film—at least not until the Gorgon of plot analysis is summoned up as has been done here. But then Leone's films do not feature character interaction in response to a situation or an environment, the way that conventional narrative cinema does. Things happen the way they do in Leone's films because they cannot happen otherwise. Watching most movies, a viewer reaches a certain point and says, "Now *anything* can happen; this film can go in any number of directions." But we never get that feeling with Leone; he does not make that kind of film.

I've already said that the joke is the basic structural element of *The Good, the Bad and the Ugly*. That is apparent not only in the wit that informs the entire film but also in the fact that the plot is built upon a series of crosses and double-crosses. Betrayal is the darker side of the joke, reversal of expectation being the operative form of both. The tone is set in the very beginning when Angeleyes is willing to murder the host whose food he's eating and then is ready to turn on the man who employed him to do the killing (both in order to improve his own chances by narrowing the field of competition). Tuco's warning that "whoever double-crosses me and leaves me alive understands nothing of Tuco" seems less credible when, as the film unreels, Blondie double-crosses Tuco several times, always leaving the bandit alive and never seeming to underestimate him.

The pattern of betrayal continues to evolve from the climax of the introduction, when Blondie abandons Tuco in the desert. The sweetheart of "Bill Carson" is willing—albeit under duress—to betray his whereabouts to Angeleyes, just as the half soldier is willing, for money, to give away anything he knows. Tuco catches up with Blondie and tries to kill him, failing primarily because of the grandiosity of his scheme. Tuco's sense of justice requires that the punishment fit the crime, that he put Blondie through what he has been through—first the noose in the hotel room, then the trek through the desert. By contrast, Blondie—like Manco in *For a Few Dollars More*—cares little for the poetry of revenge, only for the practical. He does what will balance the odds, what will get the job done. When Blondie "betrays" his new partner, Shorty, by failing to shoot through the rope at the crucial moment, Shorty loses out only because Tuco's gun is at Blondie's head.

Blondie further double-crosses Tuco by getting the second half of the secret from Carson before Carson dies. Tuco and his brother accuse each other of having betrayed their parents. They call each other cowards. Each says the other has betrayed himself. Tuco lives in a world in which betrayal rules. Neither he nor Blondie nor the viewer ever doubts that Tuco will double-cross Blondie if the Mexican can get the secret from him. That is why Blondie maintains his silence. He is smart enough to know that talking won't save him—and that not talking just might.

Angeleyes violates the mythic host-guest relationship by murdering Stevens while he sups with him. Though from a different angle, he commits the same crime when he tortures Tuco and sends him down the river after hosting him to a sumptuous meal. Blondie betrays Angeleyes by unilaterally dissolving their "partnership" and rejoining Tuco. Angeleyes tricks Tuco and Blondie by staying a jump ahead. Teasing them, he leaves a cryptic note—"See you later, idiots" ("It's for you," Blondie tells Tuco)—after they have gunned their way through the town, obliterating Angeleyes' henchmen.

The soldiers are betrayed by their short-sighted leaders, who "waste" energy pursuing a patently insignificant military objective. Blondie scores the best betrayal of the film when, giving up his share of the secret, he actually manages to foist off another lie and buy himself time and security. By having already unloaded Tuco's pistol to balance the odds in the big gundown, he's managed a double betrayal. The question of what would have happened if Angeleyes had won the draw isn't really a fair one. Blondie has hedged his bet; he alone knows Tuco's gun is empty, so he can concentrate on Angeleyes while Angeleyes and Tuco must divide their attention between Blondie and each other. The outcome is predetermined; that is why Blondie wrote nothing on the bottom of the rock. Tuco, of course, deserves the trick Blondie has in store for him—after all, he ran off without Blondie as soon as he thought he had both halves of the secret. Blondie's final betrayal of Tuco is to leave him, hands tied and head in a noose, balanced on the arms of a rickety grave-marker and unable to reach his share of the gold, which Blondie has neatly left for this new Tantalus.

The entire pattern of betrayal is undone by the climactic reprise of the film's central image: Blondie shoots through the rope, freeing Tuco; then he puts nothing but distance between himself and the feisty Mexican. Betrayal is the way of life of the film's characters, and the Joke is Leone's basic approach to his audience.

Other jokes: the purchase of a pistol that turns into a robbery of the store; Blondie's beckoning Tuco to his bedside only to splash him with water; the only really *funny* antiwar joke in the film, when what Tuco takes to be a detachment of soldiers in gray turns out to be a Union cavalry regiment whose blue coats have become coated with desert dust; and, Blondie's joke in telling Tuco the wrong grave (plus our temporary confusion over how he could know the name on one of the graves at Sad Hill Cemetery if, in fact, it was the wrong one).

But the film's ultimate joke is this: Tuco looks up from the mass of gold coins he's unearthed, and the camera pulls back to frame his head in the noose Blondie's prepared for him. "It's no joke, Tuco," Blondie says. "Stand on that cross and put your head in the noose." And so, as Blondie rides away with only his own half of the gold, Tuco is left precariously balanced atop an unsteady gravemarker. There, at the edge of a forgotten cemetery, one injudicious move can put an end to everything. When calling out to Blondie causes him to nearly hang himself, Tuco must at last learn the virtue of silence.

The creaky cross is a fitting emblem. In Tuco's world, conventional Christian ethics are nowhere to be found, and a personal code provides only the shakiest moral support. The cross restates emphatically the pattern of religious

Tuco (Eli Wallach) on the cross, as Blondie (Clint Eastwood) sets up the final joke of *The Good, the Bad and the Ugly*.

imagery occurring throughout the film: Tuco's frequent sign-of-the-cross gesture, his priest-brother, the mission, the ruined church where a young Confederate soldier dies, Tuco's comment to Blondie that "even when Judas hanged himself there was a storm, too" (though the "storm" turns out to be the Union cannonade that saves Blondie), the repetition of threes, the survival of a trek through the desert, the giving and taking of water.

The cross image is also a translingual pun—"double-cross"—that echoes the spatial geometry of the film. People continually "cross" one another: In the opening scene, a coyote crosses the path of one man approaching two others, and then the three in turn meet and head in a new direction, forming another cross; in a pivotal scene the path of the carriage of spirits crosses Blondie's and Tuco's path in the desert at the moment of Blondie's rendezvous with death; also, the path of Tuco and Blondie keeps crossing that of Angeleyes; and the final scene is set in a cemetery where rows of crosses form circles around a big empty space, literally creating an arena of death.

Blondie does what he does to Tuco not only as an elaborate joke (a punishment that fits the crime by tantalizing the bandit with the very device he and Blondie had used in their deadly confidence game), but also as a partial revenge for torments suffered and as a means of putting distance between himself and Tuco, who is left with four heavy saddlebags of gold and no horse.

In the opening of the film long shots and closeups are intercut, with little or no reference to the middle distance. This technique is echoed in the cemetery finale. Close shots of Tuco in his predicament are intercut with the long shot of Blondie's ride away from Sad Hill. After a moment, Blondie slows, turns. Leone cuts in a closeup of Blondie, who aims and fires. The rope breaks, and Tuco tumbles onto the sacks of gold. Though he has been a capable tracker in the past, Tuco has no reason to pursue Blondie now. The Mexican has a hundred thousand dollars in gold to call his own and one must assume that the relationship is severed at last. Blondie gallops off, crossing almost the entire screen—a great, great distance in a Leone film, especially in high-angle long shot. Tuco's crucifixion is done and undone, and Blondie's galloping horse repeats the graphics of the main title sequence's animated horsemen.

Lest there be any doubt that we have come full circle, the camera deliberately pans with Blondie's ride until Leone gets the composition he wants, then holds on it as Blondie rides on, and on, not managing to escape the frame before the scene fades, but becoming all but lost in—what else?—a landscape.

6

"A Nice, Quiet Country Life"

Once Upon a Time in the West

The West is never "the West" in *Once Upon a Time in the West*. It is always "the country"—just one of many touches that seem authentic in Leone's most celebrated film. It failed resoundingly at the box office; and if it later became a *success d'estime* and is today widely recognized as a masterpiece, it was not so at first. Most of the initial reviews found the film as ponderous and dull as they had found Leone's first three films raucous and offensively violent. The film was "discovered" largely in retrospect.

At first glance, *Once Upon a Time in the West* appears to be a move toward a more "authentic" view of the West than the fanciful one created in the three Clint Eastwood films. Buildings, costumes, conversation, and character relationships seem at times to be carefully studied replicas of real life in the American West. The use of dimly lit taverns instead of gay, noisy dance halls to represent the western saloon; the mud streets; desolate clusters of buildings instead of bustling boomtowns; people wearing long johns, duster coats, and suspenders ("Ford and Wayne tried as long before as *Stagecoach*," says Andrew Sarris, apropos of *The Searchers* in his book *The John Ford Movie Mystery*, "to introduce suspenders to the standard Western costume, and they failed ignominiously")—all these seem to be realist reactions against the glossy conventions of the Hollywood B-Westerns of Leone's youth.

But those old conventions pretty much had vanished by the mid-1960s anyway: "Cowboys" in fringed leather jackets and shiny spurs and pretty, powdered dancers in well-lit music halls were encountered only in parodies by then. Even in the mid-'50s a certain amount of architectural, cultural, and habilimentary realism underlay the Westerns of Ford, Boetticher, and Mann. Besides, it is worth recalling Christopher Frayling's admonition in *Spaghetti Westerns* that "emphasis on detail should not be confused with authenticity of detail." Leone never does more or less than will serve his own vision. If "the country" in *Once Upon a Time in the West* seems more like the West "as it really was," the sets and costumes are still only a background for the stark overprint of Leone's parabolic primitivism. His staging of character-groupings against a limbo of amoral—or perhaps pre-moral—experience has nothing at all to do with the historical reality of the American West. There is no question that *Once Upon a Time in the West*, by very virtue of its self-consciousness, its sometimes ponderous sorties into film poetry, its layering-on of so-called privileged moments, its insistence on the ritualistic expressiveness of a cinematic style as frozen and formalized as Japanese drama, represents Leone's most personal vision.

At the time Leone made the film, *Once Upon a Time in the West* was to be his last Western (and so it may still be regarded, though the Mexican Revolution of *Duck, You Sucker!* is hardly free of Western overtones, and Leone's hand is more than a little evident in Tonino Valerii's *My Name Is Nobody*). It is therefore legitimate to read the film as Leone's farewell to the genre and its conventions, a deeply personal song of parting, both sendoff and heartfelt tribute.

Never is Leone's acknowledgment of his own roots in the Hollywood Western so direct and explicit as in *Once Upon a Time in the West*. To begin with, the movie is solidly grounded in the tradition of the Western melodrama. It comes complete with its implacable villain in black, its land-grabbing businessman menacing the struggling landholder, who is defended by a strong, silent type. Even the harlot with the heart of gold appears. And the driving force of the film is an amplification of the oldest revenge-motive in the genre: "You killed my brother."

But it's the era of the so-called adult Western of the '50s to which Leone most frequently refers, using broad echoes as well as specific quotes from such films as: *High Noon* (three men waiting for a train and an appointment with a man named Frank), *Shane*, *Gunfight at the O.K. Corral*, *3:10 to Yuma*, *Last Train from Gun Hill*, *Johnny Guitar*, *Run of the Arrow*, *The Searchers*, *The Magnificent Seven*, and Ford's latter-day, end-of-the-cycle *The Man Who Shot Liberty Valance*. His choice of actors is richly resonant: Henry Fonda played Wyatt Earp in Ford's version of the O.K. Corral gunfight, *My Darling Clementine*, he starred in *The Ox-Bow Incident* and his portrayal of Frank James in *Jesse James* (1939) was strong enough to spawn a sequel, *The Return of Frank James* (1940). Charles Bronson had played Indians in *Apache* and *Run of the Arrow*. He'd become visible as the gentle-hearted Irish-Mexican gunfighter Bernardo O'Reilly in *The Magnificent Seven* (in which he conspicuously whittles on a stick, turning it into a flute to give to a little girl). Jason Robards was Doc Holliday in *Hour of the Gun*, John Sturges's 1967 remake of his 1957 *Gunfight at the O.K. Corral*. Claudia Cardinale had done creditable service as a desirable western wife in *The Professionals*. Even the expendable gunfighters dispatched in the opening sequence are deliberate referents to three distinct Western styles: Jack Elam, the unforgettable Face of the Hollywood Western, sometimes menacing villain, sometimes crusty comic, had figured importantly in *Gunfight at the O.K. Corral*, and he was support in scores of ether films. Woody Strode, a key Ford player in *Sergeant Rutledge*, *Two Rode Together*, and *The Man Who Shot Liberty Valance*, had also appeared in *The Professionals*— one of the first American Westerns to demonstrate the influence of the "spaghettis." And Al Mulock was the derelict gunman whose mug replaced a landscape in the opening shot of Leone's own *The Good, the Bad and the Ugly*.

More specific antecedents exist: In Michael Curtiz's *The Comancheros* (1961), Texas Ranger Jake Cutter (John Wayne) goes briefly under the alias "McBain," a town named Sweetwater appears, and Lee Marvin portrays an offbeat half-breed named Kelly Crow who could easily be an influence on the Cheyenne character here.[1] The Man with the Harmonica in *Once Upon a Time in the West*—particularly once we see the final flashback in which he begins his lonely, embittered existence as a Boy with a Harmonica—cannot help recalling *Silent Tongue*, the mute Indian boy of Sam Fuller's *Run of the Arrow*, who communicates by sawing on a harmonica: In the film's most gripping scene, discordant harmonica tones are the boy's cry for help when he falls into quicksand. Cheyenne's comment specifically acknowledges this interchange of music and voice in the Man with the Harmonica: "He plays when he ought to talk, and when he'd better play, he talks." (Bronson's character is further associated with music-making progenitors when Leone has Cheyenne call attention to his "whittling on a stick," a visual—though not aural—recollection of Bernardo's flute in *The Magnificent Seven*.)

There is much more, of course. But there's no denying that the single spirit that most haunts *Once Upon a Time in the West* is John Ford's. One doesn't need Monument Valley to sense that, though Leone can scarcely be blamed for leaping at the chance to film there. It was an opportunity made possible by a contract with Paramount, which was the result of the high profits gained from Leone's first three films. The not-quite-seamless fusion of Italian interiors and Spanish exteriors with this most evocative of cinematic landscapes proclaims *Once Upon a Time in the West* as an audacious mongrel of a movie; it is both Hollywood and "Spaghetti" Western.

The chief Ford referents are *The Searchers* and *The Man Who Shot Liberty Valance*: From the former, Leone quoted the raid on the homestead (specifically citing the birds flying up from the brush as prelude and the small child looking up apprehensively but bravely at the subjective-camera adult intruder). He made a working motif out of backlit doorways and out of costumes featuring dusters and suspenders. The latter movie contributed to the character of Frank, who seems to step largely from Liberty's boots. Frank's amoral power and the hold his men have on Flagstone (best seen during the auction sequence that parallels the election in the Ford film) recall the preeminence of Valance over the town of Shinbone. But the child-killing Frank has a personal code and is not the figure of riot that Valance is. Also from *The Man Who Shot Liberty Valance*, Leone has taken the use of light and dark milieus. These he uses to identify characters as either public (Jill, Frank, McBain, Morton) or private (Cheyenne, Harmonica).

Central to the Fordian vision is, of course, the notion of family and the family's expansion into community. In Leone's films, family is equally important, though distinctly less visible: The "Holy Family" rescued by the Man with No Name in *A Fistful of Dollars* is largely a foil to the chaotic existence of San Miguel and the anti-families that run the town; similarly, the destruction or absence of family defines character in *For a Few Dollars More* (Indio a destroyer of family, Mortimer the survivor of a destroyed family bond) and in *The Good, the Bad and the Ugly* (Angeleyes a destroyer of family, Tuco's confrontation with his brother over familial responsibility).

Leone, in this, his most Fordian film, portrays community arising from the dissolution of family (and, implicitly, the replacement of natural family with the establishment of bonds among strangers). The centrality of family to Leone's films is ever as victim rather than protagonist. Ford's families survive their funerals, even become stronger through them; but Leone's cold graves put an

amen to natural families altogether, forcing instead, in the wilderness, the forma-
tion of surrogate families.

None of the major characters in *Once Upon a Time in the West* has a family: The massacre of the McBains leaves Jill homeless and loveless; Cheyenne
talks of his dead mother and unknown father; Harmonica, as we learn in the climactic flashback, had a brother once; Frank and Morton are distinctly loners in
the world; even the garrulous barman in the first tavern speaks of a distant sister,
whose invitations to join her in New Orleans he consistently declines. Most of
these people are simply a-familial; but Frank is the Indio/Angeleyes reincarna-
tion here, a distinctly anti-familial type, and a child-murderer.

Nevertheless, he is not without his nobility. In one sense Frank is the protagonist of *Once Upon a Time in the West*, since his education is one of the main
things the film is about. "Morton told me once I could never be like him," he
tells Harmonica as they face each other at the climax: "Now I understand why. It
wouldn't 'a bothered him knowing you were around somewhere alive." The
Man with the Harmonica responds, with a satisfied smile, "So you found out
you're not a businessman after all." Frank returns the mirthless grin: "Just a
man." "An ancient race," agrees Harmonica.

In the more primitive ethos of *The Good, the Bad and the Ugly*, those who
dig work for those with loaded guns. But in the incipient modern world of *Once
Upon a Time in the West*, the gunman is hired boy to the businessman. Money
talks; Morton says it is the only weapon that can stop a gun. But he's right only
up to a point. He and McBain are both visionaries, albeit at opposite ends of the
capitalistic scale, and both are doomed to fall victim to men with loaded guns.
Nevertheless, it is their values that survive: both the town and the railroad continue to grow.

Morton, the arch-capitalist, whose power is all purchased, is not treated
kindly by the film. His "tuberculosis of the bones" makes him almost literally a
"spineless" character. Cheyenne compares him to a snail: "You leave a trail of
slime behind you whenever you go—two beautiful shiny rails." Frank is more
brutal: "When you're not in your train you're like a turtle out of its shell ... I
could crush you like a wormy apple." Morton's actual death is attended by
heavy irony: having announced early his intention of seeing the railroad from
the Atlantic to the Pacific, Morton is discovered, after the raid on the train that
liberates Cheyenne, crawling through the mud snail-like, struggling to reach not
the ocean but a puddle of filthy water. As Morton reaches the puddle, he dies,
and Leone overlays on the scene the sound of crashing waves that earlier accompanied Morton's yearning as he gazed at the painting of the Pacific coast in
his train car office.

Money and power notwithstanding, it is not the Mortons who built America. To some extent it is the dying breed of men like Cheyenne and Harmonica—and strong but flexible people like Jill. In the end, though, credit goes to
the diggers, not to the heroes. The West is built by the Boys who occasionally
need a drink and the touch of a woman.

Another victim of the gun is Wobbles. He is the film's most important minor character, the proverbial attendant lord who serves to set a scene or two. Wobbles sets up the meeting at Cattle Corner between Harmonica and Frank. Frank fails to attend the meeting; in his place he sends three gunmen in dusters. The meeting between Frank and Jill is also set up by Wobbles. Bringing word of the encounter to Frank at Morton's train, Wobbles clumsily leads the Man with the Harmonica to Frank's headquarters. Frank doesn't like this: "You should learn to live as if you didn't exist," he tells Wobbles. But it's too late for the hapless go-between to take the advice to heart since Frank is about to make him really cease to exist. "How can you trust a man who wears both belt and suspenders?" Frank asks his henchmen (a Ford icon here showing contempt for the details of dress associated most with characters in Ford films!). "Man can't even trust his own pants," he says, shooting Wobbles once through each suspender, and then through the belt buckle. Wobbles is the kind of man who tries to have it both ways and gets caught in the middle between forces too big and powerful for him to play off against each other. He is not a survivor.

Morton and McBain have names, public identities. Their dreams, however private, point to distinctly public goals having to do with wealth, power, and property development. In the very different world of Frank, Cheyenne, and the Man with the Harmonica (who pointedly tells Jill, "I don't invest in land"), identity is associated with death; anonymity, with life. Frank first knows Harmonica as "The Man Who Makes Appointments" (and Harmonica calls Frank "The Man Who Doesn't Keep Them"). When Frank asks Harmonica, "Who are you?" an intense sense of destiny hangs over the question, as it did when Indio asked Colonel Mortimer the same thing in *For a Few Dollars More*—as it always does in the world of Sergio Leone. Harmonica answers Frank's question by citing a litany of names. Frank notes that the names are of dead people. "You ought to know, Frank," Harmonica replies. Later Frank asks again and hears more names: "More dead men," he says, and the Man comments, "They were alive until they met you, Frank." Harmonica emphatically uses Frank's name when addressing him. In this way, he underscores his refusal to reveal his own name, while ironically connecting Frank with the named dead rather than with the nameless quick. Indeed, nothing could be further from the point than Harmonica's name, for what Frank really wants to know is why Harmonica is dogging him. One suspects that the revelation of Harmonica's actual name would be no help at all.

Once Upon a Time in the West carries Leone's obsession with anonymity to the extreme; we can see it as an attack on the cult of identity. Both Morton and McBain want fame for themselves and their names. Cheyenne, though, a wanted criminal, finds it convenient to hide under an alias,[2] and the Man with the Harmonica achieves the greatest security in escaping, rather than reaffirming, the pain of his true identity. In this light, again, Frank stands at the center of the film. He has half a name and wavers between identity and anonymity, just as he rides between Morton's train and Flagstone and Sweetwater and vacillates between the world of business and the world of mythic heroism.

The climax of the film has as much to do with identity as with Harmonica's grudge and Frank's comeuppance. "I have to know who you are," says Frank, "and I know now that you'll tell me." "Only at the point of dying," says the Man, and Frank nods, "I know." Leone pulls from behind the eyes of the Man with the Harmonica the flashback that reveals his reason for stalking Frank. The memory becomes, by extension, a shared flashback, like Indio's and Mortimer's memories of the outrage in *For a Few Dollars More*. When the harmonica is jammed into Frank's mouth, Leone intercuts a final flashback of Harmonica-as-a-boy crashing to the ground, the harmonica bouncing out of his mouth. Then he cuts back to Frank's own collapse into death—a look of recognition in Frank's eyes; he remembers. In Leone's world, no answer can be the most eloquent answer of all.

The Man with the Harmonica, certainly, has a name. If he chooses to be "Harmonica" to Cheyenne and "The Man Who Makes Appointments" to Frank, it is because, for him, identity means more than being called something in particular one's entire life. Indeed, it almost seems as if Leone and his anonymous protagonists regard having a name as a weakness, or at least as a distraction from true self-assertion. It's hard to forget that this attitude sprang from a man who achieved overnight success as "Bob Robertson." The world is upside down. Nicknames and aliases convey honest revelation of character ("Harmonica" is certainly more the style and identity of the Man than any name could ever imply), while real names are associated with disguise and pretense.

The Man with the Harmonica and Cheyenne treat each other in a certain way during their first meeting in the roadside tavern (cut from the original American theatrical release prints). They act the way they do because of a spontaneous mutual recognition of the kind of man they both are. As spare and cryptic as their dialogue may be, they wear their characters on their sleeves; unlike the ironically named Frank, they do not claim to be what they are not. By contrast, Frank, in order to pass suspicion onto Cheyenne's gang, disguises himself and his men when doing a killing; he deludes himself that he can be a businessman, that he can challenge Morton on his own terms.

Cheyenne is the Tuco of *Once Upon a Time in the West*: he's odd-man-out when it comes down to the ultimate confrontation. A known bandit, Cheyenne differs from Frank just as Tuco and Blondie, working for their own profit, differ from the soldiers at the bridge who die for someone else's idea of right. Frank works for someone else's profit—that is, until he discovers he can't be a businessman, and then it's too late for him to be anything else. Harmonica, on the other hand, serves not profit but a higher sense of justice—a sense of justice so personal that he keeps it secret until after he has shot Frank. Cheyenne, part profiteer and part gunman, is of neither world; yet he understands both Frank and Harmonica.

Just before the shootout, Harmonica tells Frank about the "ancient race" they share in common. "Soon other Mortons will come and wipe it off the face of the earth." Frank acknowledges the remark, but he says, "None of that matters now—not the land, not the money, not the woman." It is the suspension of all but the most basic system of behavior. These men are beyond the petty motivations of most of us (and most characters in Westerns). They stand above the usual codes of ethics and values. They operate in a realm of their own. As Danny Peary has suggested, Harmonica and Frank represent a privileged race of supermen who stand to normal men—morally and historically—as Titans to Olympians: They are older, tougher, simpler, less flexible, and doomed. They face each other even as Morton's railroad reaches Sweetwater, and the McBain station rises to greet it. Their way of life is at an end.

So is Cheyenne's. He can't stay in Sweetwater with the builders (those who dig, in Blondie's terms), because he's essentially an asocial personality. He tells Jill, setting out with Harmonica: "I gotta go, too." But he can't ride away, like Shane or Ethan Edwards. Leone again turns a time-honored Western motif on its head. Ignominiously gut-shot with the dying Morton's muff-derringer, Cheyenne tells Harmonica moments later, "I gotta stay here."

In the film, Cheyenne and Harmonica are treated briefly as potential lovers for Jill. When Cheyenne tells Jill, "You deserve better," she replies, "The last man who told me that is buried out there." But the implied comparison of Cheyenne with Brett McBain comes to nothing, despite the quirky domesticity of his two "Didja make coffee?" scenes with Jill.

The romance is doomed partly because of Jill's deeper interest in Harmonica, though Cheyenne warns her off him, saying, "People like that have something inside them—something to do with death." As she looks out the window just before the gunfight, Cheyenne cautions Jill about having any romantic notions involving Harmonica. "If that man lives, he'll come in here, pick up his gear, and say 'Adios.'" And that is almost exactly what Harmonica does, except that his valedictory is an earthier "I gotta go," which is followed, just before he exits, by the comment, "It's gonna be a beautiful town." Jill says, "I hope you'll come back someday," and Harmonica replies, "Someday," though no one in the film or in the audience believes it.

Sweetwater and Jill are left to the builders, and it falls to Cheyenne to celebrate them as the real heroes of the West, if not of the film, when he tells Jill, "If I were you, I'd go give those boys a drink. You can't know how good it makes a man feel to see a woman like you … And if one of 'em should pat your behind make believe it's nothin'. They earned it." The men with shovels and hammers even get the girl.

Knowingly or otherwise, Cheyenne and Harmonica have prepared the way for the builders—and they yield to them, having committed themselves to a higher motive than private gain (Cheyenne), the profit of another (Frank), or even the self-justification of a well-wrought act of revenge (Harmonica). The alliance of Cheyenne and Harmonica with Jill is not only an extension of their claims against Frank and their opposition to what men like Morton do to the world but also an out-and-out conspiracy to do some kind of good. As with Mortimer's revenge, a value higher than personal profit is served here. We are back to Tuco's division of the world between people with ropes around their

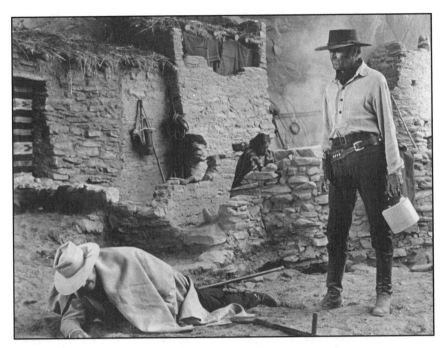

Two kinds of men: Above, Mortimer (Gabriel Ferzetti, left) abused by would-be businessman Frank (Henry Fonda, right); below, Frank and The Man with the Harmonica (Charles Bronson, right), two exemplars of an ancient race, at the moment of reckoning in *Once Upon a Time in the West.*

necks and those with the job of doing the cutting; but there's a difference. Harmonica and Cheyenne may be rope-cutters, but theirs is a supreme self-sacrifice because they help create a world that has no room for men like themselves.

For that reason, despite its engaging sense of nobility of purpose, *Once Upon a Time in the West* is not an optimistic film. Those who inherit the West—and, implicitly, the earth—simply are not as interesting as the departing race of heroes. When interviewer Noel Simsolo suggested to Leone that *Duck, You Sucker!* is a pessimistic film, Leone replied, "*Once Upon a Time in the West* was just as pessimistic. You had there the end of a world: the birth of matriarchy and the beginning of a world without balls." No consciousness-raising here: Jill is an independent woman of the world, molded gradually into a coffee-making, house-cleaning, water-carrying, semi-respectable, dependent "lady." She is always treated well by the film, but this manifestation of Goethe's "Eternal Feminine" is no ethereal, romantic, saving force; Jill is an earth mother (Cheyenne continually compares her to his own mother), whose contributions are as elemental as the fecundity of soil.

Jill is the only person with a name who survives; those who dig remain a faceless mass. The real personalities die or dissipate. Throughout the film's dialogue, numbers stand for people: "Once you've killed four, it's easy to make it five." "First three, then two." "There's one more bastard left."

If the "new world" born at the close of *Once Upon a Time in the West* is neither very brave nor admirable, the message seems to be that it is our world nonetheless and that deeds done for private motives sometimes have very public results. Morton's railroad survives both Morton and Frank; it continues its westward push, even with the passing of Harmonica and Cheyenne. Yet the railroad is never seen as an inevitability in the same way that Harmonica's vengeance is. The mythic necessity of Harmonica's dogging and destruction of Frank is, indeed, seen as the central motivating force of all the film's action, to the point that we suspect even the railroad might stop its progress ware Harmonica not to face Frank as he does at the appointed hour.

Harmonica's vengeance is a double triumph. Not only does he win the final duel with Frank but also foils Frank's effort to wrest control of McBain land from Jill, thereby gradually discrediting Frank with Morton and with Frank's own men. All of Leone's first four films arc concerned to some extent with revenge, but in *Once Upon a Time in the West* the theme plays a more important role than in *A Fistful of Dollars* and in *The Good, the Bad and the Ugly*—and the revenge is more richly developed and satisfyingly concluded than in *For a Few Dollars More*. In fact, Harmonica's single act of vengeance serves to vindicate every major character in the film—at the expense of Frank, however. And that is one reason he so carefully chooses the moment of truth.

Once Upon a Time in the West is about vindication, just as *A Fistful of Dollars* is about avarice, *For a Few Dollars More* is about obsession, and *The Good, the Bad and the Ugly* is about betrayal. By the end of the film, Cheyenne, circumstantially held responsible for the McBain killings, is vindicated; Harmonica's own claim on Frank is vindicated; Jill's abandonment of her old way of life and her embracing of a new world are vindicated by the confidence Harmonica and Cheyenne place in her; and, McBain's dream for Sweetwater is vindicated through Jill by Harmonica and Cheyenne. Most of all, the Western, an increasingly out-of-favor genre during the '60s (particularly the Italian Western, the target of simple-minded reviewers and critics), is vindicated.

Yet these vindications are achieved more in sadness than in triumph. Watching Harmonica's lonely ride away from Sweetwater we sense—as we sensed in Colonel Mortimer's tired departure from Agua Caliente—that the burden is not really lifted. People like Harmonica have "something to do with death" inside them. In *Once Upon a Time in the West* the "death wish" that became so much a part of Charles Bronson's screen image (it's observable in *The Magnificent Seven* and *The Great Escape* as well as here, in *Death Wish*, and several other more recent Bronson films) is related not so much to the need for revenge as to the phenomenon of survivor guilt. The memory of what happened to the little boy who became the Man with the Harmonica haunts us long after the satisfaction of Harmonica's revenge on Frank has faded. It's a grim variation on the considerably lighter denouement of *The Good, the Bad and the Ugly*. Tuco's rickety cross becomes the shoulders of a child. When he falls—and he will fall, it's only a question of how soon—his brother will hang from a noose affixed to the peak of an arch in the middle of a desert limbo. And this time there is no "good" hero to shoot the rope in half.

Leone gets into this drama by tracking in to extreme closeup on the Man's face as the Man confronts Frank for the final gundown. He then cuts to the recurring flashback motif of the blurred form walking toward the camera. As the form materializes into a young Frank, proffering a harmonica, Leone cuts back to the Man, tracking further in to the most extreme closeup yet: The eyes are what fill the entire Techniscope screen. Cutting to the flashback, Leone repeats the track-in on the face of a little boy with a harmonica in his mouth. But instead of coming into an extreme closeup, the camera stops. It begins to move upward and outward, revealing the boots on the boy's shoulders, and the man standing atop him, and finally the noose and the arch. From *The Good, the Bad and the Ugly* to *Once Upon a Time in the West*, Leone's interest has shifted from the plight of the man with his head in the noose to the dilemma of the boy on whose shoulders he stands—and the Man that boy will become. Rarely in cinema have past and present been so painfully and inexorably linked.

Leone's use of flashbacks here (and less successfully in *For a Few Dollars More* and *Duck, You Sucker!*) bear witness to a continuing interest in the flexibility of real time, the persistence of memory, and the permanence of mythic time. The film's title specifies "Time" and names a place as well; yet the film's manipulation of both time and space is distinctly un-concrete. We have seen in earlier films how Leone deliberately protracts time in montages that freeze the final moments before a shootout, repeating the frozen images in endless variations until violence breaks the pattern. The violent moment comes abruptly, almost anticlimactically. The sense of time is similar to that seen during the climactic duel in Kurosawa's *Sanjuro*: The two men, in profile, face-to-face, much closer than one would expect even for swordplay, stand poised, motionless, for what seems like an eternity. When the blow comes, it comes fast—more felt than seen—and the adversaries freeze once more. Then one of them slowly topples over. But where Kurosawa holds the shot to catch the horror of the swordplay, Leone cuts on the gunshot to an angle from behind Frank, to catch the expression on his face as he spins around, fatally shot and not believing it.

Gradualness to suddenness is the progression in *Once Upon a Time in the West*. The familiar, ritualistic path is plodded slowly by the characters whose behavior is necessary and inevitable. Like Camus's Sisyphus, the characters must relish the progression in order to face the undoing that must come—and they are all undone, the victors no less than the vanquished.

Leone uses slow but accelerated montage throughout his films. The technique highlights the relentless progress leading toward the fatal moment; it captures the will of his characters both to embrace the coming moment and to cling to the time that is necessarily passing. The characters use devices to discipline themselves, to force their wait, and steel their nerves: "When the chimes stop, pick up your gun." "I got a feelin' when he stops whittlin', somethin's gonna happen." Both Mortimer and Indio carried watches—identical watches. When Harmonica helps Frank escape being ambushed in Flagstone by his own men (a way of protecting his investment in Frank and the kind of justice he demands), he calls attention to a handless clock painted on a wall, behind which a gunman hides. "Time sure flies!" Harmonica calls out. The clock in the station at Flagstone has hands but isn't running. After the traitorous gunmen are finally dispatched in Flagstone and Frank is left alive to fight another day, Harmonica tells Jill, "It's time to go home now." The awareness of time pervades the film—and always with the sense of "It's getting late." All these clocks and time references are another wry subversion of the cinematic grammar of *High Noon*. The characters of *High Noon* are time's slaves; the titans of *Once Upon a Time in the West* are its masters.

Leone's directorial credit concludes the long main title sequence at Cattle Corner, dropping in an arc from screen right to horizontal, like a gate falling to stop the advancing train. *Once Upon a Time in the West* has been called Leone's slowest film, but time always seems to be moving too fast to suit Leone and his dying race of titans. There's a lot more than meets the eye and ear when a railroad worker, in momentary medium close, calls "Slow down!" to Sam, who buzzes the surveying crew with his buckboard, then rolls peacefully into Monument Valley, as yet untouched by the relentless fingers of "progress."

Some characters—notably the lesser ones—perceive time differently from the principals who are thrust toward a destiny that concludes even as it culminates. Jill is impatient when Sam wants to stop at the roadside tavern to water his horse (and whiskey himself). Inside, Jill has her conversation with the bartender. For him, all the excitement (the entire escape of Cheyenne from the law, his encounter with Harmonica, Cheyenne's release from his handcuffs, the mutually accusatory conversation between Cheyenne and Harmonica, the arrival of Cheyenne's men, and the departure of the gang) constitutes little more than a cumbersome, pesky parenthesis to his story about his sister in New Orleans, which concludes with his comment that he refuses his sister's invitation to join her because "I don't think I'd get along in a big city. ... I'm used to a quiet, simple country life." Then there's Wobbles, whose spectacular ability to be in the wrong place at the wrong time amounts to a case of terminal bad timing.

As Richard Jameson has pointed out, the characters of *Once Upon a Time in the West* have an equally remarkable relationship to space. In the two "Dollars" films people and things relate to one another in a frequently confusing way—although the confusion begins to be transformed into studied ambiguity in *For a Few Dollars More* when Colonel Mortimer strangely manipulates Manco's geographic intentions. Tucumcari, Alamogordo, Santa Cruz, and El Paso may be found on any map; Agua Caliente exists only in Sergio Leone's imagination, but its location is not hard to surmise. It is the layout of individual streets, houses, and rooms that remains unclear. In *The Good, the Bad and the Ugly* the reference to troop movements—and the constant comparison of these movements with those of Blondie and Tuco—help to establish a sense of geography, though not always of screen space within the individual shot.

Still, by *Once Upon a Time in the West*, Leone is already a master of cinematic space on both the panoramic geographic level and the interior set level. He is able to sustain the comings and goings of his characters through credible physical space and through mythical (or, as Mircea Eliade would have it, "sacred") space as well. Morton's train comes and goes along the completed portion of railroad track; Frank ranges away from it, ever returning as if held in its sphere of influence, until, near the end, that center is destroyed and Frank is drawn into the circle of the Man with the Harmonica. The movement of the train depicts the progress of the railroad toward Sweetwater and away from Flagstone, making the already thriving community of Flagstone a metaphoric "East" against Sweetwater's just-sprouting West. Jill journeys from Sweetwater to Flagstone to meet with Frank and to auction her land; but by the end of the film Sweetwater is "home." We see that coming from the way Jill is defined, visually, in terms of community. She's a city lady—we already know that from what Brett McBain has told his children. The Flagstone she comes to near the beginning of the film is a panorama of frontier life. We see Indians, slaves, carpetbaggers, businessmen, and workmen unloading the train. Barrels and crates are lifted off (including two huge casks conspicuously marked "OLIVE OIL"—Leone's joke on himself and the "Spaghetti Western" genre?). Snatches of conversation give us a pastiche of life in Flagstone, while putting us in Jill's position as she tries to determine who Brett may have sent to meet her. The noises die away. They are replaced by the majestic music associated with Jill as her loneliness is confirmed and she takes matters into her own hands. She goes into a station, gets directions, and, as the camera rises over the roof, emerges from the other side of the building into the bustling town. By the end of the film, through Jill's agency and fortitude, Sweetwater, too, will begin thriving.

Cheyenne and Harmonica always seem most comfortable coming from—and disappearing into—nowhere. The entrance into Jill's affairs seems the result of a mystical juncture of the mythic realm with real space and time. Cheyenne has a particularly improbable agility for moving through Leonean space, his specialty being the almost imperceptible slide from exterior to interior. Examples of this ability can be seen in scenes of the roadside tavern, the McBain house, and most memorably, the sequence featuring Cheyenne's transit from the underside of Morton's train car to its roof, then from outside the car to the inside via the toilet's flush-chain.

In contrast to Morton, McBain, Frank, and Jill, who nearly always are seen in full natural light, there is an almost Promethean overtone to the way Cheyenne and Harmonica are often introduced in shadow and illuminated by fire. In the roadside tavern, Cheyenne ceremoniously shoves a hanging lantern along its wire across the room to discover the source of the harmonica wail emanating from the darkness in the corner. Harmonica draws Jill's shotgun fire by striking a match outside the McBain house at night. Cheyenne is lighting the fire at the McBain house for Jill to make coffee when she opens a drawer and contemplates the knife she sees there, thinking of it as a means of ridding herself of the menacing bandit she suspects murdered her husband. "Of course, if anyone was to take a mind to kill me," says Cheyenne, "it would fire me up. And a fired-up Cheyenne ain't a pretty sight to see." The fire roars to life. Jill closes the drawer. Cheyenne smiles.

Doorway backlighting—the underlying visual motif of John Ford's *The Searchers*—attends the intrusion of both Cheyenne and Frank into the world mystically shared by Jill and Harmonica. Jill and the Man are both inside the roadside tavern (though they haven't met yet, and the Man is hidden in darkness) when Cheyenne enters, silhouetted in the doorway. Later, Jill and Harmonica are together in the saloon in Flagstone when Frank enters in an attempt to buy Sweetwater from Harmonica: the scene is lit in the same way. Similarly, Frank's form during the flashbacks is first a hazy silhouette that becomes gradually more distinct as Harmonica's memory makes what he's remembering for us. Frank, because he is a public figure, is usually associated with daylight. Cheyenne and Harmonica, however, retain private motives. Even so, all three of these mythic characters emerge from indistinctness to stark prominence, as if entering the world via almost supernatural means.

When we get our first glimpse of the Man with the Harmonica near the end of the long opening sequence, we see him from a distance as the train, from which he did not visibly disembark, pulls away to reveal him standing on the other side of the tracks. But the first real look at the Man comes during a long, slow crawl up his body in a medium-close shot. It starts at ground level and, daring an emphatic musical crescendo, comes to rest on that calm, implacable face.

The same music and the same general relationship between camera and subject recur in the introduction of Frank, near the end of the second sequence at the McBain ranch. We see Frank first from a distance, and cannot make him out clearly. Having killed three of the four McBains, Frank and his men materialize from the brush. They move toward the camera-viewpoint of Timmy McBain, acting nothing like the complacent Harmonica who enters his introductory shot standing still as an entire locomotive moves aside to accommodate his presence.

As the killers approach the little boy, their measured steps are accompanied by a different orchestration of the same musical theme ("As a Judgment"). The camera follows them, closing in on the boy from behind the left shoulder of one of the men. When the men stop, the camera keeps moving forward toward the boy, just a little more, then describes a clockwise semicircle and comes to rest on a stark profile of Frank—the baroque camera movement providing buildup and impact to the startling iconic reversal of heroic Henry Fonda in an uncompromisingly villainous role.

What goes around comes around and in the final confrontation the circle is described again, to the same music (finally taking on the full implication of its title—a phrase from the law courts for the assignment and exacting of a payment for a debt or suit finally settled). But this time, the camera's not moving around Frank; instead both camera and Frank are circling the Man with the Harmonica; it is he, not Frank, who now controls the situation. Frank and Harmonica begin their confrontation by entering the frame from the same side. This approach violates the stylistic convention of Westerns and twists the rules of the classic cinematic opposition; however, the reversal of expectation stresses a point: Frank and Harmonica are the same "kind of man." They both enjoy the willful mastery over space that befits an archetype. But in the event, the relative positions of the dominant, menacing Frank and his boy-victim at the McBain ranch are now reversed—Harmonica is at the center of the moving circle.

No mere window, this camera. Rarely in film has its presence been so obtrusive, yet so appropriately manipulated. It is almost as if the camera were a character—the "third man" in the showdown. And why shouldn't that camera be a character? It signals the most dominating presence in any Leone film—that of Leone himself, tracking wide-eyed through the (Hollywood) West.

The order of the film, needless to say, is a perceptibly Leonean order; familiar motifs recur from his earlier films, though woven into tighter unity than Leone achieved before or since. One of the most familiar motifs is the use—particularly during opening scenes—of parallel situations. Just as the Mortimer and Manco introductions in *For a Few Dollars More* carefully paralleled each other and as the "Good," "Bad," and "Ugly" announcements did likewise, the first two sequences of *Once Upon a Time in the West* are carefully balanced.

The two shootings, occurring in different atmospheres and for different reasons, are deliberately juxtaposed (joined in an Eisensteinian way) by the "bridge" of conflicting images. One image is the opening eye of the Man with the Harmonica as he is resurrected after the encounter with the three men in dusters at Cattle Corner (his eyes will become very familiar, and very important to us, by the end of the film); the other image is the crash of Brett McBain's shotgun as he rustles up some dinner for his wedding banquet.

The first sequence begins ominously, moves to violence, and ends on a note of resurrection, carrying with it a new sense of portent. The second sequence begins on a note of violence (the shotgun), proceeds through a domestic interlude to the multiple killings of McBain and his older children, and ends on the shot with which Frank kills Timmy. Sandwiched between these explosions of sound and violence are shots of the idyllic domesticity of McBain's home life, which is jarred only slightly by the brief tiff between Brett and his elder son, just as life at the remote train station in the opening goes on peacefully, soothed by the gentle creaking of the windmill, unperturbed by the menacing presence of three men in dusters as they, in turn, are unperturbed by dripping water and a pesky fly (well, relatively unperturbed).

Train whistles figure critically in both sequences. In the first, it picks up from the fly's buzz to herald the arrival of the Man. In the second, it emanates from the sound of the shot that kills the last McBain, and heralds the arrival of Jill in Flagstone. The train whistle, harbinger of progress, is always a reminder that "it's getting late"—that the appointed time approaches.

There are other parallels. In both the opening and the McBain massacre, men in dusters appear as the forces of evil; the Man with the Harmonica faces a gundown at the beginning and at the climax; Jill's association with water balances Harmonica's (and Cheyenne's) with fire. Overriding everything is a parallel between the mythic world and the real world; and this parallel is paralleled in the frequent comparison of large images with miniatures.

When we—with Jill—first see the tiny buildings in Brett McBain's trunk, we take them for children's toys, but the buildings are the stuff dreams are made on. Cut from the McBain house to a shot of a chessman in the window of Morton's train car. The chessman makes the real trains and buildings it's juxtaposed against look like toys or gamepieces on a shelf, and for a moment we are almost tricked into perceiving them on the same scale as McBain's models. The link is clear: Though real, these trains and buildings are as toys to Morton, and the difference between Morton's dream and McBain's is the difference between reducing the world to a plaything and building a world from ideas conceived in miniature. The film is about the fulfillment of McBain's dream. Morton's dream of the Pacific, in contrast, ends up miniaturized in a mud puddle.

If the trains and buildings are seen as the toys of Morton and McBain, they are, by extension, the "real" toys of Leone, as is this entire world. Jameson has compared Harmonica's comment, "You don't sell the dream of a lifetime" to the inability of Leone and Paramount to sell *Once Upon a Time in the West* to an audience. Accustomed to the wit, blood, and thunder of the first three Leone films (and, possibly, to the presence and persona of Clint Eastwood), the masses did not take to Leone's brooding exercise in mythmaking. Paramount, assuming that the problem was with the film's length or figuring they could make back some of their losses by including the film on the bottom half of double bills, hacked out nearly twenty-five minutes of the film's running time, including the entire crucial roadside tavern sequence—the scene that first brings together Jill, Harmonica, and Cheyenne. This important scene establishes Harmonica's and Cheyenne's mutual respect as well as their mutual suspicion; it also provides the important information that, to cover up his own killings, Frank is trying to frame Cheyenne's gang. Thus shortened, the film played no better; that's because it played no faster and made a lot less sense. (It was not until 1985 that a complete U.S. version of the film was again available for theatrical exhibition. Today, the most complete edition available can easily be had on DVD.)

The fact that Leone's first three films remain on *Variety*'s all-time rental champions list, while *Once Upon a Time in the West*, though extraordinarily popular in Europe, never earned back its cost in this country makes it tempting to wonder if the film might have fared better with Clint Eastwood in the Bronson role. It's hard to imagine the film's having the same mystique, however, without the very different Bronson persona at its center.

It is a slower, less plot-centered, and generally talkier film than the East-wood-Leone films and, despite its humanity and emotional depth, it is, until *Once Upon a Time in America*, Leone's coldest film. Of the lead players, only Jason Robards can sustain the kind of balance between self-parodying wit and deadly seriousness that Eastwood developed in the first three films (and that Van Cleef and Wallach extended in their respective personifications of the Leone mythos). Despite its quirkily witty moments (which remain the province of the lesser players—including Elam, Strode, and Stander), *Once Upon a Time in the West* is humorless in comparison with the first three films, and its sense of importance always overrides its sense of a good time, a direct reversal of the atmosphere of the Eastwood films.

A further problem is that the film fails to show us a single character that, even in fancy, we'd like to be. People were engaged by the style and witty dialogue of the Man with No Name. The Man with the Harmonica with his burden of guilt, his "something to do with death," his numbed emotions, ambiguous motivation, and icy distance holds little attraction for the audience that cheered No-Name's clever repartee and sly double-dealing. Frank is a child-killer, and—no matter that he's played by Fonda—there's no identifying with him. Cheyenne, the most likely (and likable) candidate, is too long kept a mystery to us to win our hearts; we fall for him only when he's finally dying, and then it's too late. So we're left with Jill, the person to whom, indeed, our sympathies are most readily extended. But sympathy isn't the same thing as identification, and Jill certainly isn't the person we'd like to be or would leave the theatre imitating and quoting. The end of the film suggests to us that we should have been with Harmonica all along. But even on repeat viewings, we never see him developing the infectiously appealing style that Eastwood's No Name did. Even Sean Mallory in *Duck, You Sucker!* invites the identification of admiring screen-dreamers more than Harmonica does, despite the fact that *Duck, You Sucker!* is a pale film beside *Once Upon a Time in the West*. People were ready for epic from Leone, but they weren't ready for poetry—even if that was what Leone had been giving them all along.

So the masterpiece was rejected, as, in a way, all truly personal masterpieces are. The final credit in the long main title sequence—Leone's, of course—is superimposed over the advancing front of a train, and is balanced with the title of the film, first seen only at the very end of the movie, turning in a circle and receding slowly from our grasp. Stories normally begin with that phrase "Once upon a time," and here this one's kept until the end. The end as beginning? The past as prologue? So what if nobody bought it? It's only, after all, a fairy tale.

Notes

1   There is also, incidentally, a shot in which Cutter, with a loaded gun, makes "Monsewer Regret" dig a hole.

2   According to Christopher Frayling, identification (via a "Wanted" poster) of Cheyenne as "Manuel 'Cheyenne' Gutierrez" was cut from the film when the first release print was assembled.

"All I Want Is the Money"

Duck, You Sucker!

The proliferation of reviews and comment about *Duck, You Sucker!* demonstrated that *Once Upon a Time in the West*, though having lost Leone his American box office standing, studio support, and mass popularity, had won him the interest, if not always the esteem, of the critics. He was now at last being taken seriously.

The reason for the seriousness was, alas, ideological. Ideology has ever been the last refuge of the bankrupt film critic, particularly where the American coterie of daily reviewers is concerned. It's so much easier to judge a movie on the rightness of its position than on its cinematic values and on the importance of its vision. Leone had been written off by the American critical establishment as irredeemably pro-violence (the term "fascist" had slipped in here and there, as it often seems to do in discussions of film-makers who attempt to deal seriously and honestly with power and the use of force).

Once Upon a Time in the West had softened the violence, which was less graphic—more deliberately poetic, and subordinated to a higher purpose—than was the primitive morality that so repulsed critics in the Eastwood films. *Duck, You Sucker!*—known in Europe as *Once Upon a Time the Revolution*—was critically popular because it had something for everybody. Leone *seemed* to be dealing with ideology, without really doing so. He managed to be political and apolitical, both revolutionary and anti-revolutionary. Juan Miranda's (and the film's) distrust of politics and politicians touched something in the hearts of the largely liberal critical community, coinciding as it did with the final chapters of America's Vietnam fiasco and the dawn of what would soon be called the Watergate Era. *Duck, You Sucker!*'s simple ideology is anti-cruelty, even at the audacious risk of seeming pro-ignorance.

Critics were cued to overemphasize the political atmosphere of the film. Here, for the first time, Leone was placing his characters in a definite historical-political context. The lawless frontier of the "Dollars" films and the coming of the railroads in *Once Upon a Time in the West* are clear-cut fantasy environments. Even the Civil War of *The Good, the Bad and the Ugly* seems an ethereal, abstract version of the historical reality of that war.

But the film's Mexican Revolution background was not simply a pretext for sociopolitical commentary, as many presumed. It had become, in fact, a convention of the Italian Western, exemplified in Damiani's *A Bullet for the General*, Sollima's *The Big Gundown*, Corbucci's *Compañeros* and *The Mercenary*, and Petroni's *Tepepa*. There is a long-standing Hollywood tradition of using—

and whitewashing—the Mexican Revolution as a vehicle for action films that avoid any real sensitivity to the Marxist cause that underlay the revolutionary struggle. Italian Westerns, by contrast, while no less guilty of simplifying historical context for their own purposes, could not help approaching the matter more honestly, given the realities of the peasant class and the communist movement in Italian life. It may be, in fact, that the "spaghetti" directors' development of the Mexican Revolution as a plot background led American filmmakers toward the rediscovery of that rich historical tapestry in such films as Brooks's *The Professionals* and Peckinpah's *The Wild Bunch*, both of which tap a number of "spaghetti" devices. Certainly there is give-and-take between Italian Westerns and American Westerns of the late '60s and early '70s. This influence is best represented by Peckinpah's revisionism of the Italian Western in *The Wild Bunch*. Also, an awareness of Peckinpah pervades later Italian Westerns, particularly *My Name Is Nobody*.

The important plot motivation of *The Wild Bunch* is not complicated. With the American West getting more settled and the forces of law and order becoming more efficient and omnipresent, the bandits who make their living working against society must move south to find an atmosphere more commensurate with their lifestyle. (The same device figures importantly in *Butch Cassidy and the Sundance Kid* and in a number of lesser Westerns of the early '70s.) But in moving south, the displaced American outlaws find themselves forced to reinterpret their own profit-oriented brigandage in the new context of political-military conflict.

The same dilemma faces Juan Miranda, the small-time Mexican dirt-bandit who becomes the hero of *Duck, You Sucker!* Juan dreams of a reverse process; he wants to leave Mexico and go to America to get rich robbing banks. But by the time that dream becomes possible, Juan's criminal activities have been redefined in terms of revolutionary activism. Almost as if *Once Upon a Time in the West* had never happened, we here find Leone again opposing the ethic of self-interest to the ethic of service to a cause, vindicating profit motivation at the expense of politics and the war mentality.

But *Duck, You Sucker!* isn't *The Good, the Bad and the Ugly* all over again—for three major reasons. First, devotion to a political cause is, for the first time in a Leone film, represented by one of the leading characters and not relegated to the background and spoken of by minor players in a scene or two. Second, the major characters are seen to change their viewpoints—to grow—something that happens to no one in the first three Leone films and only to Frank and Jill in *Once Upon a Time in the West*. Plot is not a function of conflict between personifications of established, unchanging attitudes and motivations (as it is in the earlier films); there is no gradual revelation of a static character (as in *For a Few Dollars More* and *Once Upon a Time in the West*). Rather, the plot grows out of genuine character development in the classic literary sense.

Third, and most important, in *Duck, You Sucker!* the alliance of the man of personal gain with the man of cause is presented as a troubling metaphor for the uneasy but inevitable interdependence of private enterprise and political opportunism in the western world. Such alliances are evident in earlier Leone films. In

For a Few Dollars More, Manco was out for profit, Mortimer for holy revenge. And Cheyenne and Harmonica stand in roughly the same relation to Frank and to economic realities as the two bounty killers did to Indio. But never before has the polarity between strange bedfellows been so great as with Juan Miranda ("All I want is the money!") and Sean Mallory ("There is only one revolution.").

Democratic revolution (which began the modern history of most western nations, including the United States, Leone's Italy, Miranda's Mexico, Mallory's Ireland, Marx's Germany, Marat's France, and Bakunin's Russia) here comes into the gun sights of Leone's cynical vision. Corruption—or at least corruptibility—is assumed to be universal, and moral rectitude is assigned only in terms of that context. Ironically, it is Sean, the apparent revolutionary zealot, who aphorizes the whole Leone vision. Trying to persuade Juan to go through with the proposed raid on the National Bank of Mesa Verde, Sean says of the chaotic frenzy that has seized the city, "It's just the way we like it. If it's a revolution, it's confusion. ... When there's confusion, a man who knows what he wants stands a chance of getting it."

There's more ambiguity in this than even Sean recognizes. He's deliberately taking advantage of Juan's confusion to get what he himself wants, but, as the film progresses, it becomes clearer and clearer that Sean is not, after all, so sure about what he wants. Indeed, confusion seems to win the day in this carefully structured film that begins and ends in a haze of gunsmoke. This implication is epitomized late in the film when Juan, for his own private reasons, performs the ultimate revolutionary act—assassination—then seeks egress from the train, the revolution, and the country. He's finally persuaded Sean to go to America with him to form a bank-robbing partnership, and then he asks, sheepishly, "Which way is America?" Looking out one door of the freight car they're concealed in, Sean sees firing squads mowing down their victims, and replies, "Well, not that way." He rolls back the opposite door, saying, "That's the way," and brings into view a crowd of cheering rebels who bear Juan off on their shoulders. If there are two "sides" to this revolution, they are as confused and ultimately indistinguishable as the two sides of the train car.

If it's odd that Sean's equation of revolution with confusion aims to justify self-interest, it's equally ironic that the illiterate peasant-bandit Juan draws the key, long speech about revolution and politics. In an interlude occurring between the liberation of the political prisoners from the Mesa Verde bank vaults where Juan hoped to find his fortune and the standoff at the bridge where Juan's self-interest comes bang up against Sean's higher motivation and seems to lose out utterly, Juan gives Sean an impromptu lesson in revolutionary politics. Like Tuco's speeches, this one concerns the division of the world into two kinds of people: "The people who read books, they say to the poor people, 'It's time for a change!' The revolution comes. Then the people who read books sit at tables and talk, and what has happened to the poor people? They're dead!" With a low whistle, Sean tosses down his copy of Bakunin's *Patriotism* and moves one step closer to accepting Juan's proposal to chuck politics and go to America where they will rob banks and split everything fifty-fifty. Juan, of course, numbers himself among the poor people, and his plea to go to America is the typical immigrant's dream of the land of plenty and equality. In his case, the dream is layered onto the private conviction that he can liberate himself from poverty and oppression without joining the ranks of the people who read books, simply by taking what he wants. The taking is by force of course. Ultimately there are no philosophical differences between the thief and the revolutionary, only a difference in motivation.

So what is Juan Miranda, finally? An ignorant peasant, a scroungy bandit, or a revolutionary in spite of himself? What was Villa? What was Zapata?

Throughout the film, Juan is depicted as an outsider. He's accepted nowhere except in the little community of his niños, the outlaw gang he has formed from his own sons and a few hangers-on. At the opening of the film, Juan hitches a ride on an enormous coach—as large as a railway car inside, though never quite so big from the outside—filled with exemplars of the Mexican aristocracy. Leone's camera and montage condemn the upper classes; a series of closeups of their faces and mouths reveals, while the aristocrats are eating, an overriding ugliness in even the most common of gestures.

Leone's camera work clearly excludes Juan from their number. His appearance gives rise to a discussion of the peasantry among the coach passengers; they talk about Juan and his class as if Juan himself were not present, regarding the peasants as if they were a species of vastly inferior animal (a metaphor that Juan later turns against them when, imitating a bull, he rapes one of the stuffy women).

Juan quickly is separated from Sean as well. The Irishman is literate, educated, and intellectual; he transforms his ideas and dreams into action with sophisticated systems of explosive weaponry.

Juan, on the other hand, is illiterate, unaware of the technological and political developments in the world around him, and lacking in all but the most basic wiles of the highwayman. He lives a dream that he has never been able to transform into action: "Not a bank," he tells Sean, speaking of the robbery of the National Bank of Mesa Verde "*the* bank ... like it was the gates of heaven."

When Sean gives Juan the means by which to fulfill his dream, Juan remains alienated. Following Sean to Mesa Verde, he finds himself as out of place in the city of his dreams as he was in the coach of the rich. It's no longer the town he remembers. Chaos reigns. A stranger is shot and spins into Juan's unwelcoming arms. A firing squad readies itself for another victim, a defiant revolutionary whose last act is to spit on the governor's picture. A poster is torn away from a fence, and Juan peers through knotholes—or bullet holes—his eyes replacing those missing from the governor's portrait. He watches the execution. "Papa," he asks his dead father's spirit, "are you sure this is Mesa Verde?"

Sean's circle of revolutionaries is no different from the gathering of aristocrats in the coach. As Juan looks on silently, the revolutionaries, too, talk about him as if he weren't there. When he asks to know what's going on, they ignore him until they believe it's time to give him information. "*Tierra y liberdad*" is a catch-phrase for them, despite their failure to recognize that Juan and people like him are closer to *tierra* than they will ever be. And, of course, the ultimate alienation comes when Juan sees himself as a dupe of the revolutionaries, when he is tricked into blasting his way into the Mesa Verde bank vaults in search of gold, only to find he has freed a mob of imprisoned rebels. The gold he dreamed of his entire life had been taken from these vaults long ago.

Juan, like the stereotypical Catholic peasant, seems at home only with family—and with God. He has a special relationship, a kind of understanding, with God, whom he addresses incessantly, and who has become inseparable from Juan's dream of wealth. Juan has a special shrine in his wagon-home, built around a vision of the National Bank of Mesa Verde. "It's like a miracle of God!" he tells Sean when he sees the Irishman's facility with explosives. Juan sees Sean as a Christ who has come, at last, to show him the way into the bank. Sean is shown from Juan's point of view with a banner suspended above his head; the banner bears the name of the bank while a heavenly choir amplifies the vision. Even as dreams fade, Juan keeps God on his side. He looks upward repeatedly, as if seeking guidance or confirmation of the validity of his opinions. Railing against Sean just before the battle at the bridge, Juan declaims, "I'm glad he's having fun, God, because I am not having fun."

God is the special friend whose companionship and approval give justification to Juan's self-interest and to his way of life; God is the guardian of the family. Before the bridge sequence, Juan bids farewell to his niños, telling them, "If something happens and your father doesn't come back, then I pray that the great God in heaven takes care of you." Kisses and a wink seal the bargain; but during the bridge shot, Juan's God fails him. The bridge is blown and Juan survives, returning to the rebel encampment to find his niños dead, the victims of a counterattack by the governor's *federales*. His grief is touching: "All of them," he sobs. "Six. I never counted them before." As if casting blame, he looks upward again, then rips the Christian medal from around his neck. His homely religion has served him no better than the institutionalized hypocrisy exemplified in the cardinal on the coach, who spoke mockingly of the faithful poor ("You should hear them in confession … !") while stuffing his face with rich foods. Religion, which has all along been allied with the bandit's life of criminal gain, now stands in opposition to the revolution, which Juan now embraces—at least tentatively—if only out of vengeance. The transformation is an important event in Sergio Leone's work: A character has been influenced, perhaps even changed, by circumstance.

Early in the film, on the train to Mesa Verde, the revolutionary Dr. Villega mistakes Juan for a comrade in arms. In town, looking through the eyes of the governor's picture, Juan becomes a New Wave revolutionary statement, the peasant-bandito who wears the politician's mask, albeit unwittingly. Whether or not Juan consciously opts for revolutionism, he suffers the penalties of the revolutionary. His children are massacred and, with a growing sense of the ridiculousness of his situation, he himself faces a firing squad. Juan Miranda is the dupe of history and of the would-be history makers; he's the "sucker" of the film's title. Leone tempts us—though not with too much insistence—to conclude that Juan was better off as an ignorant bandit

The conceit of *Duck, You Sucker!* is to crisscross the moral and motivational polarities represented by its two characters. While Juan tentatively accepts

Johnny and Johnny: Juan Miranda (Rod Steiger) bids farewell to his niños, above; Sean (James Coburn), the "Firecracker," below, in *Duck, You Sucker!*

his circumstantial role in the war (if only to avenge his murdered children), Sean grows more cynical about revolution. Indeed by the end of the film, his motivations are so opaque that we wonder what he ever stood for. He only seems to be idealistic at the beginning of the film. Later words and actions show him to be interested in the challenge of revolution for its own sake. Political convictions, either concrete or abstract, seem lacking in his makeup. "One revolution was enough for me," he says. But was it? If he cannot return to Ireland (all is changed, changed utterly) why does he continue to pursue revolution rather than find a less dangerous, more profitable occupation like the one Juan proposes? Perhaps it is for the same reason that Dr. Villega, confronted by Sean with his guilt as an informer, refuses to jump from the doomed train—a kind of self-destructive atonement, shared in Leone's world, by such similarly haunted men as Mortimer, Indio, and Harmonica.

Sean Mallory certainly belongs to that class of Leone titans to whom dollars do not matter and for whom land holds no attraction as an investment. The role of these titans is to invest the external world with a higher importance based on interior reality; in Leone films the inner reality is usually represented by memory. Like Mortimer, Indio, and Harmonica, Sean has flashback visions that gradually reveal the source of the burden he carries. Five times in the film Sean is visited by memories of Ireland, memories that establish only very sketchily a three-way relationship involving Sean, a young woman, and another man. At the beginning of the film, the three are seen happy and motoring together along an Irish country road. At the end of the film, during the final flashback, which occurs just before Sean's devastating suicide, Sean and the girl enjoy a near-kiss in an idyllic field. The three intervening flashbacks deal with Sean and the other man (Sean's brother? the woman's?). In the second flashback, Sean and the man stand on a street corner passing out revolutionary literature. In the third, Sean is drinking in a pub when two British soldiers enter; the man, beaten, is a prisoner between them. The man begins pointing out IRA members at the bar. The Tommies arrest the men, working their way down the bar toward Sean. In the fourth flashback, which is cut into Sean's confrontation with the traitorous Dr. Villega, Sean raises a weapon wrapped in newspaper. He fires, killing the Tommies and their prisoner.

The significance of the memory is summed up in Sean's quick bit of self-analysis to Villega just after the fourth flashback: "When I started using dynamite, I believed in many things. Finally I believed only in dynamite. I don't judge you, Villega; I did that only once in my life." Despite the fact that shooting the informer saved many lives, Sean clearly regrets the act, viewing it as the event that destroyed him. Like Indio or Mortimer or Harmonica, he is now a walking dead man, with nothing left to lose. Even at the beginning of the film, Sean is seen as a person who delights in taking suicidal risks. After demonstrating nitroglycerine to Juan, he gets ready to leave. When Juan moves to stop him, Sean opens his coat and reveals the ammo dump he wears in the linings. "If I fall, they'll have to redraw all the maps," he says. "When I go, half this bloody country goes with me." The dialogue predicts the ending of the film (and also presents another sardonic way of dividing the world in half).

A great, grand, glorious hero of the revolution: Juan Miranda (Rod Steiger) disembarks the train to greet crowds of cheering rebels, as Sean (James Coburn) enjoys the momentary success of the revolution.

The confrontation with Villega in the train engine has been crucial for Sean. After all, Sean had started out as Villega's accuser and executioner, but quickly had reformed as a result of the flashback vision. When Juan asks the wounded Sean about Villega—who, ignoring Sean's offer of redemption, has gone to his death in the train crash—Sean smiles: "Villega: A great, grand, and glorious hero of the revolution." It's the payoff of a running gag that begins with Sean's telling Juan rather earnestly, after the liberation of the prisoners of the Bank of Mesa Verde, "You're a grand hero of the revolution now." Later, after Juan has shot the governor, and Juan and Sean discuss going to America, Villega tells Juan he is favored by Pancho Villa. "I think we should get out of here," Juan tells Sean, who replies, this time with thick sarcasm, "Well, you can't leave now. You're a great, grand, glorious hero of the revolution." The tragedy of Sean Mallory is the tragedy of the Mephistophelian manipulator who finds himself inexplicably turning into Faust before the Fall.

But if Sean's inner voice finally speaks a kind of insatiable self-hatred, his redemption is already implicit in the affection and loyalty Juan bears him, long after the grubby bandit has lost all reason to expect profit from the relationship. Juan's devotion to Sean—won with dynamite—gradually erodes the simplistic right-vs.-wrong attitude. No longer is this attitude the prerequisite for revolutionary activism, just as the cruelty of revolution itself shakes whatever sociopolitical convictions Sean may have originally embraced or affected, and just as his confrontation with Villega makes him end up questioning and judging himself, not the informant.

The friendship that develops between Juan and Sean is the central event of the film. With a failed male relationship behind him in Ireland, Sean is offered, in this new revolution, a new country—and a new friendship—to test his strength of character. Sean recognizes, in the scene with Villega, the extent to which he has failed again, and this in part accounts for his judgment against himself. (In the crucial, interdependent, gradual merger of the relationship between Sean and Juan, it is tempting to see a homosexual subtext—which may be why Leone is at pains to establish the heterosexuality of both men early in the film, while sustaining the importance, to both, of male camaraderie.)

The duo, not the trio, is the operative structural metaphor in *Duck, You Sucker!*, but it is not entirely a case of opposites attracting. In fact, part of what the film is about is the recognition from the outset that—superficial differences aside—Sean and Juan are brothers under the skin. They share a sentimentality for children and for family ties, a sense of justice and independence, and a belief in a moral center that has more to do with freedom and personal loyalty than with law, justice, and politics. Juan calls Sean's nitroglycerine "holy water" and sees him as a savior. These allusions, combined with Juan's ongoing conversation with God and Sean's often repeated "for Christ's sake," emphasize the fact that we have here two archetypal Catholics, each from a country where revolutions are built upon the shoulders of Catholic peasantry (all of this viewed, of course, by a man from yet a third such country). Juan and Sean also share the dream of going to America—the land of freedom and opportunity. This wish unites Mexicans with Irish with Italians in the great American immigrant experience. Melting-pot anonymity prevails in the name Juan coins for the bank-robbing firm he hopes he and Sean will establish: "Juan and Sean, the two *especialistas* in banks—we'll call it 'Johnny and Johnny.'" It's easy to see these two guys named John as parts of a single composite personality and to guess that maybe that's the reason Juan can never bring himself to leave.

For Juan, the decisive moment occurs on the hill overlooking the bridge. As the ragtag revolutionary detachment withdraws and Sean opts to stay and defend the bridge, Juan has every reason for ending their relationship then and there. He doesn't, out of some unshakable conviction that something good (i.e., profitable) will come out of their being together. Juan looks through one end of the binoculars at the bridge. Then he flips them over, looks through the other end, and says, "No matter how I look with them, I am still too close to the bridge." Sean isn't looking at all. Supine, his hat pulled down over his eyes, he seems to be asleep. "Look at him!" says Juan. "Like a tourist who is going somewhere, only he is staying—he's having fun! I'm glad he's having fun, God, because I am not having fun." And Juan starts to leave. He actually is ready to go. But, below, a *federale* detachment appears at the other side of the bridge; the troops are accompanied by a mighty and terrible tank.

Juan tries to awaken Sean, who refuses to budge; but a low-angle shot reveals to us that Sean has been awake all along. He's bluffed long enough to prevail upon Juan's sense of loyalty and belonging, to subtly coerce Juan into staying. Together, they win the battle of the bridge for the forces of the revolution.

Juan's binoculars and Sean's open eyes, ways of looking and not looking, seeing and refusing to see—these are key images throughout the film. The smoke of Sean's engineered explosions creates an omnipresent haze that externalizes the moral and political confusion of the characters. Juan's "two-way" binoculars emphasize the relativity of viewpoint. Juan's eyes peer through the picture of the governor; Sean's eyes intercut with the eyes of Juan's dead boys. Sean's pretended sleep, the persistence of the visions of his memory, his cry to Villega to "close your eyes and jump" (Villega does the first but not the second)—all this imagery of seeing creates a complex and disturbing matrix that reflects the film's ambivalent vision of the blindness of justice-vs.-the blindness of expediency and the willingness to see and accept responsibility-vs.-the pain of seeing.

As in all other Leone films, *Duck, You Sucker!* is about how we see as well. The film is rivaled only by *Once Upon a Time in the West* in its use of broad closeups, its insistence on expansiveness of time and space, and its emphasis on magnitude rather than on speed and multiplicity. The peculiar mixture of comedy and atrocity—much more jarring than in the other Leone films—is Chaucerian in scope, juxtaposing the lowest of low humor with the highest of high-minded themes and intentions; simultaneously, Leone ridicules both. His abiding interest in betrayal, revenge, and judgment is evident, but these themes take a less important role here than in the earlier films. There is no sense of a moment of reckoning attending either Juan's confrontation with the governor or Sean's with Villega (none, at least, that ever seems as important as Sean's final judgment of himself, and the last, apocalyptic, cosmic vision of absurdity at which Juan, pointedly, does not laugh). The governor tests Juan's convictions by offering him a fortune—exactly what Juan has wanted all along—but he is spared the agony of choice when the governor dives for the door of the train car. Juan perfunctorily shoots him dead. Then he wipes his hands, as if he has done something filthy. Sean congratulates himself for not judging Villega, yet sets up the circumstance in which Villega can only judge—and condemn—himself. Both moments, rich in possibility, are disposed of fairly quickly and without the characteristically Leonean buildup and climax. There's been a shift in tone and interest from the earlier films—partly because of the different generic conventions of the "revolution" variant of the Spaghetti Western, and partly because Leone is trying for something different, something he hasn't satisfactorily achieved.

Leone had planned to supervise *Duck, You Sucker!*—not direct it. Only after a planned collaboration with Peter Bogdanovich proved unworkable did Leone step in to direct his fifth film. This change of plan may account to some degree for the lack of conviction and the relative flaccidity of "the Leone touch" in *Duck, You Sucker!* In terms of characterization, the movie is Leone's most ambitious effort, an attempt to go farther beyond the stereotypical than he had ever ventured before, all the while preserving the stereotype as a referent and starting point.

All of Leone's film characters are eccentric. In this film, though, oddity doesn't have to signify depth; there is more than the superficial colorfulness of character. In fact, one of the greatest problems in the film is Rod Steiger's inability to bring out the complexity inherent in the Juan Miranda character. For all the haunting poetry of his self-damnation, Sean remains largely inscrutable, even though we are privileged to share his flashback visions. This is because we meet and take leave of Sean wholly from Juan's viewpoint. The film begins and ends with Juan Miranda, and more's the pity that Steiger didn't do a better job with him. (Leone told Noel Simsolo, on the other hand, that Steiger "thought of the film as very serious and intellectual, and had a tendency to come off in the style of Zapata or Pancho Villa. Once he understood his mistake, everything went well." It is possible that the whole disorienting nature of Steiger's portrayal of Juan is due not to failure on Steiger's part, but simply to the inability of Steiger and Leone to see Juan in the same light. Leone's remarks to Simsolo certainly imply that he was happy with precisely those aspects of Steiger's performance that seem least satisfying in the finished film. It's possible, too, that Leone, not having wanted or planned to direct *Duck, You Sucker!* in the first place, simply didn't give the matter as much attention as it needed.)

In a sense, though, the noncommittal nature of the performance is appropriate to the film. *Duck, You Sucker!*, unlike Leone's other films, is not about resolution; it's about the lack of resolution, the failure of things to come together and make sense in a way consistent with the mythic justice of the titans of the Eastwood films and *Once Upon a Time in the West*. But those heroes have passed, after all.

Duck, You Sucker! is Leone's first film about the modern, post-mythic world, the world of Jill and the diggers rather than of the rope-cutters and the men with loaded guns. In this world, Sean Mallory is an anomaly. He appears as a cockeyed redeemer; he departs in self-sacrifice, returning, Christ-like, to the cloud of smoke whence he came, leaving his followers more powerful but befuddled and alone.

The importance of Sean's going is stressed by the cosmic silence that follows the two shots that lay him low (the same kind of sudden silence that follows the calling out of the name "York!" at the beginning of Ford's *Rio Grande*, a silence that amplifies the echo of what has gone before). It's a silence as absolute as the blast that comes a few moments later, when Sean, having sent Juan out of the way, willfully destroys his own world (and a lot of Juan's, too). It's an explosion of nuclear proportions (there may even be a veiled reference to the nuclear age in Sean's earlier line about coming to believe only in dynamite) that gathers up the whole complexity of issues in the film, crumbles it into the tight ball of a single question, heard, rather than spoken, in Juan's voice. "What about me?" Juan says as we watch his drained expression. The film's title appears on the screen as answer.[1]

Juan's future, like Sean's past, remains an unanswered question, as does the problem *Duck, You Sucker!* poses about politics and revolution in human affairs. Juan's world is as chaotic at the film's end as it is at the film's beginning. Leone's vision fills us with cynicism. What chance do we have that the revolution will improve the world for Juan's kind—or for anyone? The most peaceful moment in the film has to be the last flashback, the final memory-vision of Sean Mallory—implicitly "shared" by Juan in a strange mystic awareness that stirs him, too late, to turn back to Sean. The sequence is a Leone effort to recapture lost innocence—to return, perhaps, to the sweetness of life "before the revolution." Like his countryman Bernardo Bertolucci, who borrowed that phrase from Talleyrand for the title of his remarkable film adaptation of *The Charterhouse of Parma*, Leone has taken an equally complex and honest view of the motivations of human behavior in revolution. *Duck, You Sucker!* shares with *Before the Revolution* the quality of being simultaneously satirical and compassionate. Like Bertolucci's film, it hangs in the memory as a gradual, relentless journey from light into darkness.

Notes

1   It is because of the resonance of this moment that I insist on the film's original American title. The Leonean joke doesn't work in prints where the title that rolls onto the screen is *Once Upon a Time the Revolution* or *A Fistful of Dynamite*.

8

"There Was Never Any Good Old Days"

My Name Is Nobody

My *Name Is Nobody* is special in that it wasn't directed by Leone and in that Leone did not take as large a part in the writing as he did in the five preceding "Leone films." Leone receives neither screenplay nor story credit though the story was his idea. On the other hand, his name appears three times in the opening titles (director Tonino Valerii's appears only twice): "Sergio Leone presents," "From an Idea of Sergio Leone," and "Supervised by Sergio Leone." Reportedly, Leone directed some of the sequences in the film and closely supervised Valerii's direction of many other sequences. Quite a few critics and reviewers saw it as a Leone film, in the same way that Christian Nyby's *The Thing* is unfailingly regarded as a Howard Hawks film.

When *My Name Is Nobody* was released in the United States, Valerii seemed to many critics to stand in the same relationship to Leone as Nyby stands to Hawks: a fledgling director whose tutelage and eventual "big break" came under the aegis of the master. Unlike Nyby, however, Valerii was a credited director several times over, before directing the film that made his reputation; *My Name Is Nobody* is Valerii's fifth movie. Nevertheless, though Valerii had been pretty much his own man ever since acting as assistant director on Leone's *For a Few Dollars More*, he was still a child of the "Spaghetti Western" genre, maintaining close association with Leone and other Leone collaborators at Rafran Cinematografica. *My Name Is Nobody* remains, from an auteurist vantage, a problematic film, if only because it is so hard to separate Leone's own hand from Valerii's, and to distinguish among parody, *hommage*, and mere imitation.

Another good reason for considering *My Name Is Nobody* generically rather than in accord with auteur theory is that it is the most unabashedly self-referential of all the major Italian Westerns—perhaps of the entire Western genre. The film is a comment on, as well as an extension of, the Leone vision, and that atmosphere is intrinsic as much to the screenplay as to Valerii's direction.

A perceptible subtext of self-reference is always present in the work of the best directors; from the very beginning of Leone's film career, this subtext is observable in his movies. But not until *Once Upon a Time in the West* would Leone make a movie that was so overtly and audaciously about the myth and creation of Western films. *My Name Is Nobody* does more; it out-Leones Leone. Less subtle than even *Once Upon a Time in the West*, it is a film about Westerns, not about the West.

Persistent Nobody (Terence Hill, left) urges partnership; Beauregard (Henry Fonda) is having none of it.

In one of the film's many Leone references, the admiring wanderer Nobody has his hat shot off by the object of his obsessive enthusiasm, aging, legendary gunfighter Jack Beauregard. Nobody holds his hat tightly on his head as Beauregard continues to drill it. Then Nobody takes the hat off and looks at it: "Four shots—one hole! Just like the good old days!" Beauregard scoffs, "There was never any good old days." We're talking fiction here.

Asked who he is, the lead character says, "Me? I'm Nobody." The character of Nobody is all about the self-satisfaction of a character who realizes he is a character, not a real person. This attitude is what explains the seemingly self-contradictory passion with which Nobody maintains his lack of identity while insisting that he wants to be famous.

Jack Beauregard, by contrast, is a character who thinks himself a real person; it is Nobody who has to show him how he can serve history and legend as well as self-interest. Beauregard is played by archetypal Western figure Henry Fonda. Though only the second most important actor in the Western film tradition, Fonda carries a broader wealth of associations than John Wayne. That's because Fonda played villains as well as heroes and embraced historical as well as fictional characters with a plain man's down-home conviction that transcended incidental distinctions between good guy and bad guy, liberal and conservative.

Fonda's Beauregard, the flip side of Fonda's Frank in *Once Upon a Time in the West*, is a man who has no time for destiny and who displays no sense of personal myth. What interests him is making—and keeping—appointments. He serves no higher cause—though Nobody remembers dreaming of him as "the only hope for law and order in the West"—and he isn't "in it" for the money. Dollars are, to him, only a means to an end, the end in this case being booking passage aboard a ship (named the *Sundowner*, no less!) that will carry him away to Europe and welcome retirement. Just as Sean and Juan sought to reverse the geographic route of American outlaws and go north across the border, so Beauregard reverses the direction of western peacemakers, moving steadily eastward, back to the Old World. His series of appointments includes meeting a train in order to meet a ship. But first, like it or not, Beauregard must meet his destiny, even if Nobody has manufactured that destiny for him out of boyish dreams.

Nobody has this idea—call it an obsession; it's never as gut-wrenchingly serious as Indio's, but it won't go away—that before Beauregard moves on he must cap his career by standing alone against the legendary Wild Bunch. "I always dreamed of you like that: an open plain and a hundred and fifty purebred sonsobitches on horseback, and you facin' 'em alone ..." Beauregard is nobody's dummy—even if he does eventually seem Nobody's dummy—and he sees that the admiring country kid with the fast gun is setting him up: if Beauregard does face the Wild Bunch in glory, that much more credit will accrue to Nobody when Nobody finally shoots Beauregard down.

Jack resists, of course. He works against the myth. He avoids shooting it out with Nobody. When he draws against the kid, it is only to shoot holes in Nobody's hat. Beauregard continues his eastward progress, divesting himself of the moral and spiritual accoutrement of the Western hero. He accepts money from the corrupt Sullivan and agrees not to investigate the shady dealings Sullivan is involved in with the Wild Bunch (they've been operating a goldmine formerly run by Beauregard's brother and a partner). Beauregard takes only enough money to reserve his cabin on the *Sundowner*. He rides away from a classic opportunity to do good and avenge his brother. He wants to behave as unlike a legend as possible. He's the Hollywood Western trying to be realistic, adult, contemporary, and anti-mythic.

And, of course, Nobody is the Italian Western, forcing the Western hero right back into the mythic mold. The ride of the Wild Bunch is pulled out of a desert Nowhere. The horsemen's forward motion is slowed—frozen and reaching—by the long lens. Accompanying the sequence is a Wagner-parodying, self-parodying musical set-piece from Morricone, deliberately evoking the self-conscious mythic obtrusiveness of the Italian Western. Ghostly referents in the Leone oeuvre include the flashbacks in *For a Few Dollars More*; *Duck, You Sucker!*; and especially *Once Upon a Time in the West*. And, of course, there is the miraculous—and miraculously timed—appearance of the carriage of the spirits in *The Good, the Bad and the Ugly*. The confrontation between Nobody and Jack Beauregard in the cemetery is undercut by the hat-shooting and the semicomic banter between them; when Sullivan pays Nobody off in the hope that he'll gun down Beauregard, a second confrontation is forestalled by further hat-shooting, and finally by the arrival in town of that same ghostly Wild Bunch, none of whom we ever see too clearly.

"Sometimes you run smack into your destiny on the very road you take to get away from it," Nobody tells Jack. This bit of Oedipal lore is not incidental when one thinks of Beauregard as Nobody's father-figure, whom Nobody must kill in order to achieve his own end. "If you go away," he tells Jack, in an earlier bit of dialogue that contains one of his many punning self-references, "who's gonna be left? Nobody." Jack either doesn't get or doesn't like the pun; he ignores it: "Maybe—but a man's gotta quit sometime." "Yeah," Nobody agrees, "but a man like you's gotta go out in style."

Style seems considerably more appealing to Beauregard than the idea of going out in it. Nevertheless, a sense of finality hangs over the whole film. The year is 1899—the end of a century (but the month is April, a time of rebirth, renewal, or, in this case, replacement). Appointments with a train and with a steamship are reminders of the intrusive technology that is shrinking the world and making time a more demanding, less relative consideration. The bustle of a New Orleans street scene presents the way of life that is fast encroaching on the pre-moral fluidity of the West; and the proverbial country yokels were never such rubes as the faceless onlookers who stand witness to Nobody's gundown of Beauregard. They are unaware not only of what they're seeing but of what they're supposed to think they're seeing.

The camera doesn't validate reality—it creates it. The photographer who records the moment of Nobody's "victory" over Beauregard (framed very much like Frank's death in *Once Upon a Time in the West*) fires off his flash powder like a gun, and the blast of the powder is more real than the gun Nobody uses to fake Jack's death. Tonino Valerii is taking a shot of a photographer taking a shot of Nobody taking a shot at Beauregard, and none of it is real in the same sense that all of it is. What's significant is the reaffirmation of John Ford's oft-quoted lesson in *The Man Who Shot Liberty Valance*: "When legend becomes fact, print the legend."

Valance is one of the names recited by Nobody in a litany of men laid low by Beauregard (again, it's a reversal of the situation in *Once Upon a Time in the West*, because here the dead are bad guys, and their killer admired as a demigod). The recitation occurs in the windswept, dustblown graveyard in Navajo territory, where the name "Pekinpah" is also visible on a crude grave marker. (Valerii acknowledges his roots as surely as Leone had acknowledged his in *Once Upon a Time in the West*. Leonean sequences include graveyards, dusters, trains, objects being stuffed in people's mouths, slow accelerating montages of closeups, hat-shooting, a prophet hiding his head and railing against progress, echoes of "As a Judgment" in Morricone's "gundown" music, and a sense of fairy-tale justice and moralism. There are Peckinpavian slow-motion deaths, the "Wild Bunch," train-chasing soldiers, and the decisive turning of Ford's West into the Westerns of the '60s and '70s.) Valerii is discriminating in his choice of monuments. Certainly, if ever two men changed the face of the Western—while continuing to celebrate the vision and spirit of the master, John Ford—those men were Sergio Leone and Sam Peckinpah.

The character relationships explored in *My Name Is Nobody* are rich in allegorical implication about the Western film tradition. Nobody is to Beauregard as the Italian Western is to the American Western (Beauregard "goes to Europe" and gets replaced by a blue-eyed Italian Nobody who becomes a somebody). Nobody is to Beauregard as Leone is to Ford. Literally a "Nobody" in his use of a pseudonym on his first film, Leone is as concerned with the perpetuation of Ford's glory as he is with overhauling the Western mythos in terms of his own vision. In Beauregard's farewell letter to Nobody (read voice-over by Fonda), the outgoing champ tells the kid, "You can preserve a little of that illusion that made my generation tick. Maybe you'll do it in your own funny way, but we'll be mighty grateful just the same." It's easy to see this as Valerii (or Leone himself) imagining the spirit of John Ford addressing Sergio Leone (and company).

When the letter goes on "Seems t'me we were all a bunch o' romantic fools," there's as much an element of Fonda-as-Beauregard-as-Fonda, as there is of Fonda-as-Beauregard-as-Ford. The barbershop scene in the beginning of the film, an obvious evocation of Fonda's Wyatt Earp getting a shave in Ford's *My Darling Clementine*, is emphatically repeated with the new kid, Nobody, at the film's end. The torch is passed to a new generation (and nationality) of actors in the Western iconography, as surely as it has been passed to new directors.

Nobody is to Beauregard as Terence Hill is to Henry Fonda? Why not? Particularly when one recalls that the pseudonymic "Terence Hill" is also a "nobody" that masks the Italian named Mario Girotti. It's as much "Terence Hill" as it is "Nobody" who shoots the giant down to size (revealing him to be a dwarf on stilts) and then takes the cigar from the little guy's mouth, affecting it himself for the rest of the scene. Terence Hill isn't just replacing Henry Fonda—he's replacing Clint Eastwood as well!

Nobody is to Beauregard as Valerii is to Leone? There is, after all, more than one director of Italian Westerns, and no reason why the new breed shouldn't have its chance to topple the giant (or, remembering Leone's apprenticeship, the Colossus). The carnival sequence that begins with Nobody's shooting-away the dwarf's stilts and appropriating his cigar is a series of trials—tours de force of cinematic technique—planned as much for Valerii to show his stuff as for Nobody to impress both us and Sullivan.

Leone, though rarely subtle, always justifies his audacity by using development, pacing, and drama—the mythmaker's sense of inevitable destiny. Valerii is not always so successful. He seems to lack confidence in the comedic value of audacious set-ups and situations on their own terms and flees into the arms of a lower, blunter kind of comedy than Leone uses, even in *Duck, You Sucker!* The film's Sennettesque slapstick and fast-motion scenes are funny more because they seem so out of place than because they are inherently inventive. Whereas Leone overstates—exaggerates for emphasis—Valerii often merely repeats himself (and Leone) to the point where he loses his sense of expansion and drama. A preponderance of anal humor suggests a homosexual, or at least adolescent, environment that poorly serves the womanless plot and risks alienating the viewer. Yet it is integral to the film's concluding jape: In the final scene, Nobody settles in for a shave, just as Beauregard did in the film's opening, knowing full well that the "barber" is out to kill him. But where Beauregard steadily held a pistol at the barber's crotch to ensure no slip of the razor, Nobody holds a stiffened finger at the barber's backside, just below the crotch. Indexing how the stylized whimsy of the comic Spaghetti Westerns has replaced the stylized drama of the mythic Spaghetti Westerns that went before it, Nobody's reputation and audacity have eliminated the need for the pistol.

In Beauregard's words, "If the risk is little, the reward is little," and Valerii takes some big risks. The most notable is the climactic confrontation of Jack and the Wild Bunch. Valerii is more interested in the moment of action turning instantly into history, while Leone continually stresses his own interest in the moments before the action obliterates memory. Thus, there is no Leonean "showdown" in *My Name Is Nobody*. Instead, Beauregard fires shot after shot into the advancing horde as Nobody keeps tally, waiting aboard the train (transportation to his steamship in New Orleans will be Jack's reward for seeing through, to the end, Nobody's dream of his destiny). Moving shots are intercut with frozen frames and still shots on the turning pages of the book of history. Again, it's the camera conferring validation on history—or what passes for history. The photographic record of this moment, and of the moment when Nobody "kills" Beauregard, is as artificial as the impossible broad ellipticality of the widescreen iris with which Valerii satirizes Leone's own mastery of the Techniscope frame. The history books to which Nobody and Beauregard constantly refer turn into the movies, and they're all a pack of lies (Nobody and Beauregard conspire to create one of the biggest ones). Freeze-frames and elaborate opticals are one more way of printing the legend.

"People need somethin' t' believe in," Beauregard says in his letter, and the statement stresses once again, as in *Duck, You Sucker!*, that we are in a post-mythic, post-*Once Upon a Time in the West* world—perhaps a world without balls. Never before did Leone, or any of his followers, express interest in—or even an awareness of—what "people" need. Indeed, a concept of "the people" enters Leone's vision only at the end of *Once Upon a Time in the West*—and there only implicitly. Much of *Duck, You Sucker!*, however, is dedicated to discrediting the self-appointed servants of the people—both elected officials and revolutionary spirits—who achieve their own ends at the expense of the public they pretend to serve. (A strong *Duck, You Sucker!* atmosphere pervades *My Name Is Nobody* in its modern milieu—its low comedy and animal imagery, its awareness of the passing of mythic time, even its structure. In *Duck, You Sucker!*, a professional engineers the circumstances whereby an uncommitted amateur accepts a suicidal risk and becomes a hero in spite of himself; in *My Name Is Nobody*, an anonymous but talented amateur, a kind of gunfighter groupie, manipulates a reluctant professional into fulfilling an obligation to history.)

My Name Is Nobody is seldom informed by a sense of "the people," but there's no doubt about what Beauregard means: when the masses appear, they are the unquestioning witnesses to the lie of history. That dull crowd on the street doesn't really seem to "need something to believe in." But we, the audience, do. God, how we do.

"Go Look at Yourself"

Once Upon a Time in America

At first, *Once Upon a Time in America* doesn't seem like the kind of movie Sergio Leone would even consider taking on, much less devoting a decade or more to planning and making. The differences, more than the similarities, strike you first: The movie's not a Western; it's not widescreen; it features more big-name actors (and more American actors) than any previous Leone film; it's made in the American studio system; it features a lead actor who is a deep-character player, not the stark, archetypal presence Leone usually relies on.

And then there's that elaborate narrative structure: Leone's other films take place in straightforward story. Their action spans a few weeks or, at most, a few months. The specter of the past intrudes through cryptic dialogue (*A Fistful of Dollars*, *The Good, the Bad and the Ugly*) or through a single, gradually self-revealing flashback sequence (*For a Few Dollars More*, *Once Upon a Time in the West*, *Duck, You Sucker!*) cut into the action at key moments. But *Once Upon a Time in America*—based on Harry Grey's novel *The Hoods*, of which Leone says virtually nothing remains in the film—is a sweeping narrative, spanning three generations, moving so freely in time that the term "flashback" no longer applies; in this movie, Leone refrains from peeping through a door to the past.

The Ladd Company's initial theatrical release of the film was a hideous distortion of Leone's intent. Its cutting of the film's running time from nearly four hours to under two and a half wasn't the tragedy; every film, after all, gets shortened. (Certainly, every one of Leone's has appeared in a shorter general release version than was originally envisioned by the director. Some of these shorter versions have had Leone's approval, some have not, though Leone was as emphatic as Sam Peckinpah was in insisting that none of his films has ever been seen the way he wanted it to be seen.) The Ladd Company's sin lay not in cutting down but in rearranging the film.

As conceived, the movie begins in December 1933, then takes a time jump to 1968, then slips into 1924 for the story of four teenage hoodlums. There's a jump back to 1968, then to 1933 for the picture of those hoodlums at the height of their Prohibition-era success—another jump to 1968, then back to 1933, then a return to 1968 for the final confrontation of the two protagonists—followed by a disorienting and haunting slip back into 1933. There's method to this madness: The 1933 frame (accompanied by Kate Smith singing "God Bless America" and by shots of Noodles Aaronson in an opium den) suggests that, perhaps, the film never really gets out of that time, that it's all half-memory, half-pipe dream. In the last 1968 sequence, Noodles's childhood sweetheart, Deborah, still looking impossibly young, says, "Age can wither me, Noodles. We're both getting old. All we have now are our memories. If you go to that party you'll lose those." The subject of the film is time—time and memory.

Leone's time-jumping structure shows us David Aaronson, simultaneously, at three distinct stages of his life, thus giving us a full picture of his fundamental character. "I brought back the key to your clock," Noodles tells Fat Moe when he enters his deli late one night in 1968; and as Moe starts the clock it's as if time has begun again for David Aaronson. That clock-key and the pocket watch that Max Bercovicz steals from a drunk are the central symbols of the film (recalling the chime watch in *For a Few Dollars More* and the many timepieces in *Once Upon a Time in the West*) and play an important part in its action. In the first 1933 sequence, with its incessantly ringing telephone, we get a collection of fragments whose significance we cannot yet fully understand—an image cluster like those that haunt the films of Nicolas Roeg, forming patterns of memory, symbol, and objective correlative. But with those fragments, we get the sense of a life fragmented—and that's crucial. Later, for a few minutes of screen time, when Noodles walks from the station to Fat Moe's in 1968, we get the opposite impression; what we sense is a life starting to come together again. Just a little longer than we might expect him to, Leone holds on a welder that Noodles passes in the street (fragments being rejoined, the same way a movie is put together, from pieces), and a second or two later we see a gravestone climbing over a wall. The moving of the cemetery has something to do with the film's literal plot, but it's also a perfect image for the digging up of the past, the haunting power of roots—an image that has been used in films as diverse as John Boorman's *Deliverance* and Tobe Hooper and Steven Spielberg's *Poltergeist*. In the world of *Once Upon a Time in America*, we will find, there are again two kinds of people: those who run with time and those who try to hold it back, those who are its co-conspirators (like Max and Deborah) and those who are its victims (like Noodles)—in short, the winners and the losers.

The Ladd Company's myopic approach to this mad but magnificent scheme was to recut the film into a chronological narrative. The time frame begins in 1924, jumps to 1933, and leaps to 1968 for the resolution of a "mystery" that, in this arrangement of the film's events, is established only minutes before it is solved. Never mind that the Ladd cut eliminates such inspired transitional devices as the whirring Frisbee and the outstretched hand which, occurring in the 1968 sequence, becomes Max's welcome to Noodles as he leaves prison in 1933, or that it omits the 1933 "splashing-into-the-harbor" car that becomes, in 1968, a burned car, hosed off on a television news report on Syndicate violence. The truncated version destroys the film's reality as a single moment of consciousness. It destroys the illusion Leone created of being free in time. The shortened version removes the emphasis on time and memory as the keys to human character, demolishes Leone's substitution of expansiveness in time for the expansiveness in space that characterizes his widescreen films. Furthermore, the Ladd cut plants a gunshot on the soundtrack of its last scene that makes obvious and material what is subtle, symbolic, and appropriately hallucinatory in the climax of the full version.

Admittedly, the use of the term "full version" is misleading when commenting on *Once Upon a Time in America*: There's a European version of 250 minutes, an American version of 226 minutes, and of course, the Ladd Company's cutting of 144 minutes. Structurally, however, the two longer versions are the same—the European version containing mere detail about the activities of the Hoffa-based character identified as James Conway O'Donnell (and called Jimmy Conway throughout the film) and a 1968 conversation between Noodles and a funeral director played by Louise Fletcher. The European version played Cannes to mixed reactions. When I speak of the "full version," I'll be talking about the full American version of 226 minutes, which the Ladd Company made available for limited theatrical release in late 1984-early 1985, and which became the basis for the standard 229-minute version now available on DVD.

Though Leone did some things in *Once Upon a Time in America* that he hadn't attempted before, it's only at first look that the film seems atypical. What we see is an older, more mature, and still daring Leone at work, not some new man whose presence can't be sensed in the Westerns. It's a more cynical and despairing Leone, as well; but our recognition of that cynicism and despair bring new light to our vision of the earlier Western films. Thematically and stylistically, *Once Upon a Time in America* is very much a Leone film, and perhaps the culmination of the "Sergio Leone Film."

A few points of comparison: In this movie, as in all the Leone films, the killing of a child is seen as the heinous act, the unforgivable sin that moves even the weak-spirited Noodles to an act of reprisal. And that child-murder is presented in all its enormity as a stylistic set-piece recalling the buildup to the confrontation between Timmy McBain and Frank in *Once Upon a Time in the West.* Having sealed their partnership with the first deposit in their locker cache, the boys are returning home from the station. Their mood is playful, high-spirited. Suddenly little Dominic, who's ahead of the pack, turns and heads back toward it. He's sighted Bugsy, and he shouts, "Run!" Leone slams into slow-motion on the first ominous note of Morricone's shrill pan-pipe theme, which is counterpointed by heavy orchestral punctuation and imparts an operatic weight to the moment. Bugsy fires, fires again, and Dominic falls as Noodles looks on in helpless horror. We are back to normal motion as Dominic dies in Noodles's arms, saying only, "Noodles—I slipped." Now, as the remaining members of the Max-Noodles gang hide, Noodles begins to stalk Bugsy.

Bugsy has a pistol and Noodles only a knife, but that doesn't matter now, any more than Ramón Rojo's Winchester mattered to the Man with No Name. The music squirts discordant, percussive takes as Noodles and Bugsy play peek-a-boo with each other and Leone plays peek-a-boo with us. Once Noodles is on Bugsy he is on him so fast that the bigger boy hasn't a chance to fire a shot. Noodles stabs Bugsy repeatedly, this the most intimate, personal killing in the entire Leone oeuvre, broken off only when a pair of mounted cops come riding down on Noodles (an image whose anachronism in the streets of modern New

York Leone must have relished) and place the boy under arrest—a pivotal event in the film.

Leone remains interested in two-character confrontations, as well as in the breathless minutes that precede reckoning. *Once Upon a Time in America* is essentially a long buildup to the climactic confrontation of Noodles and Max in 1968, which is handled with a ritualistic sense of inevitability. Harbingers to this moment of truth occur throughout the film, from Noodles's first face-off with Max over the stolen drunk and the pilfered pocket watch, to the quarrel they have the last night of Prohibition—a quarrel that precipitates thirty-five years of guilt for Noodles.

Often, the confrontations are avoided by changing the subject or suggest-ing "a swim." But the two men's face-offs are always attended by a characteris-tically Leonean stylistic weight—nowhere more intensely felt than in the throne scene. Noodles has returned from the oblivion of the Chinaman's opium den, where he has spent we know not how many days smoking away the pain of his failed affair with Deborah. There's never been a suggestion that Max's and Noodles's gang had a leader—in fact, much has been made of the fact that Max doesn't like bosses, and Noodles applauds this notion. But when Noodles comes in the door, Max is seated on a throne. "What's that?" "It's a throne. It was given to a Pope. Cost me eight hundred dollars." Carol volunteers the informa-tion, "It's from the seventeenth century." Noodles: "So what're you doing with it?" Max: "I'm sitting on it." The music stops dead in midnote. Ominous silence takes over, and Noodles proceeds to take just short of forever to stir his coffee. Leone creates a delicious bit of self-parody here, in addition to stressing the time disorientation that underlies the scene: we don't really know how long Noodles has been absent, and neither does Noodles. The scene also lends moment to Max's implicit takeover of the gang, as represented by his sitting on the throne.

The power of the past remains a key motif from Leone's earlier works—in fact, Leone's use of flashback to suggest the dominion of a traumatic event over a person's subsequent life is here broadened to a time structure that suggests we shall most assuredly be time's slaves if we are not its masters.

Other images and ideas in *Once Upon a Time in America* echo earlier Leone. The interrogation and abuse of Eve in the opening scene recall Angel-eyes' assault on Bill Carson's girlfriend in *The Good, the Bad and the Ugly*. Detroit Joe's story about cock-insurance (and an unlikely informant who tipped him to a certain diamond shipment) is in the same mode as Indio's "sermon" to his men about a certain cabinetmaker in *For a Few Dollars More*. Leone's shooting of a street scene is reminiscent of Jill's arrival in Flagstone in *Once Upon a Time in the West*: The crane-up, the swelling music, the pullback to re-veal—and celebrate—the bustling streets that signal the beginning of a new way of life. Deborah is defined in terms of community. She is shot against the street, as Jill was and in a way that Noodles and his confederates never are.

There is the Leonean feel for detail, too. To casual filmgoers, Leone's name, if it's familiar at all, hearkens up a sense of excess—broad, primitive bluntness. But in all of his films, Leone has shown himself equally capable of the occasional subtle touch, set in at exactly the right moment. One of Leone's finest gestures of this type occurs in *Once Upon a Time in America*. A number of critics noticed it: Noodles has left the Prohibition "wake." He's hidden himself in the office to make the fatal phone call that will alert the police to Max's most recent shipment of illegal alcohol. Noodles is trying to get Max arrested so his old friend won't go through with the self-destructive idea of trying to rob the federal reserve bank. He thinks he's ahead of Max—and he thinks he's betrayed his friend—so he's feeling pretty guilty. Max walks in and asks what's wrong. Noodles gives a shilly-shally answer as Max advances toward him, pausing a moment to reverse the phone receiver in its cradle. In that moment we know: A man who cares which side of the phone the cord hangs down on will also know that the phone has been used. It's Max, not Noodles, who's on top of this situation.

Even subtler than this—so subtle in fact that it's easily missed first time around—is Leone's "thrown away" explanation of how the money disappeared from the locker on that fateful night in December 1933. Remember that, after Eve's death, Moe advises Noodles to get out of town, and Noodles takes the clock-key, which is on the same ring as the key to the locker at the depot. When Noodles opens the locker, he finds the suitcase empty. In 1968, he returns this same key to Moe. But later, in the mausoleum where Patsy, Cockeye, and "Max" lie interred, Noodles finds a key hanging on the wall, a silent message to him. The key opens the locker, in which he finds a suitcase full of money and a cryptic note. We're so interested in the money and the note at this point that we may miss what we should have learned: that there was a second key to the locker all along, and Max must have had betrayal on his mind from the very beginning. He's hedged his bet just as Blondie hedged his in unloading Tuco's gun.

Another Leone hallmark lies at the heart of *Once Upon a Time in America*: friendship and the betrayal of friends. Present throughout all his films, and a major theme since *For a Few Dollars More*, betrayal here becomes, for the first time, the central theme of a Leone film. There's more, of course: Noodles's guilt at having betrayed Max and caused his death is made a mockery of when Max shows Noodles up at the end of the film—the betrayal was Max's all along. Noodles only thought he had betrayed Max, only thought Max was dead. Who knows how long Max had this plan in his head?

But despite an interest in character psychology (unseen since *For a Few Dollars More*), and despite the insistence on the group of four characters (which Leone so emphasizes that, when Dominic is killed and Noodles is taken into prison, he adds Moe to the trio of Max, Patsy, and Cockeye just to keep it four), the film that *Once Upon a Time in America* most resembles is *Duck, You Sucker!*

And that's as it should be, especially if one wants to cue off the "Once Upon a Time" formula in each of their titles and view Leone's last three films as a trilogy. Using violence as metaphor, all three films deal with politics and business and with the gradual institutionalization of violence—the preemption of primal conflict between individuals of honor and strength. By the end of *Once Upon a Time in America,* the greatest act of violence Noodles can perform to avenge himself on Max is to refuse to recognize him and to refuse to kill him—a deliberate reversal of the "big gundown" toward which the first four Westerns all aim.

It's easy to take *Once Upon a Time in the West* somewhat simplistically as a tribute to the values that won the West and made America great—the strength, dreams, and pluck of the frontier entrepreneur. But with *Duck, You Sucker!* an uneasiness begins to make itself felt. A Vietnam connection? A presage of nuclear brinkmanship? By the time *Once Upon a Time in America* comes along, bracketed with choruses of "God Bless America," the irony and bitterness are apparent enough. We are no longer seeing the America of wonder and opportunity depicted in *The Good, the Bad and the Ugly*, and *Once Upon a Time in the West*; in front of us is an America of treachery, disappointment, and shattered dreams—an America observed by the man who made *Once Upon a Time in the West* for Paramount, and saw what they did to it and to him.

It's also important to note that, more than being about a real, observed America, *Once Upon a Time in America* is concerned with the *image* of America. Leone has made it clear he is less interested in the historical West than in the West's movie image. And he is also on record saying about his gangster epic that he was little interested in the lives of real underworld figures but enormously interested in the films of Richard Conte.

Leone's rejection of the Techniscope frame in *Once Upon a Time in America* was dictated by the practicalities of a video-market consciousness. But Leone also could have been emphasizing that the world of this film is a more limited world—a world, in fact, in which most of its characters are trapped, or trap themselves, far from the expansive spatial possibilities of the Westerns. The film has more of an interest in realistic character than in mythic character-type; it displays more psychological depth. People fail more interestingly, less starkly. But looming throughout is the same inexorable sense of destiny—magic and terrible—that haunts all of Leone's work.

Very well, then: What is it, this America that Leone charts in his first modern-world film? It is, first and foremost, a world where dreams go awry, becoming either lies or self-deceptions. Noodles dreams of Deborah, an exemplar of the ideal in woman, but she is never really his because he won't make the commitment. His frustration over repeated near-misses leads him eventually to rape her, putting a distinctly dark edge on Deborah's fulfillment of her own dream.

Max's dream is something else again. On the beach in Florida, he draws a cartoon image of the federal reserve bank, and when Noodles asks, "What's that?" Max replies, "It's a dream—a dream I've been dreaming all my life. I swear to God, Noodles, you and me together, we could make it come true." The dream is described in passionate, obsessive terms. It recalls Indio's "crazy idea that wouldn't go away" about the Bank of El Paso in *For a Few Dollars More*, Harmonica's secondhand recollection of Brett McBain's "dream of a lifetime" in *Once Upon a Time in the West*, and Juan Miranda's dream of robbing El Banco Nacional de Mesa Verde in *Duck, You Sucker!* McBain's dream is genuine; it is realized through the grit of true heroes like Harmonica, Cheyenne, and

Jill. Juan's dream is a lever by which Sean Mallory tricks Juan into performing a revolutionary act in spite of himself. And Max's dream, finally, is a hoax, the trick by which Max sets up Noodles's imagined betrayal of the gang to mask his own real act of betrayal. "That was a Syndicate operation, Noodles," Max admits in the friends' final conversation in 1968. Only then do we place significance on the brief shot of Frankie Minaldi, arriving—just as Max and Noodles leave—at the hospital where the political boss Sharkey attends the wounded union leader Conway.

It is Frankie who drives the first wedge between Noodles and Max in 1933, when Noodles, newly returned from prison, finds Max, Patsy, and Cockeye working for Frankie. "I thought you were the guy that didn't like bosses," says Noodles, recalling Max's resistance to working for Bugsy when the boys were teenagers in the old neighborhood. "That sounded like a good idea then and it still sounds good now." Each time this issue comes up, Max shrugs it away, but by the end of the film we know that Max had something going with the Syndicate all along. Unlike Noodles, Max is a man with a plan.

"Doesn't it make sense to have plans?" Deborah asks Noodles during their evening at the seaside club; and Noodles replies, "You sound just like Max. You's are both alike. That's why you hate each other so much." By the end of the film, Deborah will have borne Max's child, and each of them will have succeeded where Noodles has failed. "You can always tell the winners at the starting gate," Noodles broods to Moe in 1968, looking at a photograph of Deborah (all this while the film is scarcely out of its own starting gate). "You can always tell the winners—and the losers." Noodles might not have guessed Max for a winner, but he has pegged himself a loser from the very beginning. He takes offense when Deborah calls him a cockroach, is put off when she chants, "He'll always be a two-bit punk, so he'll never be my beloved—what a shame." But by 1933, Noodles is defiantly proud of his self-condemnation: "I like the stink of the streets," he tells Max and Sharkey. Claiming their belittling of him as a badge of distinction, Noodles seems to work scrupulously against his own freedom.

Although he outwits and kills a Syndicate thug at Fat Moe's by using the elevator as a decoy and coming up by a different entrance (cf. Tuco getting the drop on Blondie by coming in the hotel window in *The Good, the Bad and the Ugly*), Noodles never really has the mastery over space that Leone's godlike heroes normally command. In fact, Noodles consistently denies the freedom of choice presented to him by alternative exits: The Chinaman has to show him the safe way out of the theatre; Deborah insists on his making a choice between two exits from her dressing room; "Bailey" offers him an alternative exit from his office. These choices are always offered by others. Noodles is led by necessity, not by free will. Freedom is associated with Deborah: "It wasn't my choice," says Noodles in 1933, talking about his years in prison; and she replies, "Yes, it was. It still is." For Noodles, it's never a matter of choice. Like the archetypal American gangster of the Hays Code era crime movies, he's determined by his environment. There's even a nod in that direction when Noodles tells his friends, "My old man's praying and my old lady's cryin' and the lights are turned off—

Where life has no value, death, sometimes, has its price—and it is increasingly cheap as the New World enters the twentieth century in Sergio Leone's *Duck, You Sucker!* (above) and *Once Upon a Time in America* (below).

what the hell should I go home for?" To remain a loser, a two-bit punk, is, for Noodles, almost pridefully, a matter of fate.

Max alludes to the game of fate when, in order to extort Police Chief Aiello into calling off his cops, the gang members switch babies in the hospital nursery: "Better than Fate: We give some the good life; others, we give it to 'em right up the ass." Getting it "up the ass" is, in fact, an expression used by the gang throughout the film to define their victimization by circumstance; we espe-cially hear the phrase during scenes involving the street cop "Fartface."

Noodles never faces a situation; he only escapes situations. In 1924, when he tries to choose Deborah over Max, his decision is cut short by the arrival of Bugsy's gang. After he and Max have been beaten, he calls to Deborah to open the door, and she won't. He's had his chance. Noodles seems to learn from this. At the beginning of the film, the first thing we see him do is escape from the Chinese theatre, and, afterward, escape from New York altogether, buying a ticket for as far away as his pocketful of money will take him. In 1924, after the successful test of the salt-bag smuggling invention, Max and Noodles take a spill into the harbor. From that time on "going for a swim" becomes, for Noo-dles, a way not of renewing things but of avoiding unpleasant situations. After the argument about working for Frankie, Noodles suggests a swim and drives the car off the pier into the water. When the question of tying into the Syndicate is brought up by Sharkey, and Max seems interested, Noodles avoids the fight by suggesting another swim: This time he and Max go to Florida.

Water, then, takes on an aura of ritual escape. But the water imagery is broader than that, more deceptive. During the first fall into the harbor, Max dis-appears, leaving Noodles to call out and search, his panic rising. Then Max shows up lying on a barge and quips, "What would you do without me?" Noo-dles responds by spitting a mouthful of water into Max's face. But this brief disappearing act resonates spookily when, in 1968, the facts of Max's more seri-ous disappearing act are revealed. More water: the bodies in the rain, December 1933; Max's taunting reference to Noodles's "face full of tears"; Noodles and Deborah on the beach, between, as it were, the devil and the deep, blue sea; and, on a Florida beach, Max walking alone to the water's edge after Noodles calls him "crazy."

The opposite of water: Fire—the candle that lights the opium pipe. And where there's fire, there's smoke—Noodles's ultimate escape. Water and fire make steam, and repeatedly Noodles is seen emerging from clouds of rising steam—a recurrent reminder, perhaps, of the pipe-dream frame in which the film is set. When Fat Moe, in 1968, asks Noodles, "Whaddya been doin' all these years?" Noodles's cryptic reply is, "Goin' ta bed early." It's unlikely that Noodles would quote Proust; somewhat less so that Leone would. But in any event the comment is apt for the moment, and nicely defines a film that is about the potency of memory, even if it is more appropriate to the screenplay than to the character. Could the "bed" he refers to be a correlate of the opium crib? Could the entire film be an opium dream, moving backward and forward from 1933, mixing memory and fantasy? There's certainly plenty of evidence for that—all those clouds of steam, the hallucinatory quality of sound (the incessantly ringing telephone that finally turns into a metallic shriek, the train whistles, toots, rings, and sirens that sound moments of crisis in the film), and the specific visual images (the closing mausoleum door, the whirring Frisbee, the impossible youth of Deborah in 1968, David Bailey a dead-ringer for the young Max, the garbage truck, the 1933 revelers who drive through a 1968 street). The film's skewed sense of time also imparts the atmosphere of a dream. In fact, when Fat Moe restarts his clock and life becomes real again for Noodles, it's as if the world is being created anew. It's as if Noodles really has been asleep for thirty-five years. Isn't he aware that Deborah has become a big star? And he knows nothing of Jimmy Conway's notoriety or of the mysterious Christopher Bailey's success until he hears of them on Moe's television.

Those 1968 scenes with Moe are filled with images of looking—seeing—as validation: Noodles is in the phone booth looking at Moe in the deli looking back at him looking; Noodles looking at a photograph of Deborah; Noodles climbing onto the toilet to frame his eyes in extreme closeup through the Techniscope ratio of the peephole he enjoyed as a boy; Noodles watching television and learning about Conway and Bailey. The exchanged look with Moe sets up a gesture reminiscent of a scene from *For a Few Dollars More* when Manco's and Mortimer's eyes first meet. The "looking" image is repeated when young Noodles sees Deborah see him seeing her, and later when, after the rape, Noodles's eyes meet Deborah's, just once, before her train takes her out of his life and the screen fills with smoke and steam. There are other images of looking: the peepholes in Moe's speakeasy and in Peg's whorehouse; the viewfinder of Max's camera. All this emphasis on looking imparts a certain passivity to the looker, Noodles, the opium dreamer, who—happy, at last—flashes that broad, frozen smile in the very last frame of the film.

What's Noodles looking at? Not, apparently, at himself, for he never seems to follow Deborah's admonition that he examine himself: "Go look at yourself, David Aaronson!" The emphasis in the line delivery is interesting. Deborah could have said, "Go look at your*self*," since she has just caught him looking at *her*. But instead she says, "Go *look* at yourself," almost a curse, the intonation much the same as a popular insult. Just after Deborah says this to Noodles, Leone sees fit to allow little Dominic to inherit a moment of screen time. And what's Dominic doing? Looking into a mirror. This is Leone's way of underlining Deborah's admonition to Noodles, and also of harking back to the mirror in the train station, where we discover an older Noodles looking at himself in the film's first jump to 1968. Self-examination, as well as the difference between self-assessment and reality, is a key concern in the film.

Noodles, throughout his life, seems to be a compulsive looker. When Moe, in 1968, tells Noodles to take the money he found in the locker and disappear again, Noodles insists on staying around, on pushing the mystery to a solution. Moe asks why he's doing this, and Noodles's only answer is, "Curious." Noodles says this as the two of them sit looking at television. Just before, Leone has moved in on the TV screen to emphasize Jimmy Conway on the newscast. He has Conway say into an interviewer's microphone, "If any guilt at all exists in this situation, it lies elsewhere." Noodles, perhaps, begins to suspect that the guilt he's lived with for thirty-five years is a cheat.

Certainly, by this time, the film is filled with deceptions enough to make that recognition likely. Scarcely a character in the film is without an alias or a nickname of some sort; masks are worn in several crucial scenes (the diamond heist, the baby-switch, meeting Carol at Peg's); and it is Max's deception of Noodles that is the underlying plotline of the film.

But all deception is ultimately self-deception in Leone's world. In *For a Few Dollars More*, Manco told Indio to go in a different direction from that suggested by Colonel Mortimer, and Indio chose yet another direction; but when they arrived in Agua Caliente, there was Mortimer. Max's multiple trickeries, similarly, have led him to a trap of his own making; he seems to feel that his only chance for escape hinges upon his calling Noodles to life once more. When Noodles determines to go to Secretary Bailey's party—already half-guessing the truth—Deborah tries to dissuade him: "All we have now are our memories. If you go to that party, you'll lose those." She as much as tells Noodles that his life to this point has been based on a deception; like any mortal man, Noodles responds with curiosity. He'll pursue the course to its end to find out the truth, even if all he finds out is another lie. (It may be that Noodles refuses to accept Bailey's "job" because he suspects yet another deception.)

The relationship between Noodles and Max is, in fact, a variation on the relationship between Ransom Stoddard and Tom Doniphon in John Ford's *The Man Who Shot Liberty Valance*—a film whose influence on Leone is apparent throughout Leone's career (especially in *Once Upon a Time in the West*). Like Bailey's, Stoddard's rise to success has been built on a lie. But it's a lie about which he is unaware until Doniphon tells him about it; in this respect he is more like Noodles. When Stoddard, now a successful and influential politician, tells his true story to a journalist (the frame in which the flashback narrative of *The Man Who Shot Liberty Valance* is set), the writer is intrigued, but decides, finally, to print the fiction, not the truth: "This is the West, sir. When the legend becomes fact, print the legend." The line could be a working credo for Sergio Leone's exploration of the American film mythos. Certainly Noodles's staunch refusal to recognize Max in 1968—to call him anything but "Mr. Bailey"—is an insistence on "printing the legend." Noodles holds onto his version of what happened—guilt and all—because, true or not, it means more.

In the end, it's the friendship with Max that Noodles values most, even though the friendship was a lie from the beginning, even though it was fraught with double-crosses and betrayals every step of the way—beginning with the pilfered pocket watch and climaxing with Max's taunting announcement that he has stolen Noodles's entire life from him. There's truth in that. Noodles seems to recognize that he has been nothing without Max, that he has had no life apart from life with his "friend." His nine years in prison and his thirty-five years in Buffalo are offscreen, lost years, of little interest to us or to Noodles. His dependence is acknowledged when Max, after Max's faked drowning, greets Noodles with "What would you do without me?" In this sequence, there's a clear echo of Juan Miranda left without his Sean: "What about me?"

Noodles and Deborah, as kids on the street (above, Jennifer Connelly and Scott Tiler), with gang members Dominic (Noah Moazezi, behind Noodles), Cockeye (Adrian Curran, in wide cap), and Patsy (Brian Bloom, in stocking cap) … and as grownups on the beach (below, Elizabeth McGovern and Robert De Niro).

The homosexual subtext is inescapable in—and appropriate to—this "world without balls." In fact, all of Leone's films since *A Fistful of Dollars* have been "buddy movies" of a sort. At the end of *Once Upon a Time in the West* Harmonica rides off with Cheyenne! No one ever gets the girl in a Leone film; in fact, there's often no girl to be got (*For a Few Dollars More*; *The Good, the Bad and the Ugly*; *Duck, You Sucker!*). When there is, she's given away in a community-affirming gesture (*A Fistful of Dollars*, *Once Upon a Time in the West*). Leone never dealt with "real" man-woman relationships. In *Once Upon a Time in the West*, the male characters' relationships with Jill are intentionally allegorical, not psychologically realistic. In *Once Upon a Time in America*, which turns the near-spirituality of male-female relationships in *Once Upon a Time in the West* into a pattern that's all too carnal, Max's and Noodles's relationships with women are never more than a mirror of their relationship with each other.

Leone emphasizes Max's jealousy when, three times in the film, Noodles seems to choose Deborah over him: in 1924, Pesach, when he calls Noodles into the alley and Bugsy's boys miraculously appear to keep Noodles from going back inside to be with Deborah; in 1933, when Noodles is just out of prison, and Max won't let him stay with Deborah at the party because he wants to introduce Noodles to Frankie Minaldi and Detroit Joe, who are waiting in the back room; and, later that year, after Noodles's seaside tryst with Deborah, when Max's assumption of the "throne" seems prompted by petulant jealousy over Noodles's absence. In the first two instances, Deborah calls attention to Max's attitude with the repeated, "Go on, Noodles. Your mother's calling you."

Max protests that he doesn't need Carol ("We do our fuckin' business together an' fuckin' broads don't get in the way!"); to emphasize his loyalty to Noodles and the gang and to stress the difference between Noodles and himself, Max summarily throws Carol out of the house. For most of the film, Noodles persists in chasing an unattainable dream and ends by destroying Deborah for himself (though not for Max, as he learns when he calls her back into his world in 1968).

The two men's relationships with women begin to index their own relationship during the scene in which each of them has a go at Peggy—courtesy of the hapless, blackmailed Fartface. Noodles suffers premature ejaculation, and Max temporary impotence—and these two experiences typify the characters' business styles and sexual styles throughout the film. The events also emphasize the lack of finesse, grace, and enjoyment in their sexuality. Witness the blunt urgency with which Noodles tries Peggy in the toilet scene: so desperate is he to lose his virginity that he never stops to think that sex might be *fun*, too. Or recall the brutality with which Noodles disregards Detroit Joe's admonition to "be easy wit' da girl." When Carol says, "Hit me, make it look real," Noodles rapes her instead, and to her screams Max responds ironically: "Would you put a cork in her?" Noodles finishes his rape of Carol as Max and the others finish the diamond heist, and the two misdeeds are equated in a bad joke when Max says to Noodles, "We're goin'. You comin'?" and Noodles replies, "Comin'."

It's a man-centered world—but, again, one without balls. Police Chief Aiello, a cocky, strutting parody of Italian machismo, boasts about his newborn son, makes lusty jokes about his wife's breasts, and cautions his daughters to regard their new little brother as the boss—only to remove the infant's diaper and find the necessary equipment missing.

If women have a place among these men, it's as possessions. Max always treats Carol as a possession and, when Noodles tries to treat Deborah as something more, he fails utterly. In 1968, when Max tells Noodles how he ruined Noodles's life, Max boasts, "I took your money, I took your girl." There's an echo, here: In *Once Upon a Time in the West*, just before the final reckoning, Frank tells Harmonica, "None of that matters now—not the money, not the girl." Women and money are the ultimate possessions, and it is the failure to recognize them as more than possessions (as Harmonica and Cheyenne do with Jill in *Once Upon a Time in the West*) that contributes importantly to the ball-less collapse of Leone's latter-day antiheroes.

Despite the Old Testament Judaism of the film's nominal cultural background, the attitude toward women is very much the Mary-or-Eve dichotomy of man-centered Catholic societies (like Italy). Most women are earthy, tainted with evil (Peggy and Carol for example; we don't know much about Noodles's 1933 girlfriend, but her name is Eve). But Deborah, like Jill in *Once Upon a Time in the West*, is a near-spiritual figure. Her grace and beauty are emphasized; her presence as a saving force in the community, insisted upon (both Deborah and Jill are photographed amid crowded streets, as few Leone characters ever are, and Jill's destiny in business is echoed in Deborah's destiny in art).

Noodles, both boy and man, neither escapes nor understands his fascination with Deborah. His fatal mistake is to link the fascination with sexuality—but that response is symptomatic of Noodles's terminal adolescence. When Patsy eats the Charlotte Russe Noodles had intended to use to buy Peggy's favors, Leone places unusual emphasis on the sequence, and not just for laughs. The recognition is that sweets are as important as sex to this kid (these kids, in fact). Later, in 1933, Peggy's reappearance as a full-fledged prostitute—and the gang's careful repetition of key lines of dialogue from their youth—suggest that the characters have grown older but not up. They still stand for the same things they stood for as teenagers. Their arrested adolescence is Leone's metaphor for the American way of business—and of life.

No wonder, then, that so much of the film's sexuality is tied to death—the shooting of Eve on a bed already marked with the bullet-hole outline of a man's sleeping form, a Syndicate gunman's fondling of a woman's breast with his pistol, the girl in the coffin, Carol's self-destructive pursuit of sexual humiliation, Noodles's equally self-destructive bluntness with Deborah, and Max's final plea to Noodles to shoot him. All of Leone's films are more death-ridden than life-affirming. Even the upbeat "New World" ending of *Once Upon a Time in the West* is mitigated by the dolorous presence of Harmonica. "People like that," says Cheyenne, "have something inside—something to do with death."

The characters in *Once Upon a Time in America* flirt with death, pursue it in spite of themselves. It's not just a joke when Max says of the nude woman in the coffin, "She died of an overdose," and she leaps up, chirping, "And I'm ready for another!" It's a reminder that this film and the people in it are more than half in love with death. The disorienting opening and closing of the mausoleum door implies that maybe Noodles should be there permanently, at rest with his friends—indeed, maybe he wishes to be there. And even when we know that Max's death was faked, Carol's recollection that Max "started shooting first just to get himself killed" retains significant credibility.

Noodles sums up the legend he has chosen to print; it is his version of the truth: "I had a friend. I turned him in to save him. He was killed, but he wanted it that way. It was a great friendship. It went bad for him. It went bad for me, too." Metaphor overtakes literal narrative altogether after Noodles leaves the party: Max comes out and walks toward him; a garbage truck passes between them; Max is gone; Noodles, a tear in his eye, looks at the grinding blades in the back of the truck. A life turned to garbage. On the truck is the number "35"—the number of years that Max lived as Bailey, and Noodles went to bed early. This is the contemporary America of Noodles's vision, and Leone's: Waste. Liberal guilt meets conservative greed, and they can't even do away with each other. The world is ending—and not with a bang (at least not in the full version) but a whimper.

That end has been hastened by people like Noodles and Max. Cheyenne and Harmonica brought about the end of their world in order to build a better one in which they had no place. But Max and Noodles enjoy no such nobility of purpose. They bring the whole works down with them. Remember that Jimmy Conway called them a "plague," and that Frankie Minaldi compared them to the Four Horsemen of the Apocalypse.

Some Apocalypse. Detroit Joe had it right: "Life is stranger than shit."

Part 3

THE COMPANY

10

"They Earned It"

The Crew

A lot of people besides Sergio Leone were important to getting the Leone vision onto the screen and making it work. Here, with occasional comment, is a gallery of some of the key people to whom we—and Leone—owe a debt:

Nino Baragli

Leone's best film editor. Baragli began his association with Leone on *The Good, the Bad and the Ugly*, sharing credit with Eugenio Alabiso, co-editor of *For a Few Dollars More*. Doubtless the compelling pace of the film, and the fact that it works so remarkably well (despite a plot-thread virtually ignored for the first hour of the film), is due to Baragli's genius. One need only look at the films for which he has received sole editing credit to confirm the sureness of his skill in the service of Leone's vision.

Once Upon a Time in the West is precision itself, never wavering from the relentless slow build that begins with its very first shot; even the comic moments convey the sense of its being more than comedy—they contribute seriously to what is still to come, besides providing us with a transitory chuckle of delight. *Duck, You Sucker!* though having problems with tone and style (due partly to the fact that Leone reportedly did not take over direction of the film until Giancarlo Santi [q.v.] was on the job for ten days), displays a pace that is never off; many of the cuts enhance the film's underlying vision and meaning, as well as help carry the story along. *My Name is Nobody*, minus Leone's direction, is a horse of a slightly different color, but its cumbersomeness seems due more to Valerii's failure to fully integrate some incidental story ideas than to any lack of facility on Baragli's part. Within the scene and the sequence, his cutting is marvelously crisp and always appropriate. Anyone watching *My Name Is Nobody* sees that Baragli can indulge in self-parody along with the best of them; the time-hopping *Once Upon a Time in America* is a masterwork of editing.

Baragli mounted a number of other important and unusual Italian films, including Pasolini's *Salò* (1977), the overpowering impact of which was due at least in part to his (and Pasolini's, and Tonino Delli Colli's) matter-of-fact approach to bizarre and brutal subjects.

Bernardo Bertolucci

Leone gave Bertolucci work at a time when Bertolucci needed it, and Bertolucci gave Leone a treatment for *Once Upon a Time in the West* more than three hundred pages long, quoting (so Frayling has it) from all the great Westerns, and including some references that even Leone didn't recognize. Certainly even in a film as long as the uncut *Once Upon a Time in the West*, not all of Bertolucci's mammoth treatment could have been used; the finished film contains little of Bertolucci's characteristic politicizing. The treatment of Morton is, one assumes, a vestige of a customary Bertoluccian idea: the advancement of leftist ideals not on their own merit but by means of debunking fascism (in fact, not even fascism but individual fascist personalities). By the same token, if the world of *Once Upon a Time in the West* is inherited by the workers, it is only partly because "they earned it" and mostly because there's no one else left to take things in hand. The political subtext is still there, but the superimposition of a mythic template and the turning of the building of the West into *Götterdämmerung* are surely Leone's own. At the time, Bertolucci's credentials rested almost entirely on *Before the Revolution* (whose overlapping concerns with *Duck, You Sucker!* I have already mentioned). But he went on to be celebrated for his vision (as unique and stylized as Leone's own) in *The Conformist, The Last Tango in Paris*, and *1900*.

Massimo Dallamano

The confusing day-for-night work and the often arbitrary and ambiguous delineation of geographical space in San Miguel did not help make the plotline of *A Fistful of Dollars* more comprehensible—and the same kind of roughness crops up here and there in *For a Few Dollars More*, particularly in the action sequences. But it was cinematographer "Jack Dalmas" (not "Max," oddly) who first realized the comic-book colors, the sharp depth, the exotic angles, the sweaty-close flesh landscapes, and the slow-paced kinetics of Leone's Techniscope world. After the first two films, Leone sharpened and polished his vision with Delli Colli and Ruzzolini; but Dallamano had already laid a lot of the groundwork. His was the camera that swooped in on Marisol and Jesus at the moment of reunion, that gave us the woozy, failing vision of Ramón Rojo in his last moments on earth, and that carefully paralleled the first appearances of each of the three lead characters in *For a Few Dollars More*. After that film, Dallamano himself turned to directing, with *Bandidos* (1967).

Tonino Delli Colli

Leone's mastery of the widescreen space, and of the odd things that happen to color and light now and then, particularly under the influence of dust, developed from his association with Delli Colli. Delli Colli is a master cinematographer who shot the best films of several Italian directors—including Wertmüller and Pasolini—did exquisite work for Fellini, and subsequently went international, doing especially evocative work for Polanski and Roberto Benigni's *La Vita è bella*. He attended, among other things, Leone's perfection of the impossibly close closeup, his development of circular movement, his relentless point-of-view track-ins, and such wildly experimental stuff as the dizzying swish-pans and tracks of Tuco's race through the graveyard and the ninety-degree roll and zoom-out on Frank and Jill's tryst. *Once Upon a Time in America* showed him equally capable of bringing the Leone look to urban colors and steam as to western landscapes and dust. With Baragli, Morricone, Simi, and Vincenzoni, Tonino Delli Colli fills out Leone's royal flush.

Alberto Grimaldi

In 1964, Grimaldi was Sergio Leone's attorney. By little more than decade later he had become an accomplished big-movie producer, with titles like Bertolucci's *1900* and Fellini's *Casanova* to his credit. How did this come about? Leone entrusted Grimaldi with the production of his second and third films. These not only made Grimaldi's name and fortune but also presented him with the opportunity to do something he liked doing and did well. (Grimaldi also produced some of the more notable non-Leone Italian Westerns, including *The Big Gundown*, *Face to Face*, and *A Professional Gun*.)

Mickey Knox

Knox is credited with the English dialogue versions for both *The Good, the Bad and the Ugly* and *Once Upon a Time in the West*, the only two Leone films on which such a credit appears. A rising and pugnacious young Hollywood actor, Knox transplanted himself to Italy in search of opportunity and stumbled into becoming English-language coach to non-English-speaking actors, and ultimately an author of English dialogue for films shot in Italy, as more and more such films began to find—and ultimately be shot for—American audiences. A latter-day bit player, Knox has been seen in *Bobby Deerfield*, Norman Mailer's *Beyond the Law*, *Inchon*, and a number of other films. His memoir *The Good, the Bad, and the Dolce Vita*, devoted mostly to his remarkable career in Italian film, is an entertaining and enlightening—if not always trustworthy—read. It's hard to say whether the quirky "Did I hear that right?" atmosphere of the Leone Westerns' dialogue is due significantly to Knox, or is simply a faithful rendering of the intent of Leone and co-scenarists; but it seems likely that Knox's contribution went beyond mere translation to the actual creation of lines of dialogue. Certainly these two films contain (in any language) some of the most memorable lines in cinema, and the fact that they work so stylishly well in English has to be attributed to Knox.

Ennio Morricone

Next to Leone, Morricone is unquestionably the person most responsible for the ineffable atmosphere created by Leone's films. Even *including* Leone,

Morricone is the person most frequently associated with the Italian Western, his musical compositions and arrangements having led the way to creating a style of music uniquely associated with that remarkable subgenre of film and a key to its infectious cult popularity. The impossibly long list of credits this prolific composer has amassed in just over forty years attests to the depth of his melodic resources, the versatility of his musical ideas, and the seeming inexhaustibility of his harmonic and orchestral innovations. So great was Leone's faith in this composer, and so closely in harmony was their working relationship, that in some instances Leone filmed scenes after Morricone had submitted the music. Morricone scored all of Leone's films, as well as many other Italian Westerns, including *Pistols Don't Argue*, *A Pistol for Ringo* and *The Return of Ringo*, *The Hills Run Red*, *The Big Gundown*, *Face to Face*, *A Professional Gun*, *Tepepa*, and *My Name Is Nobody*. His early scores for Leone made Morricone a hot international property, and he's become a legend (and an idol) for his wide range of hauntingly powerful film scores (*Fists in the Pocket*, *The Battle of Algiers*, *Burn!*, *1900*, *Days of Heaven*, *Exorcist II: The Heretic*, *The Untouchables*, *The Mission*, and many others). [A detailed analysis and appreciation of Morricone's scores for the Leone films appears in "He Not Only Plays—He Can Shoot, Too" (pages 189-201).]

Bruno Nicolai

Nicolai composed quite a few scores of his own, including the especially notable *Indio Black* (marketed in the United States as *Adios Sabata*) and *$100,000 for Ringo*. He is credited on several of the Leone/Morricone films and soundtrack recordings as conductor of the music, and he is sometimes rumored to have done more than conduct. To the suggestion that Nicolai, and others, orchestrated some of his scores, Morricone denies any collaboration:

> In the history of music, composition is instrumentation. A composer doesn't just write the music and then get someone else to do the orchestration. Nobody—apart from a few people in America—does this.[1]

But even if all Nicolai did was conduct the studio orchestra recordings of many of those scores, he was clearly sensitive to the vision of Leone and to the crazy auditory imaginings of Morricone, and was thus crucial to the success not only of Leone's films but of the Italian Western genre and its unique and compelling musical sound.

Giuseppe Ruzzolini

Tonino Delli Colli got famous, went international, got busy; so, for *Duck, You Sucker!*, Leone chose Ruzzolini, at that time chiefly known for his association with Pasolini. The switch was fortuitous because a new look was needed for this modification of the Leone vision. That look—darker, thicker, suggesting a character introspection beyond the comic-book starkness of the earlier films—is appropriate. The film is a venture into new cinematic, geographic, historical, and literary territory for Leone. And it is the first film he made about the world after the twilight of the gods at the end of *Once Upon a Time in the West*. The Mexico of *Duck, You Sucker!* is a fallen world—not the pre-moral frontier of the first four Leone films but Eden after the snake. As if to emphasize that theme, the unraveling of the film is a progression from brightness and simplicity into darkness and confusion. Though there are day shots and night shots, interiors and exteriors—all of which create lights and darks along the way—the overall effect is of a journey from brightest noon to darkest night. Where Delli Colli had dust, Ruzzolini has smoke: the smoke of dynamite and cigars, of train stacks and gunfire, the smoke of revolution and of a mind whose bright dreams are clouded by disillusionment and despair. Ruzzolini went on to do the American location photography for *My Name Is Nobody*, getting a little of Delli Colli's dust after all; and the look he achieved was quite different—but just as distinctive—as the look of *Duck, You Sucker!*: brighter, whiter, and enthusiastically exploring the widescreen, making the same ratio seem even more expansive than it did in the Leone film. For his own part, Delli Colli extended Ruzzolini's "new look" in his steamy work on *Once Upon a Time in America*.

Giancarlo Santi

After Tonino Valerii (who assisted Leone on *For a Few Dollars More*) headed off to direct films of his own, Giancarlo Santi became Leone's resident assistant director. He served the master during the filming of his masterpieces *The Good, the Bad and the Ugly* and *Once Upon a Time in the West*. When the collaboration with Peter Bogdanovich collapsed, Santi was deemed worthy to make his directorial debut with *Duck, You Sucker!* The story (recounted by Sir Christopher Frayling) is that Santi did ten days' shooting on the film before stars Rod Steiger and James Coburn pressed to work with Leone himself and no other. Leone, by contrast, told Noel Simsolo that Santi was "sounded out" to direct the film, "but the financiers refused." In any case, Leone directed and signed a fifth film, and Santi ended up with another assistant director credit. Some of the film's rough texture and fluctuating tone may be due to the change of directors, but it's hard to say without a tough and probably unilluminating dredging up of who-directed-what. In any event, in films as expansive as these three, the assistant director's role is a critical one, and Leone's association with Santi clearly proved harmonious.

Carlo Simi

Simi was production designer on Leone's first four films. Sometimes he was credited as "art director," sometimes as "production designer," sometimes as "sets and costumes by." Simi was, unquestionably, one of the key men of the Sergio Leone "company," and he was responsible in no small way for the look associated with the world of Leone, and of Italian Westerns in general. His was the liberal mixing of American and Mexican (and European!) affectations of dress, the insistence upon credibly dark nineteenth-century interiors, and architecture combining the Catholic and the pagan. The dwellings are Mexican, Indian, homesteader and caveman all in one—windblown, claptrap buildings housing windblown, claptrap people. The incidental details of firearms and foodstuffs are Simi's, and he decided how both were to be presented and used. Also under Simi's purview were the eccentricities of costume (ponchos, dusters, suspenders with belts, the frequently ironic use of military uniforms), the windows made to be broken, the bridges designed to be blown up, the wall signs crafted to be either noticed or overlooked. Throughout Leone's films, these touches attest to the presence of Simi and his creative genius. His was just the right marriage of accurate period detail with out-and-out fancy. Simi made sure Leone got the Never-Never Land he wanted. In *Once Upon a Time in America*, he rose to the challenge of creating not one but three specific historical periods.

Tonino Valerii

Assistant director on *For a Few Dollars More*, Valerii left Leone early on to embark upon his own directorial career. His titles include: *For the Love of Killing* (1966); *Day of Anger* (1967), with Lee Van Cleef; *Price of Power* (1969); and *A Reason to Live, a Reason to Die* (*Massacre at Fort Holman*, 1972), with James Coburn and Telly Savalas as opposing commanding officers in a Civil War siege. In 1972-1973, Valerii again worked with Leone, this time directing *My Name Is Nobody* for Leone's production company Rafran from an idea of Leone's. *Nobody* remains Valerii's best-known, most important, and most imitated film. Valerii has his own voice and style, but is so closely indebted to Leone that he seems on surest ground when dealing with avowed parody.

Luciano Vincenzoni

Writing about his brief encounter with Leone during preparation of *Duck, You Sucker!*, Peter Bogdanovich refers in passing to Luciano Vincenzoni, calling him "the writer of Leone's two best films (*For a Few Dollars More* and *The Good, the Bad and the Ugly*)." Many may argue with Bogdanovich's exclusion of *Once Upon a Time in the West* from the "best film" category, but there is no denying that Vincenzoni's writing was essential to the maturation of Leone's vision. The differences between *A Fistful of Dollars* and the two films that followed it—the cryptic, comic, aphoristic dialogue, the richer and more integrated use of comedy, the exploration of the murky pasts and motivations of apparently shallow characters like Indio and Tuco, the use of character relationships rather than plot line to unify a film story—these are almost certainly the result of Vincenzoni's influence.

Vincenzoni played no role in the development of *Once Upon a Time in the West*, which, not coincidentally, is Leone's least overtly comic film. The movie is clever—it has some nicely delivered dialogue, particularly Cheyenne's—but it does not have the deliberately comic subtext of the Vincenzoni films. *Once Upon a Time in the West* brought to fruition one of the ideas that Leone and

Vincenzoni first developed in *For a Few Dollars More*—a remembered outrage gradually revealed in recurrent, cumulative flashback.

Vincenzoni joined Leone and the co-scenarist of *Once Upon a Time in the West*, Sergio Donati, in scripting *Duck, You Sucker!* Overt comedy—even low comedy and broadly overplayed clowning—reemerged, alongside a politically oriented plot and a gradual flashback character revelation. It seems safe to say that Vincenzoni has a distinctive sense of comedy and a flair for fleshing out characters, making the most loathsome uglies interesting, pitiable, even sympathetic. The fact that Vincenzoni's credit is always shared, usually with directors, suggests that he is a script doctor, enriching with dialogue and characterization the ideas of others. (He also co-wrote *A Professional Gun* [1968] for director Sergio Corbucci.) But if there was one definitive, essential writer in Leone's films—and in the whole realm of the Italian Western—that writer was Luciano Vincenzoni.

Notes

1   Interview in *The Guardian*, July 14, 2006.

"I Have to Know Who You Are"

The Faces

He's not very good at directing actors. He's only as good as his actors are.

—Clint Eastwood on Leone,
in Iain Johnstone's *The Man with No Name*

In casting his films, Leone didn't always get the actors he'd set his sights on, but he was always careful how he used the actor he ended up with. Sometimes that meant taking maximum advantage of physical appearance, sometimes it meant deliberately calling up memories of previous performances with which a familiar actor was irrevocably associated, and sometimes it meant diabolically subverting viewer expectations. Here is an honor roll of players who made a difference in Leone's vision.

Mario Brega

Brega's roles include the greasy, sadistic Rojo henchman Chico in *A Fistful of Dollars*, the greasy, sadistic Indio henchman Niño in *For a Few Dollars More*, the greasy, sadistic Corporal Wallace in *The Good, the Bad and the Ugly*, and the greasy, sadistic Syndicate killer Mandy in *Once Upon a Time in America*. Do we have here a classic case of a typecast character player? Not for us to ask. All we need to know is that, like many less-seen but equally emphasized Leone supporting players, Brega has a *face*—pudgy, mean, low, and indescribably beautiful.

Charles Bronson

As Charles Buchinski, he rose through a variety of small supporting character parts (particularly visible as a small-time tough in *Pat and Mike* and as Vincent Price's mute bodyguard Igor in *House of Wax*). John Sturges put Bronson on the map with strong, sympathetic supporting roles in *Never So Few*, *The Magnificent Seven*, and *The Great Escape*. But his cult following began to form in Europe in the late '60s. Though still a mere footnote in the United States, Bronson was already well paid and in high demand on the Continent when *Once Upon a Time in the West* assured him a reputation with American critics and intellectuals. Leone's insistence upon Bronson for the role of Harmonica cost him the support of United Artists, who wanted Eastwood. This insistence may also have caused the film's considerable loss at the box office. Some sources have reported that in the very beginning, Leone wanted Bronson for the Clint Eastwood role in *A Fistful of Dollars*. [See also the entry on James Coburn, below.] Nevertheless, the power that Bronson brought to the role of the nameless Man Who Makes Appointments, and to the film itself, gleaned for him a following that has outlasted a half-dozen exploitive Michael Winner films. People who thought they'd never go to the likes of *The Mechanic* or *The Stone Killer* will go just to see Bronson; the quality of the vehicle in no way detracts from their enjoyment of the actor. Sometimes, in fact, viewers are rewarded with a new version of the Bronson mystique, as can be seen in *Death Wish*—one of the few truly interesting and valuable films Winner made with Bronson, though regrettably buried under a truckload of shallow and exploitive sequels.

Bronson's dark thick hair frames a swarthy, leathery face adorned with startlingly blue-green eyes. This combination of features has made him a natural for playing ethnic types, particularly hybrids. He was a Sioux in *Run of the Arrow*, a Navajo radio operator in *Never So Few*, the cross-bred Bernardo O'Reilly in *The Magnificent Seven*, a Polish officer in *The Great Escape*, and a Mexican Indian in *Guns for San Sebastian*. Leone fixed on this ethnic ambivalence for *Once Upon a Time in the West* where it further obscures Harmonica's true identity from Frank. The climactic flashback shows young Harmonica as an undeniably Latin boy with distinctly brown eyes; but that doesn't matter a bit.

Bronson's moral ambivalence is as important as his ethnic ambivalence. He's equally at home as villain or hero and is at his best in roles that hint at the impossibility of fully separating good from evil in any man. John Sturges, whose "moral" Westerns (*Gunfight at the O.K. Corral, Last Train from Gun Hill, The Magnificent Seven, Hour of the Gun*) and taut suspense-adventures (*Bad Day at Black Rock, Never So Few, The Great Escape*) had a formative influence on Leone, made a classic, strong, silent type of Bronson, who became the loner with a deep-seated, well-protected vulnerability. It may be that *Once Upon a Time in the West* works so well because it combines the revelation of Leone's vision and Harmonica's character with the gradual unveiling of Charles Bronson's actor's soul.

Claudia Cardinale

One of the most fleshly of women, Claudia Cardinale is permanently engraved in cinematic history. Her fame is due to Federico Fellini's role-reversing use of her in *8½* as an ethereal symbol rather than as the flesh-and-blood characterization her physical appearance invites. In fact, Cardinale has been more symbol than woman in her greatest films: the aptly named Angelica, emblem of the rising bourgeoisie replacing the tottering nobility in Visconti's *The Leopard*; an airy, almost untouchable rani in Edwards's *The Pink Panther*; and a fought-over expensive pearl with rarely a moment to reveal her own wishes and make her own decisions in Brooks's *The Professionals*. For this reason, she was ideally suited to the role of Jill in *Once Upon a Time in the West*: Her sex-goddess appearance combines with her more mystical iconographic associations to ease the progress of Jill from tart to town builder, from harlot to earth mother, from sinner to symbol of America—the apotheosis of the harlot with a heart of gold.

James Coburn

Tall, gray, cold, and stony as a monument, this obelisk of the cinema became in the '60s the epitome of hard heroism and sex-symbol machismo, emitting just the right amount of cool detachment. Like Bronson, Coburn is a graduate of the Sturges stable. He captured public interest with the clipped, sparse talk and poker-straight walk of the blindingly fast knife-hurler Britt in *The Magnificent Seven*. Coburn continued to contribute strong, supporting performances in community-of-men movies like Sturges's *The Great Escape*, Siegel's *Hell Is for Heroes*, and Peckinpah's *Major Dundee*. He also managed a creditable semicomic "best friend" part in *The Americanization of Emily* and was a properly menacing villain in *Charade*.

In 1966, *Our Man Flint* made Coburn a leading man. In Flint, Coburn combined his sex appeal and cool toughness with a facility for understated, self-mocking comedy. In 1967 he starred in *Waterhole #3* as one of three Civil War soldiers out to reclaim a fortune in gold buried in the desert (!). Coburn's meteor peaked in *The President's Analyst* (1967), a Flint-like spoof in which he was cast as a befuddled psychiatrist pitted against the telephone company's sinister plot to take over the world. After that role the actor's star began to wane: *Duffy* was a failed caper movie; *Candy* was a zoo full of caged cameos; *Hard Contract* was an intensely interesting drama about high-priced hit men on the Continent—but it was too European for American audiences and critics, and it made no money.

So *Duck, You Sucker!* was something of a change of image for Coburn. Here he played a more introspective, sensitive, changeable character, forced to come to terms with something inside rather than outside himself. Like Bronson, Coburn brought the right amount of iconographic ambiguity to his Leone starturn. Sean isn't a plain-and-simple good guy, and his enigmatic silences and more puzzling monologues keep the characters—as well as the viewer—guessing as to what to expect from the Irish "firecracker."

Financial and availability considerations, not inclination, were what kept Leone from using Coburn in a film until *Duck, You Sucker!* David Downing and Gary Herman report in their biography of Clint Eastwood[1] that Coburn was Leone's first choice for the Man with No Name (1964), and that only Coburn's asking price deterred Leone—twenty-five thousand dollars.

Coburn made one other Spaghetti Western, *A Reason to Live, a Reason to Die*, for Tonino Valerii in 1972. His star rose again during the later '70s when he did more work for Peckinpah (*Pat Garrett and Billy the Kid*, *Cross of Iron*) and teamed with Bronson in Walter Hill's *Hard Times*. He enjoyed a resurgence of popularity in the '90s, won an Academy Award for his performance in *Affliction*, was never without work, and was a screen legend when he died in 2002.

Robert De Niro

He's paisan, of course. And despite the fact that *Once Upon a Time in America* is about *Jewish* gangsters, he brought to it the mixed but mostly Italian-American iconographic associations of Johnny Boy in *Mean Streets*, Travis Bickle in *Taxi Driver*, Jimmy Doyle in *New York, New York*, Jake LaMotta in *Raging Bull*, and the young Vito Corleone in *The Godfather, Part II*. But he's not really Leone's type of actor, any more than Rod Steiger was in *Duck, You Sucker!* De Niro's too much the chameleon, too ready to obliterate the subtext of his own personality for the sake of the role. That's one kind of acting, but it's not the kind that works best in Leone's films, where type is at least as important as character. *Duck, You Sucker!* and *Once Upon a Time in America* are both exemplars of a new kind of character grouping: the pair rather than the trio. In both films a two-bit thief is acted on by a traveling operator with smoother style and higher ideas who ultimately betrays his low-class protégé. In both films, the smooth operator is played by an identifiable "type" player with strong iconographic associations (James Coburn, James Woods), while the protagonist-protégé is played by a method actor whose screen persona is less readily typified, more malleable (Steiger, De Niro). The approach wasn't really perfected in either film, but, as always, Leone was up to something, and one wishes he hadn't stopped whittling so soon, so we could have seen what was going to happen.

Clint Eastwood

Eastwood, a late choice for the lead role in *A Fistful of Dollars*, was a tabula rasa on which Leone would write ineradicable capital letters. Downing and Herman quote Leone as saying, "I looked at him and I didn't see any character … just a physical figure." Everything that Clint Eastwood became, he owes to two men—Leone and Don Siegel. No Name and Dirty Harry made his fortune and image, but the roles also cursed him with stereotypical associations. Within the parts he worked wonders; outside of them he ran into trouble. His more personal projects as a director are haunted by the collision between him and his image. His masterpiece, *Unforgiven*, is a gloss on the difference between fact and legend, between the old Western and the new, between the public reputation for violence and the private wish to serve higher ideals or be left alone. Working through this, Eastwood became his own man and has done accomplished work in his own right, both as actor out from the shadow of his Leone and Siegel roles, and as a director of unique vision. Unknown in Italy and virtually unknown in the United States (he was a second-stringer on *Rawhide*, and even a lot of people who watched the show regularly thought he was new blood when Leone trotted him out as No Name), Eastwood was a Western hero redressed in the trappings of violence and amorality associated with the traditional villainous gunslinger. But, of course, he turned out to be a hero after all, and audiences loved his easy manner, his unassuming superiority over all comers, his sardonic wit, and his lack of claim to heroism even when caught in the act of doing good.

We assume from the beginning that Eastwood, in *For a Few Dollars More*, is playing the same character he had played in *A Fistful of Dollars*. In fact, the advertising campaign for the film encouraged us to do so ("The Man with No Name Is Back and the Man in Black Is Waiting for Him!"). But jarring points signal character dissimilarities. Eastwood's called "Manco" in the Italian prints (and in at least one American print), he's more mercenary than he was in the previous film, and he talks about wanting to use his money to (get this) retire! His character's morality is even more pragmatic than it had been in *A Fistful of Dollars*, where at least he does what he does in order to protect the innocent. There is a certain bond of honor with Colonel Mortimer; but most of what Eastwood's Manco does in the film is consistent with the bounty-killer amorality ascribed to him from the onset.

Yet poncho and cigar, stubble and squint persist through all three Eastwood/Leone films. If the characters portrayed by Eastwood are not supposed to be the same man, it is at least fair to treat them as variations on a theme. What theme? Screen Western heroism stripped of all pretension and motivation and forced to look inward to see a truth: Show me a hero and I'll show you a villain with good excuses. There's good and bad (and ugly) in all of us, and Eastwood was the key player Leone used to mold traditional Western-movie heroism into something with darker roots—if not Hell, then at least Purgatory.

Jack Elam

My father used to say that the presence of Jack Elam is like the stamp of approval on a Western film. Elam's being in a Western makes it official. Doomed by his face never to be more than a character player, Elam turned that face into a distinctive and indispensable part of the Western movie landscape. He appears, among many other places, in Robert Aldrich's *Vera Cruz*, in John Sturges's *Gunfight at the O.K. Corral*, and in Michael Curtiz's *The Comancheros*—all key films in shaping the Leone vision. Most importantly, Elam has a splendidly Leonean face: wall-eyed homeliness to revel in, rubbery features just made to do battle with a fly, a two-way gaze to disarm even the hardest opponent, and a commitment to personal ugliness that assures us this man is capable of anything. The wonder is that it took Leone four films to get around to using Elam. The old wandering eye is perfect as one of a trio of Western icons (two from Hollywood, one from Cinecittà) who wait ominously and satirically for the Man Who Makes Appointments. Frayling and others have recounted that Leone wanted the three waiting gunmen to be none other than Eastwood, Van Cleef, and Eli Wallach, as a joking farewell to the world of his first three films, but Eastwood's price was prohibitive—doubtless a function of his unwillingness to play a cameo role and be killed off in the first scene.

Gabriele Ferzetti

A leading man in Italian films beginning in the late '40s, Gabriele Ferzetti was an eminently respectable actor and intimately associated with the Italian film industry establishment. He was also closely connected in the popular imagination with the world of culture and high art, as his roles in *Puccini* (1954), *Donatello* (1956), and Antonioni's *L'Avventurra* (1959) attest. Ferzetti, therefore, was the perfect figure to portray the culturally and commercially lavish but physically and spiritually deprived Morton in *Once Upon a Time in the West*. Whenever Morton talks to anyone there is a tone (not nasty, just matter-of-fact) of pearls before swine—exactly right from a top-billed, mainstream Italian cinema actor making his first appearance in one of the renegade undercurrent films (first the mythological epics, then the "Spaghetti Westerns") that transformed Italian movies from within. Morton would have been a plum role even if Ferzetti had not been fairly inactive for nearly a decade. *Once Upon a Time in the West* and *On Her Majesty's Secret Service* almost simultaneously brought him back to world attention. Leone could hardly have made a more appropriate choice for the role.

Henry Fonda

Opposing the Old World condescension of Ferzetti's Morton was the New World strength and drive of Henry Fonda's Frank. In Danny Peary's *Closeups*, Leone writes glowingly of his admiration for Fonda, "the idol of my youth," and recounts how he tried unsuccessfully to get the screenplay of *A Fistful of Dollars* to Fonda in 1963 (though it's hard to imagine Fonda as the Man with No Name, and even harder to imagine him accepting a lesser role). Leone talks of the excitement he felt while executing the famous and powerful shot that first discloses Fonda's face at the McBain massacre: "The audience would be struck in an instant by this profound contrast between the pitiless character Fonda is playing and Fonda's face, a face which for so many years had symbolized justice and goodness." But the "goodness" that Fonda stood for was not unqualified. True enough, he'd been a Western hero from the thirties on; he played Lincoln, and he played a Wyatt Earp with few of the vices that flawed the historical Earp. But the roles that made him an American institution were more complicated: A ranch hand who goes along with a lynching, even though it's against his conscience and his better judgment, because he's afraid he'll be a suspect if he doesn't, and better them than him (*The Ox-Bow Incident*); a gentle young idealist moved by circumstance to take up the sword of violence against social injustice (*The Grapes of Wrath*); a stylish and engaging outlaw—but still an outlaw—Frank James (*Jesse James* and *The Return of Frank James*); and a by-the-book military commander so tainted with hubris he leads his regiment in a suicidal attack rather than admit he was wrong and a junior officer was right (*Fort Apache*). Tom Dunson and Ethan Edwards notwithstanding, John Wayne always stood for "justice and goodness" much more solidly than Fonda did; but it was precisely that taint of corruptibility that made Fonda's characters more human and believable and that made him so right for *Once Upon a Time in the West* (try to imagine the Duke playing Frank!). Leone says that Fonda "designed a character so real and human that he ran the risk of having his personality overwhelm the other actors around him." Though Ferzetti, Bronson, and Cardinale never seem "overwhelmed" by Fonda, there's no denying that Fonda's performance goes far toward making Frank seem, by the end of the film, almost sympathetic.

Be all that as it may, it is possible—though not easy—to imagine someone else playing Frank. Lee Van Cleef, perhaps. Jack Palance, in a different vein. James Coburn, maybe. The end result would not have been as rich, but it could have been accomplished.

By contrast, it is impossible to imagine anyone but Fonda playing Jack Beauregard in *My Name is Nobody*. The character and performance are so intimately bound up with Fonda's specific screen image that it is inviting to wonder if Fonda made any personal contributions to the script. His letter to Nobody at the end refers as specifically to his own Western acting career as it does to Beauregard's gunfighting career. Unlike Leone, Valerii taps little of the darker side of the Fonda icon—oh, maybe the image-breaking moment when Beauregard declines to avenge his murdered brother and allows himself to be bought off for the price of a steamer ticket. But mostly Fonda's Beauregard is a man in white, an older version of the Wyatt Earp of *My Darling Clementine* (the first of three versions of the Earp-Holliday-Clanton story that fueled Leone's world with actors and images). When Jack Beauregard departs for Europe at the end of *My Name Is Nobody*, we feel the haunting sensation that a grand old man of the movies is bidding farewell to a genre and to a career.

Terence Hill

Terence Hill is the Nobody who replaces Fonda's Beauregard. A light, blond, blue-eyed north Italian, Hill is really Mario Girotti working under a *nom de cinema* that is also his wife's maiden name. It was Hill's destiny to bring non-violence to the Italian Western, a genre originally distinguished by its profuse and graphic bloodshed. As Nobody, and even more so as Trinity, Hill plays a character so good with a gun that he rarely has to use it. When he does use his weapon, normally he scares opponents off by demonstrating his skill rather than by shooting them dead. Hill was a rich choice for Nobody. He not only represents the Italian Western vis-à-vis Fonda's representation of the American, but also represents the "new" Italian Western—comic, introspective, often political, marked by surreal intellectual symbolism—vis-à-vis Leone's "old" Italian Western. Hill's Nobody and Trinity characters are so much better than their opponents they can afford to clown around. Hill did so repeatedly, usually in tandem with the big, brutish Bud Spencer as his half-trained bear of a sidekick. Leone was quoted as regretting the team identification, maintaining that Hill would have a better future as his own man. After the waning of the Spaghetti Western, Hill resurfaced in police thrillers, and has continued to work steadily in that genre.

Klaus Kinski

Now *there's* a face! Put this man in the company of Mario Brega, Jack Elam, and Al Mulock, and you have formidable fodder, indeed, for Leone's closeup lens. Well, that lineup never existed. Kinski was in only one Leone film, so he managed to get next to only Mario Brega—and, of course, to Lee Van Cleef. The two encounters between Colonel Mortimer and the hunchbacked bandit Wild remain decisive high points in *For a Few Dollars More*, as much for the electricity between the two actors as for the understated comedy of the scenes. This conspicuous performance, together with a highly visible cameo as a condemned anarchist in *Dr. Zhivago*, made 1965 a crucial year in Kinski's career. Another came in 1972, when his first of several performances for Werner Herzog, as *Aguirre, the Wrath of God*, put him on the international critical and box office map. Throughout the '50s and early '60s—beginning with a walk-on in *Decision before Dawn* (1952)—Kinski played parts of varying size and importance in many made-in-Germany films (not only German but American and British as well). Rarely, however, did Kinski use the redoubtable arsenal of his facial technology as well as he did in *For a Few Dollars More*: the hanging, quivering lips; the clenched teeth and trembling jaw; the spasmodically twitching cheek; the glaring, outraged eyes; the throbbing, engorged blood vessels—we could swear that this man is going to explode before our very eyes. And he does.

Al Mulock

Billed as "Al Mulloch" in the credits of *The Good, the Bad and the Ugly*, English character actor Mulock was the crucial plot device that reunited Blondie and Tuco the moment he was shot through Tuco's bathwater. His face is the pocked, scarred, hills-and-valleys topography that replaces the sweeping landscape in the film's opening shot. It's a terrific face, a perfect Leone face. It bespeaks toughness—not the toughness of the honorably battered hero but the bullish tenacity of the guy who keeps getting beat up yet always comes back for more. He comes back later in *The Good, the Bad and the Ugly* and still hasn't learned to shoot, just talk.

Mulock committed suicide during the filming of *Once Upon a Time in the West*, not quite finishing his memorable contribution to that film. While Jack Elam wages a war of nerves with a whining fly and Woody Strode submits to the quiet torture of a leaky tank dripping water on his head, Mulock contributes to the outré musicale by cracking his knuckles. He gets killed off by the Man with the Harmonica a few minutes later, after demonstrating once again his penchant for talking instead of shooting. He's a perennial loser, scarred with his many defeats. As the quick-learning peasant Miguel said, to gunfighter Chris's pleasure, in *The Magnificent Seven*, "The man for us is the one who *gave* him that face."

Luigi Pistilli

Inquisitive, a bit smarter, more calculating, more prudent than the other "members of the gang," Pistilli's Groggy hangs on a lot longer—in *For a Few Dollars More* he is the last to die. One standout performance deserves another, and in *The Good, the Bad and the Ugly*, Leone gave Pistilli the role of Tuco's brother, Father Ramirez—a role now wonderfully enriched for devotees of that film by the enhanced DVD version of the film, which restores in full the encounter between the two brothers.

Jason Robards

Robards has had a long and distinguished acting career onstage and in films. His parts are set mostly in contemporary surroundings or in the early twentieth-century milieu of *Long Day's Journey into Night*, *The St. Valentine's Day Massacre*, or *The Night They Raided Minsky's*. A clever poker story in which he played a part, *A Big Hand for the Little Lady* (1966)—with Henry Fonda, interestingly enough—had little to do with the Western genre, its milieu merely incidental to its story.

But it's not hard to figure out what attracted Leone to Robards. In 1967 the actor played Doc Holliday in John Sturges's *Hour of the Gun*, a sequel to the O.K. Corral story, and this crusty characterization undoubtedly had much to do with the development of the cryptic romantic-in-cynic's clothing, Cheyenne. Robards, even more often than Fonda, has played characters marred by weakness and villainy. The dipsomaniacal Jamie Tyrone in *Long Day's Journey into Night*, the dissipated Dr. Richard Diver in *Tender Is the Night*, and Al Capone in *The St. Valentine's Day Massacre* are key portrayals in his iconography. Capable of a vicious, self-abusive sort of comedy, and an uncompromising antisocial streak (*A Thousand Clowns*), Robards's image is right for the "Tuco" type in *Once Upon a Time in the West*. Accepting the role was an important decision for him, and a good one both for Leone and for Robards, who went on to build a couple more monuments in the Western landscape with Sam Peckinpah in *The Ballad of Cable Hogue* and *Pat Garrett and Billy the Kid*.

Lionel Stander

Blacklisted during the '50s, Stander made a comeback in British films during the mid-'60s. The role of the bartender in *Once Upon a Time in the West* must have looked like a way to make it back into the eyes and hearts of the American viewing audience and the U.S. film industry. But cruel fate! The film did not do well, and whoever recut it for theatrical release deleted Stander's only scene. A few people saw him, though, and he began to reappear in American films in the early '70s. As always, he was good, even when playing the household help in the television series *Hart to Hart*, but Leone and Polanski (*Cul-de-Sac*) remain two of the very few directors who used this remarkably deep character actor to advantage.

Benito Stefanelli

Laurel to Mario Brega's Hardy, this slim but strong regular of the Leone stock company looks like the archetypal Roman centurion. He's always a member of the gang, most visibly as Rubio in *A Fistful of Dollars* and Yuri in *For a Few Dollars More*. Stefanelli was in every one of Leone's Westerns, and a good number of the best and most visible films of the Italian Western genre.

Rod Steiger

An actor of good reputation, who worked with some of the best directors in the business and who was consistently visible during the '60s, Steiger may have thought himself to be slumming—or stooping—when he played Juan Miranda in *Duck, You Sucker!* That he didn't give the role his all is clear when this performance is compared with those that demonstrated what he was capable of when he took the time to examine a character seriously and think things through (Charlie in *On the Waterfront*, O'Meara in *Run of the Arrow*, Al Capone, the psychiatrist in *The Mark*, Sol Nazerman in *The Pawnbroker*, Chief Gillespie in *In the Heat of the Night*). It's no accident that these career-defining performances predated Steiger's Academy Award. Oscar seems to have marked the turning point in his career: thereafter, his performances tended toward shallow caricature, his emotionalism indulging bathos instead of pathos. Eventually, Steiger's quest for versatility left him with no identifiable screen image at all. Because Leone relied heavily on the iconography of his players to bring a sense of importance to their performances and to the film, Steiger's lack of image seriously harmed *Duck, You Sucker!* The only film in Steiger's career that seems important to his work for Leone is Samuel Fuller's *Run of the Arrow*, from which Leone drew two actors and a number of key ideas. (Steiger had also played Pope John XXIII in Ermanno Olmi's *A Man Called John*, the most important, though not the only Italian connection in his career.) *Duck, You Sucker!* is Juan's film, not Sean's, and there seems no explanation for Steiger's broad overplaying of the character to the exclusion of any kind of introspection and understanding. Steiger played the role as if he had contempt for Juan, without having taken the trouble to know him.

Paolo Stoppa

Beginning in the early '30s, Stoppa did character acting in Italian films. By the time Leone used him in a cameo as Sam, Jill's buckboard driver, in *Once Upon a Time in the West*, he had become an institution. His testy but colorful manner when explaining to Jill that both horses and people need to stop for a drink now and again, balances the overly amiable style of the talkative bartender inside the tavern. Stoppa has a throwaway part, but Leone was perceptive seeing him as an Italian Lionel Stander.

Woody Strode

One of many John Ford referents in *Once Upon a Time in the West* is Leone's use of Strode as one of the three gunmen who wait at the desert water-stop for the Man Who Makes Appointments. Strode was *Sergeant Rutledge* (1960); he figured importantly in *Two Rode Together* and *The Man Who Shot Liberty Valance* (both 1962); of all things, he was a Chinese warrior in Ford's last film, *Seven Women* (1965). Before Leone, Richard Brooks had made use of Strode's iconographic presence in *The Professionals* (1966). In that film, he is emphatically a character; to Leone he is both more and less. Standing stonily under the leaking water tank, smiling at his mastery of the fabled Chinese torture, Strode is a symbol who soon becomes one of the three exemplars of the mythic West to be knocked over by the avenging gunfire of Leone's new angel.

Lee Van Cleef

Van Cleef is another institution—throughout the '50s, a personification of villainy in American Westerns and films noir. It's the eyes—narrow, shrewd, piercing. They size up everything as if there were a center of ultimate judgment behind them. At times they almost threaten to cross as, in extreme closeup, they stare down at you over a monumental nose. If Van Cleef can't fix you with his eyes, he'll pin you with that nose. There's no escaping the relentless evil genius of this face. And the first thing Leone did with his quintessential Western villain was to turn him into a pretty nice guy. Well, not the first thing. As *For a Few Dollars More* opens, we see a hat reading the Bible, and when we discover the head beneath it, the Bible itself is subverted. In no way can this archetypal nasty be a preacher—nor even a casual student—of the Word of the Lord. But the collision of image and icon sets us up for a bigger reversal toward the end of the movie. It is then we recognize Colonel Mortimer's indignation as righteous after all and his pursuit of Indio as more than purely mercenary. The reversal is assisted by the softening effect worked on Van Cleef's image by scenes such as the hat-shooting that allow him to play his icon for comic effect.

Leone's overhauling of Van Cleef's image paved the way for the most important and lucrative phase of Van Cleef's career: he went on to play heroes, antiheroes, and aging mentors in numerous Italian Westerns, notably Sollima's *The Big Gundown*, Valerii's *Day of Anger*, and the "Sabata" films. In the meantime, Leone blithely re-inverted the Van Cleef image, making the actor a bad guy again, in *The Good, the Bad and the Ugly*. More's the pity Leone couldn't bring off the joke planned for the opening of *Once Upon a Time in the West*, in which Van Cleef, veteran of *High Noon*, *Gunfight at the O.K. Corral*, and *The Man Who Shot Liberty Valance*, could well have been one of the men waiting for the Italian train that brings a new icon into the Western landscape. That would have been a nice parting shot for Leone and Van Cleef, two men who owe each other a lot.

Gian Maria Volontè

In both *Yojimbo* and *Sanjuro*, writes Donald Richie, "the villain Tatsuya Nakadai stays around for the first fight, admires Mifune, tries to get Mifune to join his side, and is, in the end, killed by him." Gian Maria Volontè is Nakadai to Clint Eastwood's Mifune. Leone's first two films created Volontè's screen image by establishing the actor as a dangerous, sensitive type, a bad guy of such emotional intensity that he brings a pitiable sense of inner torment to even the most irredeemable, reprehensible, villainous roles. Volontè is one of those *busy* actors. Every part of him is working all the time; he makes you uneasy just watching him. Like Steiger, Volontè continually performs thespian acrobatics; working without a net, he teeters on the very brink of hamminess; unlike Steiger, he never falls. His larger-than-life style was perfectly suited to Leone's purpose of creating stark, almost comic stereotypes, then of plunging into them as if they were full-blown characters, and by doing so, making them full-blown by sheer cussedness. His work for Leone propelled the intensely political Volontè into a period of international recognition with *Investigation of a Citizen Above Suspicion* (1969), Melville's *Le Cercle Rouge* (1970), *Sacco and Vanzetti* (1971), *The Mattei Affair* (1972), and *Lucky Luciano* (1974)—after which he continued to work in less visible Italian films until his death in 1994.

Eli Wallach

Wallach, a versatile method actor like Steiger, had often handled bad-guy roles and had built a specialty of playing low-life types. His Calvera, the bandit, in *The Magnificent Seven* (1960), is the role upon which the Tuco character is built—a cocky, laughing, drooling peasant whose grossness gives him an edge by masking his superiority at tactics and firearms. A man like Tuco could not have stayed alive so long if he hadn't been smarter than he seemed, and a moviegoer who does not recognize this understands nothing of Tuco—nothing! His stock-in-trade was coming as close as possible to overplaying, but knowing when too much is just enough. Wallach appeared in several other Italian Westerns, and it's pleasant to speculate what the results might have been if Wallach had played Juan in *Duck, You Sucker!* This Actors Studio alum must have been flabbergasted to see Tuco become his most famous role, his defining performance. In 2005, his chatty, episodic memoir *The Good, the Bad, and Me* was published to wide acclaim and delight. The next year he was honored at a ceremony in Almeria, Spain, where *The Good, the Bad and the Ugly* had been shot forty years earlier, and where he remains a hero and an indelible icon.

James Woods

The feeling you get from a James Woods performance is that the actor is on the edge and capable of anything. Even when he smiles, his lupine visage suggests he could devour you in a moment. Every once in a while, he does. In *The Onion Field* Woods plays a psychopathic cop-killer and criminal mastermind who, not unlike Max in *Once Upon a Time in America*, influences and betrays a trusting associate. He was a self-destructive red herring in *Eyewitness*, a manic de-programmer in *Split Image*, a video pirate who discovered the dark side of the future in Cronenberg's *Videodrome*, and an improbable vampire-hunter with heavy ordnance in John Carpenter's *Vampires*. But his performance in *Once Upon a Time in America* is his most ambitious and accomplished work, tapping all of the dark potency of his disarming screen image.

Keenan Wynn

Wynn was a slight Western figure. He appeared in *The War Wagon* (1967) and *McKenna's Gold* (1968) (an all-star genre picture that also featured Eli Wallach in a post-Leone Western role). There's an oblique Ford connection in that Wynn played Luke Plummer in the 1966 Gordon Douglas remake of *Stagecoach*. If Wynn has an identifiable screen presence, it's as a hapless, hopeless symbol of authority who doesn't know, or doesn't care, that things are collapsing around his ears. The sheriff in *Once Upon a Time in the West* is a bad joke—a lawman where there is no law—a mainstay of the Western. He's a mellower version of that earlier, most famous Wynn persona, Colonel Bat Guano, whose protection of the moral order and the rights of the Coca-Cola Company stood firm while everything else in *Dr. Strangelove* was going to hell. Wynn's role in *Once Upon a Time in the West* was pared down from a meatier one that existed before the film was released; but by God, this man knows how to run an auction (and a town)—even if he is powerless to stop the railroad from stealing the McBain land claim and outlaws from murdering children under his very nose.

Notes

1 *Clint Eastwood: All-American Anti-Hero* (see Bibliography).

Part 4

THE VISION

"A Man Who Knows What He Wants"

The Moral Geometry of Sergio Leone

Fairy tales are concerned with right conduct and its difficulties. They are about courage and cowardice, truth and lies, hatred and compassion. They are about morals; and yet moralizing to a fairy tale is as frost to a flower. At the least breath of that frost, they wither into dull, exemplary lessens as boring as impertinent. What work they perform in the spirit is, so to speak, without benefit of clergy, felt rather than understood. They engage the whole awareness. Our reason, even in childhood, tells us the event is impossible at the very moment we feel its rightness, and we move with our will to accept a cosmos in which these things can have their own validity.

—William Golding, "Custodians of the Real"
A Moving Target

The fairy tale simplifies all situations. Its figures are clearly drawn; and details, unless very important, are eliminated. All characters are typical rather than unique.

—Bruno Bettelheim, *The Uses of Enchantment*

It's no accident that the titles of Sergio Leone's movies suggest the stark simplicity of the fairy tale. The films are hardly intended for children. They're broad, primitive, elemental enchantments—superficially simple, yet all the while betraying a dark and complex vision of morality and the psyche.

In fairy tales, variations are countless. There are few rigid plot elements, and plot itself is rarely of the essence; frequently, a plot is illogical or inconsequential. The characters, though often richly drawn, are not often objects of intense empathy. The proof of the tale lies in the telling—and so it is with Leone's films. His camera is no more (nor less) interested in human beings than in the ramshackle buildings, desolate anti-towns, and desert limbos that landscape his Western parables. Bright swatches of color recall the garish, unmixed, unsubtle shades of comic books, or the striking, often clashing hues of Technicolor Westerns of the '50s. Montage stresses incidental detail rather than overall action—stresses, Buddhist-like, the action that is in inaction. The intimacy the film establishes is not between viewer and character but between viewer and vision. Leone is interested only in showing us his way of seeing—a world that has nothing to do with realism and everything to do with style, a world of form almost devoid of "content."

Antecedents (and roots) of the Leone style are to be found in Eisenstein's colliding montage of faces and decorative details in a slowly changing milieu; Kurosawa's studied comic ritualism; the self-consciously epic scope of John Sturges's adventurism; John Ford's emphasis on landscape, character grouping, and family. "There are directors who discover the world and directors who invent it," Andrew Sarris writes in *The John Ford Movie Mystery*. "Ford and most of his Hollywood colleagues belong in the second category, where the cinema has always been more a dream than a document." So it is with Leone, who grew up watching Hollywood films and working more in the period fantasies of Cinecittà than in the street scenes of the neorealists. In Leone's revision of Ford, the graveyard replaces the funeral; there is no correlate to the wedding; dance music accompanies visions of character tension against the backdrop of a bustling town, never against the setting of an elegant cotillion; the confrontation is always more important than the action or the resolution. But the Fordian approach is there in spades. "Ford had never been a director to shrink from the obvious," writes Sarris, "and surprisingly often he brings it off by the sheer strength and tenacity of his visual style." Leone certainly shares with Ford a mastery of what Sarris calls "obviousness that transcends the obvious."

It is tempting—and perhaps illuminating—to think of Leone as the child not only of John Ford but of Sam Fuller, whose stark, obvious, underpopulated parables, shot and mounted in closeups and "headlines," provide an important stylistic precedent for Leone's own vision. Certainly Fuller's primitivism offers the "missing link" between the sentimental power of Ford and the anti-sentimental audacity of Leone. Any broadstroke, stylistic primitive, even in his greatest moments (perhaps especially in those moments) runs the risk of appearing ridiculous. The willingness to run that risk, and the danger involved in running it, is what makes great primitive cinema. Leone, like Fuller, has built a career on laughing in the face of chance.

Often, the laughter takes the form of action or dialogue that deliberately calls attention to Leone's own quirky manipulation of time and space. A good example—and one that provides one of the richest moments in Leone's films—occurs when Manco evens the balance of firepower between Mortimer and Indio. Opening Mortimer's locket watch, Manco says, "Now we start." Start what? It's not starting that Mortimer and Indio are about, it's finishing—finishing a lifelong fixation, finishing an obsessive manhunt, finishing their growing rivalry, and finishing the face-off that they had begun only a few moments before Manco's appearance. The only thing that is starting here is Leone's trademark, the "gundown" montage: Manco's line is a way of saying that the first Morricone-orchestrated, cross-cut confrontation was just a false start, and now the real one begins. Leone has jokingly stopped the rhythm of his own style—then started it up all over again—in order to call special attention to what he is doing.

That interruption is called for by the plot, of course. But Sergio Leone's plots are not exactly famous for adhering to the rules. To say his films are leisurely would understate the case. Leone takes an extraordinary amount of time to introduce his characters and their styles, paying little or no attention to the "plot hook" traditionally required within the first few minutes of screen-time. What hook there is comes up fairly quickly in *A Fistful of Dollars*, but it takes more than two reels for some semblance of a plot to develop in *For a Few Dollars More* and in *Once Upon a Time in the West*. And, though the gold is mentioned in the second scene of *The Good, the Bad and the Ugly*, the subject doesn't come up again for nearly an hour. Sergio Leone likes to take his time.

> It's a terrible pity you can't make time stand still. There are moments that you want to relive over and over, very slowly, moments that you never want to end.
>
> —Sergio Leone, in interview[1]

> "It's an Italian Western. You know: Ten minutes of people looking at each other. Americans believe in blood and gore. Leone is interested in what comes before."
>
> "That's because the Italians are more interested in the pasta than in the main course. It's no accident they're called 'Spaghetti Westerns'."
>
> —An overheard conversation

Montage is commonly thought of as a means of shortening real time, of reducing the duration of mundane, repetitious events to a crisply paced, economic presentation of highlights. The American term for the process—"editing"—emphasizes the shortening aspect. The jump cut not only saves time, it increases pace, and heightens viewer interest, excitement, involvement. But despite his penchant for some unconventional cutting procedures—Leone, in *The Good, the Bad and the Ugly*'s opening and closing sequences, for example, illogically cuts directly from a point-of-view long shot to an impossible closeup of, in the first case, two riders' faces, and in the second, Blondie aiming his rifle for the last time—Leone is generally not one for jump-cutting. Cutting out minutiae to "speed up" real time is only one use of montage, and it's not Leone's. He's more interested in saving the moment, stretching it, protracting real time by long takes and "slow" montages during which the suspense that precedes explosive action is drawn out by photographing all the details of a single event and reassembling them lineally. This is what Leone does in the buildups to his climactic gun battles. He makes the simultaneous become sequential, and thereby comes as close as anyone can to making time stand still.

The same effect is achieved in the self-parodying, coffee-stirring scene in *Once Upon a Time in America*, but that scene is atypical of Leone's use of time in his most recent film. Generally, Leone reverses his gundown montage technique, and, instead of making the simultaneous sequential (thereby stretching time), he makes the sequential simultaneous (evidenced particularly in the phone-ringing montage), compressing time so that all at once we see Noodles at three different stages of his life.

The de-emphasis on movement through time creates a greater interest in the static occupancy of space. The essence of the Leone style is geometry. Char-

acters are grouped numerically, their relationships carefully ordered. The ordering is often more important than the characters themselves, who, despite their
frequent richness, become not so much people as symbols, elements in a structure. Is it any wonder so many of them have no names, and that, in their dialogue, numbers come increasingly to represent human beings—or at least human
bodies? "Both in the conscious and in the unconscious," Bettelheim reminds us,
"numbers stand for people."

> The real conquest of modern cinema is ... not the challenging of the "classic
> shot breakdown" but that of the frame.
>
> —Eric Rohmer and Claude Chabrol
> *Hitchcock*

The landscape in which Leone chose to place his figures with their nu-
merical relationships (except in the television-conscious *Once Upon a Time in
America*) is the Techniscope frame, an anamorphic widescreen process that
saves money (over the old Cinemascope process and the younger, sharper
Panavision) by using standard 35-millimeter film on which the old 1.33:1 frame
is split horizontally, accommodating two squeezed images proportionally twice
as wide. The resulting image—of the 2.35:1 family—is then made even broader
than the Cinemascope or Panavision frame by masking or trimming the top and
bottom. Widescreen processes developed early in film history, though they came
into popular use only during the '50s as a means of combating, through spectacle, the more limited possibilities of the nevertheless ever-threatening television
set.

The initial impact of the new frame ratio was to discourage camera movement and inventive camera placement, thus creating a plethora of films in which
the framed image, though spectacular in scope, was essentially static. The softened effect of frame composition in the hands of directors and cinematographers
unused to the new ratio led Chabrol and Rohmer to write, in 1957, that "in
cinemascope films ... the extreme ends of the screen are for all practical purposes useless. The point is not that the frame contains more but that what is contained seems less oppressive." It may be that widescreen needed a new generation of filmmakers to bring its potential to fruition. Masters such as Leone,
Peckinpah, Altman, and Kubrick appear to have made the Chabrol-Rohmer ob-
servation inapplicable.

Leone recognized that the widescreen ratio more closely approximates the
actual range of vision of a pair of human eyes, and that long takes with static
camera setups are closer to the way most of us actually look at the world most of
the time. Even in the non-Scope *Once Upon a Time in America*, Leone refers to
the Scope ratio in the dimensions of the peephole through which Noodles
watches Deborah dance.

Held in place by a stationary camera, the widescreen frame actually becomes more rigid than the standard 1.33:1 frame, which is continually melting
away with pans and tracking shots. Like Stanley Kubrick, Leone doesn't move
his camera a lot. He knows how much is to be gained from allowing the viewer

to move his eyes over a static composition, how much can be done with an oppressively immobile widescreen frame, and how, when camera movement does come, it will be the more meaningful because of the attention it calls to itself.

If Leone's frame is a kind of window, its sides are most certainly walls. Onscreen action directed at an offscreen object is nearly always toward the camera, not off the sides of the frame (an indication that the give-and-take of Leone's films is conceived in terms of confrontational viewpoints, which alternate in the manner of the so-called *decoupage classique*—even if Leone doesn't always cut them that way). The result emerges partly because the Techniscope format provides a frame of action so expansive that few lateral images or movements remain incomplete within our field of vision. The screen is so wide that nothing has to be excluded from the frame unless Leone specifically wants it to be. When he does want it so, the exclusion has been used to surprise us by surprising his onscreen characters; this technique is an excellent example of the absoluteness of the frame in Leone's vision. Take for example the often recurring motif of a gun intruding into the frame: In *The Good, the Bad and the Ugly*, as Blondie waits prone on a ridge, preparing to shoot the rope from the neck of his new partner, Shorty, it is Tuco's pistol barrel that enters from the left of the frame to touch Blondie's head, and only when it does so does the bounty killer become aware of the Mexican bandit's presence. Or later, when Tuco is digging with a stick of wood at the grave of Arch Stanton and doesn't know that Blondie has arrived until the shovel Blondie throws enters the frame—the impact is echoed moments later when Angeleyes surprises both Blondie and Tuco by throwing another shovel into the picture. It's impossible that these characters, in the relatively unobstructed desert and graveyard milieus, would be oblivious to the approach of another character in real space; they wouldn't have to be physically interfered with before they became aware of the new presence. But in Leone's joking use of the frame, objects and actions are real only once they're on the screen and can be reacted to. In *Once Upon a Time in America* a hand reaching into the frame to catch a Frisbee becomes a bridge from 1968 to 1933. As Andrew Sarris says of John Ford, Leone "manipulates reality to certify the movies."

The absoluteness of the point-of-view frame corresponds to the absoluteness of Leone's characters. With the exception of the two Johnnys in *Duck, You Sucker!* and Max and Noodles in *Once Upon a Time in America*, Leone's characters don't grow or change, they merely gradually reveal more about themselves—and sometimes they don't even do that. The frame occasionally moves with a moving person; but usually a moving point-of-view shot indicates a weakening on the part of the subjective character. Reeling, shaky, hand-held, point-of-view shots destroy frame rigidity, deliberately, at certain key points in Leone's work. For example, the swaying vision of the Man with No Name and the cockeyed tilt up to the sky that is the last thing Ramón Rojo's tortured eyes see in *A Fistful of Dollars*, or the similar careering tilt-shot when Stevens's wife faints as Angeleyes rides away from his small-scale massacre in *The Good, the Bad and the Ugly*, or the wobbly viewpoint of Tuco on the rickety cross at the end of the same film.

The triangle in the circle (above): Tuco (Eli Wallach, left), Blondie (Clint Eastwood, center), and Angeleyes (Lee Van Cleef) face off in the three-way showdown at the climax of *The Good, the Bad and the Ugly*. The triangle broken (below): Col. Mortimer (Lee Van Cleef, left), Manco (Clint Eastwood, center), and the dead Indio (Gian Maria Volontè) after the faceoff in *For a Few Dollars More*.

As Richard Jameson has said of *Once Upon a Time in the West*, "Space is a constant adventure. ... To watch Leone's film is to realize how few truly wide-screen movies there have been." If such a thing as meaning enters into Sergio Leone's films, it does so in the way his characters enter and leave that implacable, ineffable frame—and how they are grouped to occupy the space while they are in it.

> Mostly ... he insists on the triangle ... through composition.
>
> —Donald Richie on Kurosawa's *Rashomon*

Three is, of course, the magic number of fairy tales, as well as of myth, Catholic orthodoxy, the Bible, and much literature. Bettelheim relates the number's mystique to Freud's division of the consciousness into id, ego, and superego. But he also notes that the number three is associated with sexuality. Original Sin—metaphorically depicted as carnal knowledge, but also called "knowledge of good and evil," as if morality, not its lack, were the true enemy—involved the invasion of a third party, the serpent, into the harmonious duo of Eden. In like manner, the basic structural proposition of Sergio Leone's fairy-tale world is: Three into two won't go.

In *A Fistful of Dollars*, each shift of the Man with No Name's weight resolves the film's triangular tension into a two-way face-off. In *For a Few Dollars More*, the shaky alliance ("Me on the outside, you on the inside") of the two bounty killers in pursuit of the bandit also gives way to a two-man confrontation as Manco is neutralized into the role of referee. Two survivors ride away, instead of the one who left the world to us at the end of the first film. In *The Good, the Bad and the Ugly*, there are also two survivors: two men's unsteady partnership is invaded by a third party and what threatens to be a three-way free-for-all is once again resolved (by Blondie's unloading Tuco's gun) into a one-on-one.

In *Once Upon a Time in the West*, there are two trios: Cheyenne-Harmonica-Frank and McBain-Jill-Morton, each of which is resolved into a two-way confrontation (Harmonica-vs.-Frank, physically; Jill-vs.-Morton, spiritually), with only one member of each trio surviving. In *Duck, You Sucker!*, Juan's and Sean's uneasy partnership suffers more from within than from without. Neither the hated Governor nor the revolutionist-turned-informer Villega is strong enough to sustain a triadic tension with the two Johnnys. So unless one wants to force the issue by claiming that the third member of the trio is the revolution itself (just as the third member of the trio of *My Name is Nobody* is nothing less than a hundred and fifty purebred sonsobitches on horseback), we have a climax in which, instead of three resolving into two, two resolve into one. In *Once Upon a Time in America*'s finale there is a similar resolution of two into one and a freeze on a single face.

> Contrary to what takes place in many modern children's stories, in fairy tales, evil is as omnipresent as virtue. In practically every fairy tale good and evil are given body in the form of some figures and their actions, as good and evil are omnipresent in life and the propensities for both are present in every man. It is this duality which poses the moral problem, and requires the struggle to solve it.
>
> —Bruno Bettelheim
> *The Uses of Enchantment*

The constant resolution of threes into twos signals a tendency to simplify conflict, to reduce matters, perhaps, to "good" and "bad"—though these, in Leone's world, are hardly associated with orthodox notions of right and wrong. In *The Good, the Bad and the Ugly* (whose Italian title, *Il Buono, il brutto, il cattivo* places "good" and "bad" at opposite ends, "ugly" in the middle), the introductions of the three emblematic principal characters are carefully balanced, each man shooting three people in his first sequence. Tuco's and Blondie's shootings are, if not defensive, at least somewhat competitive. But Angeleyes kills an unarmed, bedridden invalid, a family man ill-equipped to match him, and—most important in Leone's world—a boy (in *Once Upon a Time in the West*, Cheyenne equates killing a child with killing a priest); so even without that title reading "the bad," we'd have no problem classifying Angeleyes first time out.

Leone's anonymous heroes, however, are not "good" in a conventional sense or even in Hawksian sense (for some of his bad guys are good that way, too). It's not motivation that determines goodness, either. Those who work for a private motive of meting out personal justice are always delineated as "good guys," but there are both good and bad (and ugly) people who seem to have no higher purpose than monetary gain. What then separates the exemplars of these moral categories? Ultimately, it's little more than Leone's proclamation that they are "good" or "bad." We don't question this, any more than we question the motivations of the wicked stepmother.

But there's another key difference, and it's relevant in the fairy tale as well as in the Leone film. Moral character is defined in terms of one's attitude toward innocence. Both the "good" and the "bad" characters have long since lost their own innocence—we know that ("Were you ever young?" Manco asks Mortimer). But the "bad" characters have no qualms about victimizing those who retain their innocence. They even seek out opportunities to destroy children and families, while the "good" characters—like confidence men—victimize only those who are predisposed to treachery themselves. Only objectively "bad" people are killed by the "good" characters, and though the anti-traditional, amoral, perhaps even a little sadistic "good" guys may relish the role of judge, jury, and executioner, they do what they have to, responsibly and consistently. No Name, Manco, Blondie, and Harmonica may have fewer scruples and fewer illusions than the Lone Ranger, but protecting (or avenging) the innocent is still their motive. The two-bit thief Noodles becomes a killer to avenge Bugsy's slaying of little Dominic. Something is sacred. The balance remains.

> But why speak of enriching an image, when we crystallize it in geometrical perfection? ... Seized in its center and brevity, the mere designation of roundness is astonishingly complete.

—Gaston Bachelard
The Poetics of Space

Despite the division of the world into two kinds of people, and the subsequent delineation of characters as points along a line between two moral poles, Leone's basic element of characterization and balance remains triangulation, not polarity. The triangle, flat if viewed from above, extends into foreground and background when viewed from one of its angles. The two-dimensionality of the potentially linear widescreen is exploded by the movement of Leone's camera; whether he uses it subjectively, or intrusively the camera insists on its own presence as an invisible character. Movement into the image imparts a third dimension. Anyone's camera can do this; but few do it as emphatically as Leone during his unforgettable slow-zooms from midshot to the extremest of extreme closeups in *Once Upon a Time in the West*.

A straight linear distribution of characters across the screen pretty much dominates *A Fistful of Dollars*—people between people, people among people, people confronting people. Even the climactic showdown between No Name and Ramón Rojo is a two-character, two-dimensional affair. But the triangular climaxes of *For a Few Dollars More* and *The Good, the Bad and the Ugly* invest Leone's space with new depth. It's the advantage of the equilateral triangle that it can be inscribed in a circle. The trios of these films become neither points on a line nor corners of a triangle; they are points along the circumference of a circle—a circumference that comfortably accommodates the camera's presence (you, the viewer) as well.

Circularity is by no means absent from *A Fistful of Dollars*, but *For a Few Dollars More* announces a new awareness of its importance as image (indeed, the two Os left on the screen at the end of the main titles of the film seem, according to Leone's vision, to signal the emergence of the circle as a force to be reckoned with). The crude stone circle across whose Techniscope diameter the film's characters face one another at the climax has no logical reason to be there and every imagistic right to be. Manco, seated at center frame on the nearest edge of the circle, is at once the outermost participant and the innermost spectator at the arena of reckoning. An enlargement of the little locket-watch image, the stone circle becomes the watch as the tone and rhythm of the tinny chimes are taken up by Morricone's score.

The same balance is in effect at the climax of *The Good, the Bad and the Ugly*, but with a difference, since we don't know that one of the three adversaries is only a spectator (and, in fact, only one of *them* knows). The not-knowing underlies the tension. Eyes shift from one opponent to another, hands edge toward guns, and three men fan out across the empty circle in the center of a desolate desert graveyard. This circle is even richer than the one in *For a Few Dollars More*. It geometrizes the relationship among the three characters and provides an arena for their reckoning; it echoes the circle motif established at the beginning when Angeleyes rides up to Stevens's home, past a round stone floor and a turning waterwheel; it comments ironically on the whole situation, summing up the film's cynical view of life itself. Those countless concentric circles of graves are grouped around a large nothing, a big empty circle, a zero—the only answer to the question silently asked by all these dead soldiers. No name on the grave, no name on the rock, and nothing left to do but "shoot, don't talk"—an audience of crosses, still and absolute, attends this most final of rituals.

The circle—always the richest of symbols, with its simultaneous representation of the endlessness of infinity, the completeness of unity, the emptiness of nothing, and the incessant turning of fortune's wheel—recurs throughout *Once Upon a Time in the West*. We see windmills, wagon wheels, eyeballs, and the advancing front of the train at the end of the long opening title sequence that visually widens to take us in as it rumbles down upon us with Sergio Leone's directorial credit superimposed. And there's the advancing train at the other end of the film over which the film's title is seen for the first time, turning in a lazy circle as it spins away from us.

But just as often in *Once Upon a Time in the West*, the circle is formed in the movement of the camera, the way-of-seeing that Leone imposes on both observers and observed. As Leone pulls back his camera and executes that rarest of cinematic audacities, a ninety-degree roll, a shot of Frank and Jill facing each other across the screen is revealed to be actually a shot of the two of them in bed, Frank dominant. The shot's flashy, but it makes its point: Frank and Jill have equal power and value in the scene and in the film. Frank's position of control in the ensuing conversation is undercut by the beginning of that shot, which imparts to Jill an equality she never again loses (in fact, later in the scene, she assumes the dominant position).

Most important is the way in which the circle attends the relationship between Frank and his victims—the semicircular movement with which the camera first reveals him as he is about to shoot Tinny McBain and the way he becomes part of a circular movement around Harmonica at the climax when a young victim from his distant past returns for a reckoning out-of-time. The diametric opposition of three men along the circumference of a circle is now resolved into the balance of centrifugal and centripetal force, the center and the satellite. It's as if Leone has gone from the two-man showdown of traditional Westerns (and of *A Fistful of Dollars*), to the three-man showdowns of *For a Few Dollars More* and *The Good, the Bad and the Ugly*, only to come back to the two-man showdown and make it new again. "The end of all our exploring," Eliot wrote in the final lines of *Four Quartets*, "Will be to arrive where we started / And know the place for the first time." That, too, is what Leone's circles are about.

What about me?

—Juan Miranda

There remains the moment of leaving, that all important moment in film when the viewer is pulled out of the world he's entered and then is left to decide for himself where he's been and what he has to show for it. "The fairy tale reassures," says Bettelheim, "gives hope for the future, and holds out the promise of a happy ending." In some sense, all of Leone's films have "happy" endings; but—especially in *Duck, You Sucker!*—the happiness is always qualified.

In *A Fistful of Dollars* and *Once Upon a Time in the West*, the anonymous heroes ride away, having rid the world of a threat to its harmonious development and having left that development in the hands of simple working folk. In *For a Few Dollars More* and *The Good, the Bad and the Ugly*, the Clint Eastwood character rides off with a lot of money, having earned his wages by risking his life to entertain us. All four of these films end with high-angle wide shots.

The pull-back crane-ups used by Leone to end *A Fistful of Dollars*, *For a Few Dollars More*, and *Once Upon a Time in the West* increase the physical and visual distance between the viewer and the subject of interest—increase it to the point where the original focal object threatens to become utterly lost in the landscape. The shot takes in more space, less detail. Our point-of-view is widened, but distanced. Substituted for all those closeups that hang in the memory is a panoramic vista of the mythic West; no longer, in this shot, is the West the battleground of good and evil. Even without a pullback, the ending of *The Good, the Bad and the Ugly* compares to the endings of the other three films in its deliberately placing the viewer out of—in fact, above—the action of the film's subjects; it is as if the God's-eye view were being forced upon us. The scenes represent the release and the abstraction—if not the laughter—of Chaucer's Troilus or Homer's Gods.

The definitive Leone finale is the baroque, all-inclusive crane shot at the end of *Once Upon a Time in the West*. Frustratingly, in many "uncut" prints of the film, especially those shown on television, this final crane shot is frozen before it is even half over. In its proper composition, the shot pulls up and back, up and back, disclosing Harmonica riding away toward the top of the frame as he leads Cheyenne's body on the dead bandit's horse. While the train pulls into the soon-to-be town of Sweetwater (toward the bottom of the frame), the new station rises, and aquarian Jill moves among the thirsting workmen. Early in the shot, the title of the film makes its first appearance over the circular front of the advancing train; then it recedes in a slow circling motion. This title, which more than any other emphasizes the fairy-tale aspect of Leone's vision, is held until the end of the film, implying that the end is a beginning (after all, "Once upon a time" is an opening phrase), and that the entire film has served as a kind of prologue. And so it has, stressing as it does the passing away of the old gods and the birth of a new kind of world.

The title is also held until the end in *Duck, You Sucker!*, the one exception to Leone's customary distancing finales. Here, in the dark and the smoke we seem to move closer to Juan, to get inside him for the first time as his disembodied voice makes us part of his confusion and sense of loss. Juan's friends, niños, hopes, and illusions are all gone, and so is the revolutionary mentor who did all this for/to him. "What about me?" he asks the dead Sean, or perhaps the God who has deserted him; the film's title is his answer—funny, yes, but darkly so, a more searingly personal ending than the avowedly mythic tone of Leone's earlier finales.

The same dark mood and haunting irony inhabit the ending of *Once Upon a Time in America*. Despite the fact that he has been betrayed by his friend, Noodles feels a sense of loss at the enigmatic passing of Max. His eyes fill with tears, and, as if in answer to an unspoken sentiment of remorse, a car full of revelers speeds by to whisk him back to 1933, to the Chinaman's opium den, to the pipe, to the one moment in his life when he might have considered himself happy.

If Leone's characters begin as types and seldom become any less simplified through all the numbering and geometric reordering, Leone's approach to them nevertheless announces a new dimension of judgment, an increasingly complex moral subtext in his deceptively shallow world. More and more, moral relationships—like visual ones—depend less on a knowledge of right and wrong than on a geometric sense of balance.

Notes

1 Cynthia Grenier, "Pastalong Cassidy Always Wears Black," *Oui* #2, April 1973, p. 88.

"Shoot—Don't Talk"

Themes and Images

Even though auteurism has long since passed out of critical favor—and duly considering genre convention and collaborator contribution—there can't be much argument that Sergio Leone is one of the cinema's most distinctive and personal presences. Regardless of the authorship of initial ideas, lines of dialogue, or shooting scripts, the things that seem most important to the person behind the camera are the ones that show up in the finished film. Anyone who takes any kind of camera in hand makes choices—conscious or otherwise—about where to stand to get the picture he wants. Over time, the sum total of those choices reveals patterns that allow an objective observer to draw some conclusions about the person with the camera and about that person's attitude toward space and light, as well as toward nature and toward other people. Visual images begin to recur and form recognizable patterns. What seems incidental becomes integral. And if the ordering mind of the person with the camera has a vision worth sharing and the will to share it, the images begin to make some sort of sense, not only in themselves but in the way they bounce off one another. The persistence of theme and imagery in Leone's films makes his style and vision as immediately distinguishable as those of Hitchcock and Ford. This little catalog considers a few of Leone's salient motifs and images.

Anonymity

Anonymity is central to heroism in Leone's world. Throughout the oeuvre, nicknames, generic names, pseudonyms, and anonyms are more common than given names and surnames. It's all part of Leone's notion of silence—his development of the prototypical silent stranger of the Hollywood Western paradigm: The survivor is he who says the least, reveals the least about himself; doing that, he is the least vulnerable.

The four horsemen of *Once Upon a Time in America* all have nicknames, but we also know their full names and even their dates of birth—a situation unique in Leone's films. The characters are the very opposite of anonymous, and Max and Noodles survive the debacle of 1933 only by changing their names and adopting false identities. The two men's true names are acknowledged again only when "Bailey" calls "Williams" to a secret reunion thirty-five years later. Noodles clings to the death of his friend Max, and insistently addresses him as "Mr. Bailey" throughout the 1968 reunion. Max has styled himself a stranger and proven himself one.

Leone, who hid himself behind the name "Bob Robertson" in 1964, made his anonymous antiheroes the logical heirs of that first silent stranger who, when told, "I didn't catch your name, mister," calmly replied, "I didn't throw it."

Bettelheim writes of character-naming in fairy tales: "The fairy tale makes it clear that it tells about everyman. If names appear, it is quite clear that these are not proper names, but general or descriptive ones. ... Even when the hero is given a name, the use of very common names makes them generic terms." Leone's heroes may be types of Everyman; they make their way through the allegorical desert of life, facing obstacles filled with metaphoric importance. We spend more time, though, looking at these heroes than seeing with their eyes. Clearly, something other than simple identification is at work. Anonymity is useful in preserving an air of mystery about a person. It gives that person a protective shield against the heart-aimed arrows to which less impersonal individuals succumb. Anonymity lets Leone suggest, without insisting on, a supernatural element to the presence of his heroes. (Remember, Leone gained a foothold in cinema through biblical spectaculars and the "sword and sandal" mythological epics in which the spiritual element is commonplace.) There's nothing new in the suggestion that the Man with No Name in *A Fistful of Dollars* and Sean Mallory in *Duck, You Sucker!* are cockeyed Christs. Could *The Good, the Bad and the Ugly* be read as a Miltonian epic in which a divine and suffering Jesus (Blondie) and a calculating Lucifer (Angeleyes) engage in combat to offer redemption or damnation to the "ugly" (stained by Original Sin) soul of man (Tuco)?

Bells

There are holy times and sacred places. Surely if there is a way of sanctifying sound, the religions of the world have made that sanctification the province of the bell. It's used in religious ceremony, where it is associated with magic—white and black. It's an attention-getter, a sign of warning, a tool of music, a voice of joy. Juan de Dios in *A Fistful of Dollars* is the town bell ringer. Unlike his prototype, the town crier with clappers in *Yojimbo*, Juan doesn't have much occasion to do his job. When Colonel Mortimer stops the train in Tucumcari at the beginning of *For a Few Dollars More*, the exterior shot of the train is one that emphasizes the bell mounted on the engine. The scene in which Indio preaches his "sermon" begins with a shot of the abandoned church's bell tower; on this occasion, the bell is being rung by gunshots fired at it by Groggy's men. In the same film, the matching locket-watches play a bell tune when opened. The anomalous stone arch, which we see in the desert during the final flashback in *Once Upon a Time in the West*, has no visible relation to any buildings, or to any world beyond that desolate place; but it has a bell hanging just at its very tip. Leone uses an insistent twenty-two telephone rings to objectify the jumble of fear and remorse that haunts Noodles Aaronson (in 1933) in *Once Upon a Time in America*. It is not by accident that Morricone's scores for Leone's films abound with bell music, from tinkle sounds to clangs. Seen or heard or both, bells provide a kind of spiritual punctuation—often, but not always, ironic—to the intensely physical confrontations of Leone's world.

Bridges

A traditional natural symbol for crossing from one world or way of life to another, the bridge image is repeatedly turned on its ear in Leone's films. Leone's characters find themselves *under* bridges more often than they cross them: The little lives of the gang members in *Once Upon a Time in America* are dominated by the oppressive mass of the Williamsburg Bridge. Tuco and Blondie wire the bridge in *The Good, the Bad and the Ugly* by wading underneath it—and they ultimately wade across the river once the bridge is blown up, demonstrating that it was fundamentally unimportant. That bridge, a symbolic extension of the relationship that exists among the film's three main characters, is like the bridge in *Duck, You Sucker!* Both get blown up, and the immediate result of the destruction is that armies withdraw and "go somewhere else to fight." Bridges are important, to the military at least, not because of where they are or what they do, but only because they are bridges.

Two highly visible bridges in Leone's films do not get blown up. One is the bridge Tuco crosses as he emerges from the desert about half an hour into *The Good, the Bad and the Ugly*. The other *Once Upon a Time in America*'s Williamsburg Bridge, which overhangs the film's crucial 1924 street fight. The former has nothing under it but a dry arroyo; the latter, death.

Bugs

A roach crawls across Sancho Perez's face in the Alamogordo Jail early in *For a Few Dollars More*. He removes that roach with a pinch we can feel, and we know that the hapless creature can't possibly survive. The world-weary Indio, waiting for the bounty killers and his men to wipe each other out, externalizes his self-destructive sadism by half-smashing a bug then watching it crawl lamely around the table. Flies show up throughout *The Good, the Bad and the Ugly*, almost as if directed by Leone, almost as if the flies' presence had been planned. The actors endure the flies with stoic resignation. No one in a Leone film so much as acknowledges one until Jack Elam's extended fly combat in the opening of *Once Upon a Time in the West*. Even then, Elam's character is a model of restraint. Swat he will not, though he tries every conceivable machination of that marvelous rubber face to dissuade the fly from taking up permanent residence in the crevices of his cheek. By waiting until the right moment, Elam's character demonstrates to his—and to our—satisfaction how the fly can become his prisoner, not vice versa. (Except for one shot, the fly is a real one, and "most cooperative—a fortunate accident," according to Leone.) We expect flies to land on Juan Miranda, but we don't expect them to bother Sean Mallory. Yet there they are, marring this handsome Irish hero's features with something as embarrassing as a tragic flaw or the stain of Original Sin. Deborah calls Noodles a "cockroach." What are all these bugs? The inevitable byproducts of shooting

The Williamsburg Bridge, the most oppressive of many bridge images in Leone's films, looms over the youthful gang members as they stride toward impending doom in *Once Upon a Time in America*. (Left to right: Adrian Curran as Cockeye, Brian Bloom as Patsy, Rusty Jacobs as Max, Scott Tiler as Noodles, and Noah Moazezi as Dominic.)

film on warm days in Spain—certainly—but also a ubiquitous and grim reminder of the cheapness and paltriness of life: We breed like flies, die like flies,
make food for flies.

Carriages and Coaches

These are inevitable images in the Western genre. But Leone always manages to make his carriages and coaches contain something grotesque or unex-
pected. A pistol greets No Name when he tries to get a look inside the coach in
A Fistful of Dollars. Indio's mob uses a wagon to haul a stolen safe in *For a
Few Dollars More*. Sam's buckboard in *Once Upon a Time in the West* brings
Jill into frontier territory and flies—almost literally—in the face of the progress
represented by the railroad. The enormous carriage in *Duck, You Sucker!* is
filled with hideous exemplars of an exploitive aristocracy. But, unquestionably,
the definitive Leone carriage is the carriage of the spirits in *The Good, the Bad
and the Ugly*. It appears as a miraculous deus ex machina just as Tuco is about
to kill Blondie in the desert. It carries the dying Bill Carson, who will split his
secret between them and set the treasure hunt truly in motion; everyone else in
the carriage is dead.

Cats

Cats, another traditional image of the supernatural, make two appearances
in Leone's films, but the actions are so similar they make one think something
more than meets the eye is going on. In *A Fistful of Dollars*, a cat darts across
the scene in the small house, causing the Rojo guards to look up from their card
game just before the Man with No Name shoots down everybody—except the
cat. In *For a Few Dollars More*, a yowling cat startles Manco and Mortimer in
the streets of Agua Caliente as the pair begins their search-and-destroy mission
against Indio's gang. Again, the cat survives. What does all this mean? Well, the
whining, startling cat appears in only the first two films, thus implying that
Leone outgrew, or got bored with, easy scares. But the cats Leone filmed do
impart a sense of importance. As a Leone character might say, Where there are
rats, there are always cats, but the rats won't be there long.

Cemeteries

No Leone film is without its graveyard scene. At the beginning of *A Fistful
of Dollars*, San Miguel is called "a cemetery," and it's in the nearby graveyard
that No Name stages the ruse that intensifies the Rojo-Baxter rivalry and precipitates the eventual disaster. In *For a Few Dollars More* Agua Caliente (surely
a sister city to San Miguel) is compared to a morgue by Indio and is turned into
one by the end of the film. The carriage of the dead in *The Good, the Bad and
the Ugly* is something new: a mobile graveyard. Among the bodies is a still-
living man who carries with him the secret of a hidden treasure—buried, ana-
logically, in a military cemetery. That cemetery, once found, becomes the scene

for the film's climax-upon-climax last reel. Row upon row of crosses grouped around a single stage-like central circle turn that setting into a morbidly one-sided game of tic-tac-toe. The crosses stand for death, and the circle is a disturbing zero. In *Once Upon a Time in the West*, Jill's first vision of Sweetwater is a track-in on a knot of people grouped around bodies laid out for the burying, and the first thing she does in her new home is to put her entire adopted family into the ground. In the world of *Duck, You Sucker!*, mass deaths, mass burials, and mass graves are the norm. The violence of the earlier Leone films is escalated and the stakes are raised. The commentary is ironic since this scale of murder is justified in the name of the people. The pivotal meeting between Nobody and Jack Beauregard in *My Name is Nobody* is set in a desolate, dust-blown grave-yard—Valerii commenting satirically that the cemetery scene is obligatory in a Leone film. The mausoleum scene in *Once Upon a Time in America* is crucial. The door seems to want to close on Noodles as if suggesting that Noodles, too, belongs in the grave and is already figuratively among the dead ("going to bed early"?). And it is in that crypt that Noodles finds the literal and metaphorical key to the mystery that has haunted him for thirty-five years. There's no secret what all this is about. In a Tarot deck, the Death card doesn't really stand for death. But Leone is not so subtle or so self-contradictory. All of his films have "something to do with death." Everything, in fact.

Children

Leone has a characteristically Italian-Catholic sentimentality for children. His production company, Rafran, is an acronym for the names of his own children. Like Peckinpah, Leone fills his world with children, though in Leone's films the children often suffer for the sins of the adults, while in Peckinpah's they merely look on and learn. I give you Jesus in *A Fistful of Dollars*; at Indio's order, in *For a Few Dollars More*, a little boy is killed with his mother; a boy hires out as a spy in El Paso; in the same film, a boy knocks apples off a tree in Agua Caliente; a boy sits on a burro near the beginning of *The Good, the Bad and the Ugly*, and his older brother is shot dead trying to get the drop on their father's killer; a dying Confederate soldier can't be old enough to smoke the last cigarette Blondie offers him; Timmy McBain is shot in *Once Upon a Time in the West*, and the remembered image of the person who is to be his avenger is a boy with a harmonica; in *Duck, You Sucker!*, Juan Miranda has his niños; a boy with a toy train is the vanguard for a bank job; a cluster of slaughtered innocents look almost as if they are merely asleep in the mountain cave; there are the youthful criminals of *Once Upon a Time in America*, also their murdered friend Dominic; and in the opening scene of *My Name Is Nobody*, the barber has a son. Make of these children, and their futures (where applicable) what you will.

Churches

Churches are never what they are supposed to be in Leone's films. Though there is a church in San Miguel, it is merely a vestigial appendage to Juan de Dios's equally disused bell tower. In *For a Few Dollars More*, the church is a hideout for a gang of criminals ("You have made it a den of thieves"). In *The Good, the Bad and the Ugly*, the Mission San Antonio has become a field hospital, a charnel-house of hopeless surgery, a waiting room for Charon's passengers. There's another church in this film—the bare, ruined choir where the young Confederate soldier dies, just a little bit this side of the Sad Hill Cemetery. We never see the synagogue to which Max's and Noodles's neighbors are drawn on Pesach, 1924, in *Once Upon a Time in America*; their devotion is, for Max, only an invitation to larceny. In Juan Miranda's fantasy in *Duck, You Sucker!*, the National Bank of Mesa Verde has taken on the status of a religious shrine, and Juan keeps a small monument to it in his wagon. This is a world abandoned by God; where churches are impractical, they are turned to alternative service.

Clergymen

As with the churches, the clergy, too, are never what they're supposed to be. In *The Good, the Bad and the Ugly*, the monks have become doctors and nurses. Padre Ramirez's encounter with his brother Tuco stands as evidence that the cleric is no paragon of virtue and strength. The priest in the enormous coach in the opening of *Duck, You Sucker!* has detached himself from the bothersome business of religion to enjoy the luxury of the first estate. And if clergymen are characterized as something other than what they profess to be, it's only fair that those who profess evil sometimes find themselves portrayed as clergymen: Blondie is ministering priest to the dying soldier across the river in *The Good, the Bad and the Ugly*; in *For a Few Dollars More*, Mortimer is introduced to us as a bible-reading preacher; the Man with No Name's Italian nickname is "Manco." Leone's gunmen are a kind of wandering clergy, ministering confessions, giving penance and absolution, and offering what sacraments they and the situation deem appropriate.

Coffins

Leone goes out of his way to include not just graves but coffins in his films; coffins are more direct and personal images. The coffins of the McBains are tough to look at because we have known, if only for a short time, the people who now occupy them. "My mistake—four coffins" is comically abstract, as is the character of the coffin-maker in *A Fistful of Dollars*. But I can imagine no more achingly intimate image of death than that of the soldier in *The Good, the Bad and the Ugly*, wearing a sign marked "Thief," carrying his own coffin into town where he summarily is shot by the firing squad that accompanied him on the march. On the other hand, a coffin is the vessel of escape for the Man with

No Name when, in *A Fistful of Dollars*, the going really gets tough. And it's the repository of a fortune of gold in *The Good, the Bad and the Ugly*, the seeming contradictory image serving to remind the viewer that the profit is matched in enormity by the risk. The bodies of Juan Miranda's niños and of Noodles Aaronson's betrayed friends are laid out without benefit of coffins; elsewhere in *Once Upon a Time in America*, a covered, wheeled casket masks the quick hit-men who deal death to Willie the Ape and Chicken Joe. The dead members of the four horsemen end up in a spectacular hoax of a crypt, appropriate consider-ing their use of a funeral business as a front. Life and death are most inexorably linked in Max's joke when he welcomes Noodles home from prison in 1933 with a hearse containing a live and willing woman. Why go on living when we can bury you for $49.50? The pattern fulfills itself spectacularly in *Once Upon a Time in America*: life in death, death in life, and, finally, life as death.

Crosses

Grave markers aren't always crosses, but in Leone's films that's how they appear—most visibly in *A Fistful of Dollars*, Valerii's *My Name Is Nobody*, and, of course, *The Good, the Bad and the Ugly*. Apart from its acquired Christian implications, the cross has always been a symbol of the meeting of opposites— of opposition itself. Life and death meet in the graveyard, and never more obvi-ously than when Tuco stands on top of—instead of under—a grave marker; the means of death is above him, the place of repose is below him, and the reward of the living is just beyond him, out of reach. The graveyard filled with crosses amplifies the symbolism in *The Good, the Bad and the Ugly*, which is a film filled with double-crosses. The cross, however, is also—nonsymbolically—a crucifix in a world that has been deserted by Christ (as Tuco's frequent, hypo-critical, vain signs of the cross attest).

Deformity and Dismemberment

There are more physically grotesque people in *Yojimbo* than there are in Leone's remake, but Kurosawa seems to have provided the cue for a whole mo-tif in Leone's work, a motif that peaks in *The Good, the Bad and the Ugly*. When the film opens, Al Mulock has a cavernous hole in his cheek, and later he turns up minus an arm; Baker is a bedridden consumptive; Angeleyes gets in-formation from a legless "half soldier"; Bill Carson wears an eyepatch because he needs one—Tuco wears one to imitate Carson; amputees are painfully visible in the Mission San Antonio; Tuco baits a one-armed soldier, telling him it's bet-ter to have a price on one's head than to get nothing for one's arm; the comman-dant of the Union prison camp has a gangrenous leg that is slowly eating away at his body; Corporal Wallace has a damaged eye; Angeleyes (and in fact Lee Van Cleef) has a missing fingertip, quite noticeable in the closeup montage be-fore the final showdown. Elsewhere, we have the hunchback in *For a Few Dol-lars More*, the trio of grotesques at the opening of *Once Upon a Time in the West*, the crumbling Morton whose business sense dominates the film, ubiquitous uglies in *Duck, You Sucker!*, and, in *Once Upon a Time in America*, Cockeye's closed eye and Moe's obesity. Such dwelling on external deficiency is likely a mirror of internal disorder, even as it was in medieval and Renaissance literature. Though the deformities are nearly always those of minor characters, the disorders they reflect are presumably those of the world itself. Is it too tiresome to suggest, once again, the specter of Original Sin? Oddly, Leone's never made use of the rich image of blindness, though it's more than evident in classical myth, in samurai films, and in other Spaghetti Westerns.

Emblems

Tokens abound in Leone's films. To a limited extent, these gimmicks characterize and move the plot. A grab bag of such "emblems" includes: the poncho worn by the Man with No Name, a revolution in Western-film costuming; the suit of armor Ramón Rojo uses for target practice, which inspires the bulletproof vest No Name fashions for his resurrection near the end of the film; the matching timepieces in *For a Few Dollars More*, and the belabored and unsatisfactory image of Manco's wrist strap in the same film; Bill Carson's tobacco pouch, which works both for and against Tuco in *The Good, the Bad and the Ugly*; Harmonica's harmonica and McBain's model station in *Once Upon a Time in the West*; Juan's religious medal and his boy's toy train in *Duck, You Sucker!*; and the thrice-pinched pocket watch in *Once Upon a Time in America*.

Emergence

In *A Fistful of Dollars*, the Man with No Name leans in toward the window of a wagon to find out what it's carrying. He then draws back as a gun emerges from the window with a hand on the end of it and a soldier's face behind that. There are a lot of "coming out" images in Leone's films. They imply that Leone delights in—and takes maximum stylistic advantage of—the idea of something appearing, whether suddenly or gradually. No Name, resurrected, emerges from the smoke of a series of dynamite explosions; Mortimer emerges from behind a bible in the opening of *For a Few Dollars More*, and the cabinet that conceals a safe is pulled out of the bank (and out of the smoke) during Indio's robbery of the Bank of El Paso; in *The Good, the Bad and the Ugly*, the carriage of the spirits emerges from the emptiness of the desert, and guns and shovels keep emerging from the sides of the frame; in *Once Upon a Time in the West* Harmonica emerges from behind a train and from the darkness in a tavern or outside the McBain house, while Frank emerges from the brush at the McBain massacre and from the mists of Harmonica's memory during the recurring flashback; Sean Mallory emerges from a veil of smoke in his first appearance in *Duck, You Sucker!*; the Wild Bunch rides out of the heat-wavy, out-of-focus distance for the climactic rendezvous in *My Name Is Nobody*; and Noodles emerges from clouds of steam throughout *Once Upon a Time in America*. Emergence is the opposite of penetration [q.v.]; it's the entrance of something new into the world; more often than not it's nothing short of the approach of destiny.

Enterprise

In *A Fistful of Dollars*, the Rojos and the Baxters demonstrate that the logical extension of business competition is war [q.v.]. Mortimer and Manco in *For a Few Dollars More* and Blondie and Tuco in *The Good, the Bad and the Ugly* verify, however shakily, that a partnership has a better chance of achieving a desired objective than does solo enterprise. *For a Few Dollars More* begins Leone's series of character studies contrasting those who work for a cause with those who work for profit. In *The Good, the Bad and the Ugly* and *Duck, You Sucker!*, those who work for profit come off decidedly better than those who work for a cause (war or revolution). In *Once Upon a Time in the West*, by contrast, the man with a personal cause wins the day, even though the corporate enterprise represented by Morton and the small business started by McBain both continue to flourish. Morton says only money can stop a gun, but that's only one side of the coin. Businessmen, in Leone films, are ever the inevitable victims of men with guns, as evidenced in the humiliation and robbery of the shopkeeper in *The Good, the Bad and the Ugly*, the slaughter of McBain and the ignominious death of Morton in *Once Upon a Time in the West*, and the crime-as-business metaphor of *Once Upon a Time in America*. Guns may serve private enterprise, but they can also subvert it.

Explosions

For sheer spectacle, nothing can match dynamite. Explosions are used to prepare for, and mask, the return of the Man with No Name near the finish of *A Fistful of Dollars*; to liberate a legendary safe in *For a Few Dollars More*; to demolish bridges in *The Good, the Bad and the Ugly* and in *Duck, You Sucker!*; to advance the railroad in *Once Upon a Time in the West*; and as character index of Sean Mallory in *Duck, You Sucker!*—he emerges from and returns into violent explosions at opposite ends of the film. Two great Leone images meet when dynamite is used to destroy two trains in the climax of the same film. In the absence of dynamite, cannon fire also provides suitably smoky pyrotechnics. Civil War cannonades facilitate Blondie's escape from the hotel where Tuco is about to hang him and to punctuate the gunfight between Blondie and Tuco and Angeleyes' men that takes place in the streets of the town. Blondie's use of a cannon against Tuco only pushes the bandit to his destination—the Sad Hill graveyard.

Valerii satirizes Leone's penchant for explosions in *My Name Is Nobody*. Nobody first presents himself to Beauregard as bearer of a packaged bomb Beauregard's enemies have sent. Later, in the climactic showdown between the lone Beauregard and the entire Wild Bunch, each gang member Jack shoots down explodes. There's a reason for this, but it's more fun to see the episode as a deliberately cartoonish effect.

Faces

If the face is the mirror of the soul, there are a lot of scarred and hairy souls in Leone's world. Talking with Noel Simsolo, Leone invoked history as witness: "I have consulted historical documents and can assure you that they were a lot dirtier in reality. As to their faces, they were incredible and had a lot more character than those of my actors." Leone starts with the face as an instant index of character; then, gradually, he grows interested in its specific parts. There are relatively few closeups in *A Fistful of Dollars*, and none of them are particularly striking. In *For a Few Dollars More*, the moving face becomes the object of interest and expression: Mortimer looking up from behind his bible, Indio looking up from under his sombrero, eyes rolling significantly upward as a means of betraying a killer or confirming what the mouth denies. Then of course there is that often-noted montage that intercuts the eyes of Indio on the poster with the eyes of Mortimer looking at it. Leone's interest in the face gradually narrows to interest in the eyes (though this is matched, in *For a Few Dollars More*, by an equal interest in closeups of hands). In *The Good, the Bad and the Ugly* there are Carson's eyepatch, Wallace's hurt eye, the darting, searching eyes of Tuco, the snaky, calculating eyes of Angeleyes, and the calm, alert but relaxed eyes of Blondie. The stylistic climax of the film comes with the intercutting of these sets of eyes. In *Once Upon a Time in the West* the most extreme closeups center on the eyes as signs of life (Harmonica, fluttering an eye open at the end of the opening gundown) and as protectors and projectors of the secret treasures of the mind (Harmonica's eyes as the doorway to the flashback memory that "explains" him to us). Eyes are a crucial symbol in *Duck, You Sucker!* as well; but here Leone turns his interest to the mouth, appropriate to this film in which an imagistic concern with consumption [see Food] reaches a new scale in Leone's work. Still, the eyes continue to have it.

In *Once Upon a Time in America* the eye-deformity motif recurs in Cockeye's narrowed eye and in Patsy's shooting of Detroit Joe, right in the jeweler's loupe. And there's always a Brechtian effect when Leone comes in tight on eyes; they're what we're seeing, but they're also what we're seeing with. Add this reality to the fact that we see other people's faces a lot more than we see our own, and you have a characteristically Leonean ticket to character identification.

Fire

Despite the fact that fire's destructive force is used by the Rojos to wipe out the Baxters once and for all in *A Fistful of Dollars*, and although it obliterates the identity of Max's dead proxy in *Once Upon a Time in America*, Leone is generally more interested in it as a source of light than as a leveler. The gods of *Once Upon a Time in the West* are often revealed by fire: Cheyenne at McBain's, Harmonica in the tavern and later in the darkness outside McBain's. Firelight is important at the end of *Duck, You Sucker!* where it provides the smoky illumination by which Juan takes leave of his friend and finds himself alone in an absurd world. In the pre-gas and electric world of the old West, fire was an all-important means of cooking food. It was also a source of warmth, though Leone rarely depicts it that way, choosing—-despite his interest in historical reality—to use fire infrequently and (when it is included) almost always for its qualities of light. Light, of course, is seen—warmth only felt—and unlike many film-makers who seek to run the emotional and sensory gamut, Sergio Leone is usually content with making us see.

Food

One of the first things that strike people about Leone's films is the amount of consumption that goes on during them: the Rojos invite the Baxters to dinner in *A Fistful of Dollars*, and heavy drinking becomes an occasion by which the Man with No Name can fool the Rojos. In *For a Few Dollars More*, a bank guard sits down to munch a sandwich before he is blown away by Indio's bank raiders; Mortimer is slurping a bowl of beans in the cantina in Agua Caliente when Juan calls for satisfaction; *The Good, the Bad and the Ugly* opens with an unseen shootout from which Tuco, crashing through a window and wearing a napkin-bib, escapes brandishing a pistol and a joint of meat; uninvited, Angeleyes eats Stevens's lunch before killing him; Tuco is fed a sumptuous meal by Angeleyes before being brutally beaten by Wallace; in *Once Upon a Time in the West*, the McBains are setting up a picnic when they are slaughtered by Frank's men; Cheyenne's greeting to Jill is, "Didja make coffee?"; the lard-assed upper classes are portrayed in *Duck, You Sucker!* as a cluster of mouths eager to consume everything; when Juan catches up to him, Sean is eating in the café in Mesa Verde; Patsy's consumption of the Charlotte Russe intended as payment for Peggy's favors indexes the adolescent sexuality of *Once Upon a Time in America*; Detroit Joe tries sloppily to eat kosher meat as he tells his story about cock insurance and a secret diamond shipment; Noodles is named for a food (why, we don't know) and, in one memorable scene, he takes forever to prepare his cup of coffee.

These are only the more noticeable instances of food consumption. What's more remarkable is that eating, more often than not, is associated with violence, pain, and death. By juxtaposing life-giving consumption with death, Leone provides us with one of his more provocative and sardonic motifs. In the midst of life, we are in death. Leone may be making a deliberate comment on the relative luxury of life in today's world: we might as well be shot down as eat ourselves to death like pigs. Eating and dying are both natural animal functions, and it's one of the grimmer aspects of Leone's imagery that he so often emphasizes this similarity by placing them side-by-side.

Hats

Hats (always wide-brimmed, to conceal the face and provide an illusory sense of protection) are a key image in *For a Few Dollars More*. Each of the main characters is hidden by his hat before we first see his face, and the climactic first meeting of Manco and Mortimer occasions an event that will become a

Leone ritual—the shooting off of hats. Blondie shoots off the hats of spectators when he "rescues" Tuco from hanging in *The Good, the Bad and the Ugly*. Tonino Valerii goes so far as to substitute hat-shooting for any real combat between the two protagonists in *My Name Is Nobody*. Then there's Woody Strode's water-catching hat in the opening scene of *Once Upon a Time in the West* and the hat under which Sean pretends to be asleep just before the siege at the bridge in *Duck, You Sucker!* These are all comic, or at least semicomic, bits, suggesting that hats don't really mean anything particularly important to Leone but are instead a handy device for viewing—and instantly altering the image of—characters (the four young crooks of *Once Upon a Time in America* adopt wide-brim hats when they solidify their business association). It further suggests that, for Leone, cowboy hats, no matter how historically representative, never cease to be just a little ridiculous.

Landscape

No director of Westerns can ever be insensitive to landscapes. But Leone, perhaps self-conscious about his Spanish and Italian locations, paid minimal attention to them in his first two films, concentrating instead on actions in specific populated locales.

In *The Good, the Bad and the Ugly*, however, Leone breaks from this position and, for the first time, demonstrates that he has learned from Ford not only the preeminence of landscape but its symbolic value as well. The desert (a "hell" through which only Tuco, Blondie, and a wagonload of corpses will pass) is a powerful image, as is the permanence of the river (in contrast with the transience and illusory importance of the manmade bridge). Also effective is the ability of dust to change the apparent political affiliation of an entire column of cavalry. It's as if Leone was earning his credentials with *The Good, the Bad and the Ugly*, so that, on his next film, he would be worthy to shoot in Ford country.

Menials

The menials in *A Fistful of Dollars* demonstrate a quiet dignity. The cantina proprietor, bell ringer, and coffinmaker all survive the abuses of the Rojos and the Baxters and live to build a new town. But in *For a Few Dollars More* there begins a Leone tradition of insulting and abusing menials for comic effect. Considering its occurrence in the oeuvre, this motif may be related to the presence of scenarist Luciano Vincenzoni.

Mortimer is quietly contemptuous of the train conductor and of the telegraph operator in Tucumcari; a barber is gratuitously humiliated by Red Cavanaugh's men when they interrupt a shave to go help Red out; Manco cockily throws out a paying hotel guest so he can have a room with a view—in the bargain, he teases the man about his underwear; the Chinese bellhop is terrorized by contradictory orders from Manco and Mortimer; Mortimer baits Juan; and Manco ridicules a way-station telegraph operator who is only trying to fry himself some eggs.

The pattern's repeated in *The Good, the Bad and the Ugly* with Tuco and the shopkeeper, in *Once Upon a Time in the West* with the three gunmen and the stationmaster at the beginning, and in the treatment of Wobbles by both Harmonica and Frank; and in *Duck, You Sucker!*'s opening scene, during which the traveling aristos alternately ridicule and patronize Juan. In a sense, the rest of that film may be seen as the menial's attempt to avenge himself against this kind of abuse. Juan succeeds and keeps on succeeding—however unintentionally, and no matter what it ends up costing him. But he's still not taken seriously, even by the end of the film.

In *My Name Is Nobody* there's a twist in Valerii's variation on this Leone theme. The barber and his son, during the opening, are humiliated and manhandled by the bad guys. Nobody makes his way through the film abusing and mistreating only those who have demonstrated themselves to be villainous. The hero doesn't have time for such things as deliberate abuse of the lower orders. But in *For a Few Dollars More*, both of the heroes do have time for this, and it remains a vaguely disturbing mystery why a kind of vicious class-consciousness serves Leone's comic purpose in this film (and for a few moments in later films). Perhaps Leone is attempting a first tentative drawing of the line between those who dig (i.e., work for a living) and those elite professionals who carry loaded guns. Still, the attempt betrays a nasty (but funny) streak in Leone's generally likable protagonists. The generally unlikable protagonists of *Once upon a Time in America* get the better of a couple of corrupt cops, but Noodles's smallness is highlighted by the fact that he is always bested by menials (e.g., the train ticket agent, the waiter, and—of course—the chauffeur who scorns Noodles and his money after Deborah's rape).

Money

In Valerii's *My Name Is Nobody*, money is a means to an end. Beauregard takes a share of his brother's money to buy himself a ticket on a boat—and that's important, because in the five Leone films, money is always an end in itself, a given. The Man with No Name outstays the profitability of his enterprise in *A Fistful of Dollars* out of a kind of personal sense of revenge, but his initial and overriding purpose is to play the ruling families off against each other for money. In *For a Few Dollars More*, No Name mentions something about buying himself a ranch, but his real goal is to amass bodies, because bodies equal dollars (this belief made powerfully clear during the final shots of the film). When Mortimer reveals he was never at all interested in the money, the partnership dissolves. In *The Good, the Bad and the Ugly*, money is the only motivation, and it's seen to be a far better one than the "causes" for which war is waged—though finally the game does become more important than the prize. Despite the fact that the goals of private enterprise win out in the end, in *Once Upon a Time in the West*, high ideals override money. Harmonica "betrays" Cheyenne for the money necessary to secure the McBain land claim for Jill. In *Duck, You Sucker!*, though Juan manages to steal scarcely a centavo in the film, his privateering is seen as preferable to the dedication of the revolutionaries.

Money hidden in the station locker in *Once Upon a Time in America* is always more a plot device than an emblem of commercial success. Though emphasis is placed on it, money is never a satisfying motive in Leone's films. It is, nevertheless, often the only motive and just as often the best one.

Musical Instruments

The chiming watches in *For a Few Dollars More*, the prison band in *The Good, the Bad and the Ugly*, the harmonica in *Once Upon a Time in the West*, and the pan-pipe in *Once Upon a Time in America* are particularly rich emblems, in that they tie the film's images to the soundtrack score, and do so in a way that elucidates character, while at the same time—in the case of the first and third named films—they turn the entire plot. The harmonica is Leone's perfection of this technique. It's Harmonica's ever-present reminder of his mission against Frank: the instrument has become so much a symbol of him and what he stands for that he substitutes the harmonica's honks and wails for conversation ("When he oughtta talk, he plays"). It's the harmonica in his pocket that stops the bullet that might have killed him in the opening shootout, like the bible in Richard Hannay's coat pocket in *The 39 Steps*: Both are metaphoric emblems of the quest that keeps a man going—in Hannay's case, the will to do good, in Harmonica's, the obsession with revenge. In both cases, these tokens quite literally keep their bearers alive. We have to assume that the harmonica is the same one that Frank shoved into the boy's mouth those many years ago, and that its return to Frank completes a mythic cycle of transgression and expiation. Music, one of the pleasurable things in life (especially so in Morricone's scores for the Leone films), in Leone's vision is, like food, ironically associated with pain and suffering (this association pointing to the subtext of Christian dualism as well as to the Catholic's guilty attitude toward pleasure).

The musical instrument becomes the center of the film in *Once Upon a Time in the West*. Charles Bronson as the Man with the Harmonica (center), approached by Cheyenne (Jason Robards, right) and one of his henchmen (unidentified).

Numbers

The incessant wordplay in Leone's films makes his characters' dialogue as odd and unsettling as a Kafka parable, as mystic and sage as a biblical proverb, as opaque and mind-boggling as a Zen koan. The salient feature of this offbeat anti-conversation is a bizarre preoccupation with numbers. "Every town has a boss ... but when there are two around, I'd say there's one too many." "My mistake—four coffins." "Thought I was having trouble with my adding." "Two kinds of people in the world." "Five for you, five for me." "Once you've killed four, it's easy to make it five." This business reaches the status of high art in *Once Upon a Time in the West*:

> Harmonica: Did you bring a horse for me?
> Gunman (eying the three horses):
>   Awww, now ... Looks like we're shy one horse. (Laughter.)
> Harmonica (slowly shakes his head no):   Brought two too many.
>   *
> Cheyenne: You interested in fashions, Harmonica?
> Harmonica: I saw three dusters like this a short time ago. They were wait-
>   ing for a train. Inside the dusters there were three men.
> Cheyenne: So?
> Harmonica: Inside the men there were three bullets.
> Cheyenne: That's a crazy story, Harmonica—for two reasons. First, the
>   only men who wear dusters like these are Cheyenne's men; and second,
>   Cheyenne's men don't get killed.
>   *
> Harmonica: Well, you know music, and you can count—all the way up to
>   two.
> Cheyenne: All the way up to six, if I have to—and maybe faster than you.

That last one's even a rhymed couplet, with its rhythm a little sprung. The fascination Leone's characters have with numbers and counting evokes the numerology of ancient lore, in which simply the saying of certain numbers or combinations of numbers constituted a kind of charm or explained a mystery. The reduction of evaluation to enumeration, of course, springs from the Italian Western's conventional emphasis on money and on the more mercenary aspects of the Western myth. Reducing people to numbers goes hand-in-hand with the consideration of all ventures in terms of financial profit—the clichéd view of American capitalism reflected in Italian Westerns, and, indeed, in most European films. To the European mind (not without cause), money and violence are the two inescapable features of the American experience. In Leone's number games, the numbers nearly always refer to bullets, bodies, or bucks. And, of course, this numerology heightens Leone's essentially geometric reordering of both the physical and the moral universe.

Parables and Sayings

The Man with No Name, about to tell Consuelo Baxter about Ramón Rojo's massacre of the federal soldiers, doesn't blurt out the information quickly. Instead, he begins, "Once upon a time there was a wagonload of gold." Leone's characters don't converse; they toss stories and made-up maxims at each other. Indio sermonizes when mapping out a bank robbery plan for his gang. Blondie and Tuco keep revising their notion of what two kinds of people make up the world. Number games abound in *Once Upon a Time in the West*. In *My Name Is Nobody*, Valerii parodies the technique with an elaborate story about a bird covered with cow manure—a tale that illustrates not one but three morals, all of which have something to do with the movie. Detroit Joe sets up a heist in *Once Upon a Time in America* by telling a story even stranger than Indio's.

What all this reveals is Leone's basic self-referential technique, a hall-of-mirrors pattern of stories-within-stories that keeps us aware of the mythic nature of the film we are watching, even while it dares by extension to suggest that we, too, tend to invest our own lives with a lot of story quality.

Partnerships

The one real partnership in *A Fistful of Dollars* is never formally agreed to—that is the loyalty that binds Silvanito to No Name and makes them help and protect each other. Most partnerships, however, are sham; they exist only for profit making. These relationships are dangerous because of the ever-possible double-cross. But they are preferable to two hunters going after the same prey and shooting each other in the back. There is a certain strength in partnership that enables it to achieve a purpose that a lone individual might not accomplish. But the all-important consideration is that, once the purpose is fulfilled, the partnership must dissolve. Blondie-and-Tuco and Juan-and-Sean are examples of partnerships that outlast their usefulness; while Manco-and-Mortimer and Harmonica-and-Cheyenne represent perfect teamings that unite to bring about a key event, then separate forever. All of Leone's partnerships, from Manco-and-Mortimer through Max-and-Noodles, are based on equal parts trust and treachery. The perfect Leone partnership may well be the pairing of Nobody and Jack in *My Name Is Nobody* (based, after all, on "an idea of Sergio Leone"). The men are mock rivals of each other, but in reality co-conspirators against History itself.

Partnerships: The Bandit and the Firecracker (Rod Steiger and James Coburn as Juan and Sean) in *Duck, You Sucker!* (above); the boys (Scott Tiler and Rusty Jacobs as Noodles and Max, below left) and the men (Robert De Niro and James Woods as Noodles and Max, below right) in *Once Upon a Time in America*.

Penetration

Nearly always a comic effect, the penetration image (the opposite of emergence, which see) is omnipresent in Leone's later films. Tuco, for no apparent reason, takes the time to stuff the "Closed" sign into the mouth of the shopkeeper he's just robbed. Harmonica, for a very palpable reason, "explains" himself by shoving his harmonica into the dying Frank's mouth. In *My Name Is Nobody*, a shaving brush is shoved into a barber's mouth. This plugging of orifices sometimes has a practical purpose—the gagging of a victim—though it's always done comically, stylistically, and in any case, superfluously, in a world where a simple finger to the lips and a "ssssh!" are enough to insure a hostage's silence.

For Leone, penetration carries the force of rape. Frank clearly intended a nasty, mocking sort of rape when he shoved the harmonica laughingly into that boy's mouth. The penetration image is not seen in *For a Few Dollars More*, a film in which the central memory image is a real rape that results in the death of a woman and in the permanent dementia of her assailant.

Guns and bullets do a lot of penetrating, of course, but on a symbolic as well as on a literal level. The rifles of Juan's gang penetrate the glass windows of the luxurious coach as the put-upon peasant turns the tables on the rich (a symbolic violation of their world that is made literal moments later when he rapes one of the women). In *The Good, the Bad and the Ugly*, Angeleyes shoots Stevens through a bowl of chili and Baker through a pillow; Tuco shoots the Al Mulock character through his bathwater; only the "good" Blondie always shoots directly and honestly. In *Once Upon a Time in the West*, Cheyenne, as an extension of his gun hand, uses his boot and shoots one of Morton's men through its toe.

All this is a disguise, of course, that compares with Frank's ruse of disguising his men as Cheyenne's to frame the bandit. In *Once Upon a Time in America* sexual penetration is explicit and violent, and the image echoes elsewhere: A thug fondles a woman's breast with his pistol; Patsy shoots Joe in the eye. All of this business is a means of carrying the old gun/phallus equation one step farther: shooting is a sexual act, both assault and insult.

Posters

The "Wanted" poster is a staple of the Hollywood Western. Like the cowboy hat, it is yet another device that Leone has turned to his own purposes. The image is central in *For a Few Dollars More*. There are extra 0s on the Calloway poster that Mortimer eventually slides under the door of the hotel room where his prey is taking his pleasure; the Cavanaugh poster bridges Mortimer's introductory sequence to Manco's; the laughing Indio poster is an exponent of character relationships both early and late in the film.

In *The Good, the Bad and the Ugly* Tuco is first identified for us by a foreground "Wanted" poster that is held by a would-be bounty collector. A poster identifying Cheyenne was cut from the final release version of *Once Upon a Time in the West* (according to Frayling). During the nightmarish Mesa Verde sequence in *Duck, You Sucker!*, Juan's eyes peer through a political poster. Newspaper articles serve equally well as a kind of expository shorthand—Mortimer learns Manco's identity through a newspaper photo, and Juan finds out about Sean from papers in the Irishman's satchel. "So you can read," says Sean, and Juan replies, "You don't have to read. I see a man's picture and below it a price, and I know that man is in trouble." That's it. Shorthand. The equation of money and flesh. The commoditization of the human.

Rape

Rape is always an atrocity, and nowhere more so than in Leone's films, where it is an affront to human dignity and, indirectly, to the procreative sexuality that is the basis of family. The sexual nature of Ramón Rojo's relationship with Marisol in *A Fistful of Dollars* is kept offscreen but is no secret. The devastation this relationship suffers is what No Name avenges when he reunites and liberates the disrupted family.

In *For a Few Dollars More*, rape is the central trauma in Indio's life of crime. It looms larger than his many murders because of its intrusion on family and its resulting suicide. In *The Good, the Bad and the Ugly*, the dehumanizing brutality of war is indexed, among other incidental moments, by the introduction of Bill Carson's sweetheart—she is cast out of a wagon of carousing soldiers who have clearly gang-raped her. Frank, in *Once Upon a Time in the West*, is obviously capable of rape, but his image of himself as incipient businessman leads him to bargain for Jill's life with her flesh. In *Duck, You Sucker!* and in *Once Upon a Time in America*, however, a distancing ambiguity exists. In these films, the protagonists commit rape, and, though they do so as a violent expression of their socially imposed frustration, their acts intrude on our ability to see them sympathetically.

Revenge

Andrew Sarris says of Tom Joad in John Ford's *The Grapes of Wrath*, "His putatively proletarian becomes morosely menacing in that shadowy crossroads where social justice intersects with personal vengeance." The same might be said of the Man with No Name, if one considers the spurious prologue a legitimate part of *A Fistful of Dollars*. No Name's initially thin motivation (monetary gain and a chance for parole from prison) becomes more intense and morally defensible when the question of vengeance enters the picture. Granted, No Name's primary reason for overstaying the profitability of his mission in San Miguel is to get back at the Rojos for the physical abuse he himself has suffered. But he also wants to avenge the injustices committed against Silvanito and, before that, against Marisol and her family.

Revenge is a motif that Leone has drawn from Italian opera, the Renaissance stage, and the medieval epic (whence it descended from classical myth and literature). For him, the emotion is nearly always family-motivated. Even in *A Fistful of Dollars*, where it occurs on behalf of someone else, the act of vengeance is carried out in the name of family. In *For a Few Dollars More*, Colonel Mortimer's commitment to avenge his sister's death drives the entire film, even though it is not fully explained until the very end; Manco so respects the colonel's motivation (which even he doesn't understand fully) that he is prepared to sacrifice the lucrative bounty on Indio so that Mortimer, for his own private reason, can lay claim to it by killing Indio himself.

In *The Good, the Bad and the Ugly*, the vengeance motive is a subtext to the trading-off of betrayals that moves the story. Watching Blondie and Tuco blow so many chances to get even with each other, we finally get the idea they don't really want revenge; they're just not trying hard enough. This lack of follow-through is consistent with the comic overtone of the film; but revenge in *Once Upon a Time in the West* is a very different matter. The motive in this movie is nothing less than a holy mission, as well as what separates the passing gods from mere mortals.

Jill feels no motivation to avenge the deaths of the McBains, while Harmonica's whole purpose, like the most deeply felt religion, is a single act of revenge for the one cataclysmic occurrence that irrevocably altered his life (here, revenge is, again, a familially motivated obsession). Harmonica is avenging his brother's death as well as the inhumanity of Frank in having made him the instrument of that death. The McBains, by contrast, were Jill's adopted family— she'd never even met the children, so the impulse to redress the wrong is not so strongly felt. Jill is even willing to meet Frank on his own terms and to count herself well out of the whole business, as long as she gets away with her life. Fortunately (or otherwise), Harmonica has other plans for Jill's destiny and for the future of the McBain land claim. His plans make his revenge against Frank a doubly satisfying one. Harmonica, like Colonel Mortimer, loves with his gun, not his tears.

The notion of revenge is increasingly questioned in *Duck, You Sucker!* and *My Name Is Nobody*. Sean Mallory feels the old impulse for revenge rising in him when he sees Villega betraying the revolutionaries to the *federales*, but desire for it is exorcised during his conversation with Villega on the train when Sean at last gives up the notion of making himself a judge. Juan Miranda has a legitimate reason for wanting vengeance—his sons were massacred by government forces. Yet when Juan finally does shoot the governor, he does it because the man makes a sudden dash for freedom. Juan's act is a reflex, not the calculated premeditation of a person bent on revenge. Sean's own sacrificial suicide at the end of the film may well be interpreted as an act of revenge against his own haunted conscience.

By the time Jack Beauregard makes his boat reservation in *My Name Is Nobody*, revenge (in Westerns) is almost discredited as a character motivation. Jack does not avenge his brother's murder. He even takes money from those who have wrested the gold mine from his brother and his brother's partner.

This reversal is mostly the result of Valerii's turning of the Italian Western against itself. But it also springs from the almost obligatory atmosphere occurring in a Terence Hill film, where intimate violence is out and only epic-scale ferocity is permitted. If confrontations have no splashy historical-mythic impact, they are simply dispensed with in favor of the more comic humiliation of figures too lightweight to deserve to be the objects of so strenuous a motivation as revenge.

In *Once Upon a Time in America*, revenge is again a critical part of the fabric, though in this film it is not as explicitly significant as it is in the Westerns. Noodles adds murder to his crimes—and goes to prison—when, during a savage knifing, he spontaneously avenges Bugsy's shooting of Dominic. Max plays on the impulse for vengeance when he asks Noodles to be his executioner at the end of the film; Noodles's refusal may represent a kind of moral maturity or, more simply, another of his many weaknesses. The worlds of *Duck, You Sucker!* and *Once Upon a Time in America* no longer have room for the kind of honor that demands vengeance for an inalterable wrong. Indeed, inalterable wrongs become the way of life.

Rope Cutting

Undoubtedly inherited from the final scene of *Yojimbo* and from the climactic rescue of Vienna in *Johnny Guitar* (which—who knows?—may have inspired Kurosawa and may itself descend from the rescue from the noose at the end of both Belasco's and Puccini's *Girl of the Golden West*), the hero's cutting of a rope to free someone else is first stated (in a Leone film) in the climax of *A Fistful of Dollars*. Unlike the analogous shot in *Yojimbo*, No Name's rope-cutting rescue of Silvanito occurs before No Name's confrontation with Ramón Rojo. A similar image, involving impossible pistol skill, is the shooting (in *For a Few Dollars More*) of the apples off the tree in Agua Caliente. But it is in *The Good, the Bad and the Ugly* that Leone makes his most definitive use of this essentially comic idea. Sean's rescue of Juan from the firing squad in *Duck, You Sucker!* may be seen as a metaphoric rope cutting. So, in an even more abstract sense, may Harmonica's and Cheyenne's silent advocacy of Jill in *Once Upon a Time in the West*, and the freeing of Jimmy Conway from the gasoline bath in *Once Upon a Time in America*. Tuco's separation of the world into those with ropes around their necks and those who have the job of cutting is simplistic: He makes the mistake (a revealing one, for Tuco) of forgetting the people who put the ropes there in the first place. Without them, Leone's world would have no need of rope cutters.

Sexuality

The sexual atmosphere of Leone's films is not so much conventionally heterosexual as simply anti-homosexual. In *A Fistful of Dollars* and *For a Few Dollars More*, the Man with No Name repeatedly rejects homosexual environments ("I don't find you men all that appealing"). In the first film, he seeks other quarters—and is motivated to action—because of a sentimentality for women and family that he is too embarrassed to discuss. In the second film, No Name infiltrates Indio's monastic enclave but keeps himself suitably aloof. His sexual character is sketched in briefly; we see the quiet electricity that sparks between

Blondie at the end of Tuco's rope in *The Good, the Bad and the Ugly*—one of many rope images in Sergio Leone's films.

him and the hotel-owner's wife; we listen to his announcement that he doesn't wear long johns. In this film, too, sentimentality over a woman is again a central force. But here it is Mortimer and Indio who are plagued by it, and the woman haunting them is dead.

In *The Good, the Bad and the Ugly*, only two women's roles are visible, and both are adjuncts to the power of the male. Stevens's wife is quiet and dutiful; Bill Carson's girlfriend (introduced as the tossed-aside plaything of soldiers in what is to my mind the only bad moment in all of Leone's films) is abused by Angeleyes into revealing Carson's whereabouts.

During the early part of the film, a few women witness Tuco's two hangings, but their only role is to be prim, proper, and suitably disgusted by Tuco's record of transgressions. The three principal characters make no reference to women or to sex, though sexuality is inherent in Angeleyes' sadism and in the almost vampiric way that Tuco and Blondie feed off each other. Tuco is the only demonstrably sexual being in the film, and his is a criminal sexuality (he's accused of raping "a woman of the white race," among other things). Is Leone using Blondie, Angeleyes, and Tuco to represent ego, id, and libido in a world devoid of superego?

In *Once Upon a Time in the West*, Cheyenne, Harmonica, and Frank are all presented as possible lovers of Jill, though only Frank is actually seen to bed her. There are some implications involving Harmonica (the hotel room, late in the film—and earlier his tearing away of the bodice of her dress, an apparent prologue to rape that turns out to be partly a ruse to distract Frank's hidden snipers and partly a means of disencumbering Jill for the role she must play in what is to come), but he is consumed by his vengeful mission in a way that debars sexual activity. By the end of the film, Jill's possible suitors are gone. The workers, whatever humble nobility they may have, provide slim pickings in this "beginning of a world without balls."

Juan Miranda's sexuality is very much like Tuco's: We never see him feeling for a woman anything that even approaches tenderness, and it's easy to imagine that the horde of niños he has around him are all the products of rape. His sexual approach is defined in the early scene: "Can you make a baby?" he challenges one of the aristocrats. Getting a negative answer, he says, "We'll soon fix that," whereupon he stalks the man's wife as if he were a bull.

In *My Name Is Nobody*, sex is reduced even further to the level of a bad joke, often with homosexual overtones. Anal humor and razors to the crotch abound, and are put into perspective—just barely—by recalling that Valerii's purpose is parody. The evidence of *Once Upon a Time in the West* notwithstanding, Leone's world is a man's world. The women in it are always defined in terms of the men. And, to the men, sexuality is incidental to the more important concerns of enterprise, profit, revenge, a cause, or simply the embrace of the violent way of life for its own sake.

This is nowhere more apparent than in *Once Upon a Time in America*: The protagonists' relationships with women reveal the men's failure to grow up; the film goes on to suggest that the male preoccupation with business and violence—often the same thing in Leone's world—may be compensation for sexual failure.

Shootouts

Generally only two kinds of shootouts occur in Leone's films. They are as different from one another as the shooting gallery is different from the arena. Into the former category fall Manco's and Mortimer's "search and destroy" missions against Indio's men, Tuco's and Blondie's missions against Angeleyes' men, and Harmonica's and Frank's missions against Frank's own traitorous men. Also in the "shooting gallery" class are the fast little throwaway shootouts: No Name's killing of four Baxter henchmen as an audition for the Rojos, Manco's shooting of the men he accompanies on the decoy mission to Santa Cruz, Tuco's dispatching of the three men who come against him in the first scene of *The Good, the Bad and the Ugly*, and Blondie's shooting of three more men who come against Tuco not long afterward. All these scenes demonstrate the skill of the protagonists, advance the plot—if only a little—and rid the film of unessential minor demons; at the same time, they underscore the cheapness of life and the law of the gun.

Set against this kind of shootout is the "arena" confrontation, the moment of reckoning, the point at which one feels that a real change or resolution will come out of the encounter. These arena shootouts come but one to a film: No Name-vs.-Ramón Rojo, Mortimer-vs.-Indio, Angeleyes-vs.-Blondie-vs.-Tuco, Harmonica-vs.-Frank. It's no accident that Leone doesn't provide us with one in the post-mythic world of *Duck, You Sucker!*, and that he fakes the reckoning in the satirical world of *My Name Is Nobody*; in the contemporary world of *Once Upon a Time in America* violence is so institutionalized that both Leone and his killer-protagonist Noodles walk away from the opportunity for a climactic duel.

Sleep

Though people feign sleep a lot in Leone's films, few actually go under and those who do are generally losers. Noodles Aaronson describes his lost years in Buffalo as "going to bed early." No Name is able to trick the Rojos by pretending he has fallen into a drunken sleep. At Silvanito's, he lies under the covers with all his clothes on. When, in *For a Few Dollars More*, we're first introduced to Indio, we think he's asleep, but in a moment an eye peers up at us. Sleep is the excuse for Manco's taking leave of Indio's gang at the church. Baker is asleep in bed when, early in *The Good, the Bad and the Ugly*, Angeleyes returns to report on the Stevens job. Baker ends the scene in a deeper sleep—under the pillow, not on top of it.

Later in the film, sleep is Tuco's undoing. Only because Tuco goes to sleep during the battle is Blondie able to unload Tuco's pistol and effectively neutralize the scruffy bandit's power. The only time Blondie truly sleeps is in the Mission San Antonio, where he knows Tuco will protect him against any harm as long as he has the other half of the secret. Before the battle at the bridge in *Duck, You Sucker!*, Sean Mallory feigns sleep, for no more obvious purpose than to eavesdrop on Juan's dialogue with God and to avoid having to join in.

But the image resonates; that's because our first really important look at James Coburn in *The Magnificent Seven* found him in approximately the same position—seated, legs out, hat pulled down over eyes, as he tried to get some sleep and avoid an unpleasant confrontation. A while later in the film when we see Juan's massacred children, the sleep image is more haunting. The children look as if they're sleeping. They are—irreversibly.

Smoking

The cheroot affected by the Clint Eastwood character in Leone's first three films remains one of the cinema's most famous uses of smoking as a means of characterization. Valerii's Nobody satirizes No Name (and Leone) when he takes the cigar from the dwarf whose stilts he shoots out from under him, and then continues to smoke it throughout the remainder of the confrontational carnival sequence. Juan Miranda smokes a cigar—just one more source of carboniferous gas in that smokiest of films. Tuco tracks Blondie by his cheroot butts and doused campfires and knows his quarry is near when he is able to draw a puff of smoke from a discarded cigar. Bill Carson's tobacco pouch—a gratuitous bit of theft on Tuco's part—becomes the means by which Angeleyes discovers that Tuco and Blondie know the secret of the gold. In *Once Upon a Time in America*, Max puts on a cigar when he assumes the throne of leadership. And of course, at beginning and end, Noodles smokes from an opium pipe.

But unquestionably the film in which smoking plays the most important role is *For a Few Dollars More*: Manco smokes his cheroot; Mortimer, his gentlemanly pipe; Indio, his joint of marijuana. Even the minor character Wild smokes a cigar—the cigar and Mortimer's pipe being the means by which Mortimer, in order to test the abrasiveness of Indio's gang, effects his first confrontation with the hunchback. "In ten minutes you'll be smoking in hell," Wild tells Mortimer on their second encounter; but looking at it another way, maybe they all are doing that already. The rooms are certainly smoky enough.

Timepieces

In the mythic world of Leone's films, an unspoken notion exists that there is a "right time" for reckoning—for the payment of debts. The conditions that must exist for the time to be identifiably "right" are never enumerated—either explicitly or by suggestion—but one takes it on faith that when the time is right one feels it to be so. In Mircea Eliade's terms, this "right time" may be considered a point at which profane, quotidian time and sacred, mythic time touch, merge for a moment, just long enough for human events to move to a spiritual level. It's at these moments that, by means of montage, Leone stops time—which is simply another way of saying that he subjects character and action to a different kind of time. The locket-watches of *For a Few Dollars More* link time and the visual image of a dead woman with music. This linkage creates the central matrix of imagery in the film—and what more appropriate device than a timepiece to introduce a flashback? The stopped clock at the Flagstone station and the handless clock face painted on a building in the streets where Harmonica helps Frank protect himself from ambush testify to the frozen time so crucial to an understanding of *Once Upon a Time in the West*, a film set at the very end of sacred time.

In *Duck, You Sucker!*, time is not elemental but simply utile: Sean watches the clock and the toy train in quick alternation in the buildup to the Mesa Verde "bank job." The film takes place after the end of sacred time, when, in Leone's vision of doom, the coming of the priests of modernism leaves the world in a state of irreconcilable confusion. The one chance for a man like Sean is to act with consistency and precision. He and Juan are inexorably in, not out of, time. *Once Upon a Time in America*'s Noodles is perceived in three times, and, when we last see him, he is indulging his only way of escaping time and the string of botched opportunities it represents to him.

Toys

Indio steals a little model cabinet from his cell mate in *For a Few Dollars More*, and uses it to illustrate his bank robbery plan. In *Duck, You Sucker!*, "Johnny and Johnny" load the toy train with nitroglycerine in order to blow the main door of the bank in Mesa Verde. But, unquestioningly, the toy image (like others) reaches full fruition in *Once Upon a Time in the West*. The doll and the little model "Station" in the McBain house compare visually with Morton's chessmen, suggesting that the people and events in the film are all just the toys of someone else. And we know who.

Trains

Ever an emblem of the coming of civilization, progress, corporate capitalism, and "law and order" to the frontier, trains have been tapped by Leone more richly than they have been tapped by any other director of Westerns. Never merely an incidental image, trains consistently provide a measure of the degree to which modernism has intruded into the mythic world and replaced sacred with profane time. There are no trains in *A Fistful of Dollars*. In *For a Few Dollars More*, a train opens the film proper; it conveys Colonel Mortimer to Tucumcari, regulations notwithstanding. The old prophet, from whom Manco obtains information about Mortimer, is a comic premonition of Brett McBain: Having refused to sell his land to the railroad, he now suffers the consequences of his independence—his walls shake, his shelves empty themselves, and his shack fills with steam and smoke every time a train passes along the edge of his little plot. Heightening the irony attached to his nickname, the old prophet hides under a pillow and curses the railroads—not his own lack of vision.

Railroads are well established in the Southwest of *The Good, the Bad and the Ugly*, but they do not intrude on the characters and action of the film. Trains and people coexist peacefully. The railroad plays a major role only when Corporal Wallace takes Tuco away from the prison camp; here the train provides Tuco with precisely the kind of opportunity he needs to make his escape. The bandit even uses a train to cut the shackles that bind him to Wallace.

Men like Tuco and Harmonica have potent mastery over time, events, and objects. At the beginning of *Once Upon a Time in the West*, Harmonica uses an entire train to mask his first entrance. Mortimer, too, had used a train to get where he was going (regardless of the train's own schedule), and Tuco used a train to set himself free.

But *Once Upon a Time in the West* is about the passing of such men; we see throughout the film the emergence of people who are servants of history, of the railroads, of what passes for progress. Men of such mettle that they would blow up a bridge to walk across the river or use a cannon to stop the escape of a traitorous partner are fading fast. As they fade, the railroad becomes more in evidence, plays a bigger role. The locomotive's mechanical, quotidian mastery of space replaces the near miraculous comings and goings of the godlike "ancient race." Morton, hideously crippled, is a slave to his railroad and to his commercial ambition; he is not a master of his fate. Jill survives not only because she vindicates McBain's independence and vision but because she learns to incorporate the railroad into her future. Indeed, she is associated with the railroad in her very first appearance in the film when she steps off a train. Harmonica's first appearance is also train-related, but what is emphasized in his first scene is that he does not visibly get off that train and seems aloof from the train's presence (Morton at Tucumcari carried a step farther). The unseen train raid during which Cheyenne's men stop Morton's train—and Cheyenne kills Morton though sustaining a fatal wound himself—is a final, desperate blow against the empire. Harmonica pointedly moves away from trains, separates himself from them. He finds himself in a genuinely compromising situation only when he is on Morton's train. At the beginning and at the end of the film, trains advance on us—almost as if to run us over—before Leone cuts away or pulls back to expand our vision.

Once Upon a Time in the West notwithstanding, *Duck, You Sucker!* is Leone's most train-filled film. In this world, trains have taken over. Only a man like Sean is capable of mastering them, his fire-and-smoke being more powerful than those of a locomotive. Sean initially escapes Juan when a train passes between them. Juan is "recognized" by Villega on a train and is morally recruited into the cause when the revolutionaries kill to protect him from being discovered—all he's trying to do is get a free ride. A toy train is the instrument used to mount the attack on the bank. A train is the site of Juan's confrontation with the governor and is the arbitrary divider between firing squads and cheering crowds—two sides of the revolutionary coin. And, of course, a train engine is the scene of Sean's confrontation with Villega as well as the instrument of Villega's "execution."

In *My Name Is Nobody*, Jack Beauregard must meet a train to get out of reality and into legend, to escape the West and find anonymity in the civilized Old World. A train station figures heavily in *Once Upon a Time in America* as a gateway to the past and future, but the film's only train serves to take Deborah

One train brings Jill (Claudia Cardinale) to her destiny in *Once Upon a Time in the West* (above); another takes Deborah (Elizabeth McGovern) away from Noodles in *Once Upon a Time in America* (below).

permanently away from Noodles, this loss being the most devastating of his missed opportunities.

Trains run on fire and water. But they are not of the elements; rather, they alter and consume the elements. Their tracks carve up the land and, in Leone's films, train tracks serve much the same imagistic purpose as barbed-wire fences do in cattle-oriented Westerns. In *Once Upon a Time in the West* and *Duck, You Sucker!* (and, satirically, in *My Name Is Nobody*), train tracks form the kind of moral and spiritual dividing line that rivers represent in much classic literature (and in Western films like *Red River, Rio Grande, Major Dundee, The Wild Bunch*, and the trainless *A Fistful of Dollars*). The dividing line separates the world in which men control themselves and their milieu from the world in which they are the subjects of tyrannical machinery and social regimen.

Violence

Leone made a for-the-record statement that he wanted his films to show "what serious violence, ending in death, really is." Noting the remark, John L. Wasserman of the *San Francisco Chronicle* cracked of *Duck, You Sucker!*, "This film is going to stamp out violence like Sophia Loren is going to stamp out sex." But the exposure of violence and a campaign against violence are two different matters. Wasserman (and many others) never took the time to examine how Leone used depth and ambivalence to approach the subject. What Leone is against is cruel, impersonal, organized mass violence: war, revolution, firing squads. But there's a kind of poetry in violence that is intimate, personal. It's ironic that it took Sam Peckinpah (who learned much from watching Leone's films) to create in the United States the kind of critical atmosphere which allowed film violence to be looked upon with the same objectivity as violence in literature or painting. (Nearly a decade later, Leone's films would come to be seen for the important mythic visions that they are.)

Violence doesn't decrease as one moves through Leone's films—quite the opposite, in fact—but it becomes less graphic, less direct and personal, and consequently more absurd. All the deaths that occur in *Once Upon a Time in the West* and *Duck, You Sucker!* are astonishingly clean and bloodless in comparison with the intimate brutality of the violence in the Eastwood films. Yet it is precisely this intimacy, this personalism, that makes violence meaningful. The difference between, for example, *For a Few Dollars More* and *Duck, You Sucker!* is the difference between the world of the face-to-face duel and that of the faceless slaughter of Hiroshima. One of the most palpably Leonean notes in *My Name Is Nobody* sounds in Beauregard's letter to Nobody at the end, when Beauregard says, "Violence has changed, too—it's crueler; got organized." More than explicitly summing up Leone's ambivalent view of violence, this statement suggests a transition to the gangster world of *Once Upon a Time in America*, where violence is so brutalizing and commonplace that Noodles's one hope for redemption may be in not killing the traitorous friend who has wrecked his life.

War

War is the logical extension of competitive free enterprise (be it in politics or in economics or both). San Miguel is in a metaphorical state of war in *A Fistful of Dollars*. The only alternative to this ordered, rule-less piling up of bodies is partnership, which is the thesis of *For a Few Dollars More* ("We don't want to end up shooting each other in the back"). In *The Good, the Bad and the Ugly*, war is simply a poor alternative to self-centered profiteering. The same view holds in *Duck, You Sucker!*, except that in this film it is harder for the profiteer to avoid joining the state of war that has become a way of life. In Leone's world, the only legitimate wars are the private ones.

Water

Water is incidental in the first two Leone films: Ramón Rojo's massacre of the gold shipment escort occurs on the bank of the river, and Indio's gang hides out in a town called Agua Caliente, which may or may not be an intentional play on the American idiom for "in trouble."

In *The Good, the Bad and the Ugly*, however, water becomes central. The desert landscape highlights the inherent brutality of Leone's pre-moral wasteland. The waterwheel at Stevens's little farm is an emphatic and memorable image because it contrasts so sharply with the absence of water in the world inhabited by Tuco and Blondie: the dry riverbed across which Tuco emerges from his ordeal in the desert; the subsequent ordeal to which he subjects Blondie; the spilled canteen; the deliberate withholding followed by the desperate giving of water once Blondie's life becomes more important to Tuco than his own revenge. The battle is waged over tactical control of a bridge that crosses an apparently critical body of water, and that river must be crossed by Blondie and Tuco (and, presumably, by Angeleyes) before they can reach Sad Hill Cemetery and undergo the final test. Blondie offers water to the dying Confederate soldier on the other side of the river—a stark contrast to Tuco's having denied water first to Blondie and then to Bill Carson.

Once Upon a Time in the West is the Leone film to which water imagery is most central. The whole plot hangs on the inherent value of McBain's land claim, "Sweetwater," an invaluable source of water in the middle of a desert. (The same kind of discovery would, in the next few years, make an entrepreneur out of Sam Peckinpah's Cable Hogue and a monster out of Roman Polanski's Noah Cross.) One of the functions of that creaking windmill, the water dripping on Woody Strode's head, and the wheezing locomotive getting a drink in the opening of the film, is to fix in our minds the fact that trains need water. Jill's buckboard driver reminds her that horses and people both have to stop for a drink now and then. So do railroad builders, and Jill's function as water bearer—artificial, early in the film, to work a ruse on Frank's men, but central and necessary by the end—ties her to the workers and the water in the desert, pointing the way to the future.

Leone throws water in front of us at every turn: Sam stopping at the tavern because the horse needs a drink, Wobbles's laundry, the flush-toilet in Morton's train car. Valerii seems to have cottoned to this, considering the way he stresses Nobody's mastery of the water in the fish-catching scene at the beginning of *My Name Is Nobody* (itself patterned after a similar scene in *The Magnificent Seven*), and Beauregard's departure by water at the end of it.

Water is, of course, the very stuff of life. Only people like Harmonica do not need to concern themselves with it; they're above life. In *Once Upon a Time in America*, ritual immersion takes on vital importance by providing friends with a way of renewing their partnership from time to time and, perhaps, of symbolically cleansing their guilt. That the criminals are Jewish makes Leone's insistence on the periodic baptism even more suggestive.

Weaponry

Weapons systems are an important index of character in Leone's films. Ramón Rojo debates the virtues of a Winchester over the Man with No Name's pistol in *A Fistful of Dollars*. Colonel Douglas Mortimer's professionalism is in part defined by his saddlebag gun rack in *For a Few Dollars More*. Tuco manufactures an intensely personal dream-pistol in *The Good, the Bad and the Ugly*, which Blondie (impossibly, as I have pointed out) identifies by the sound of its timing. On the other hand, a less personal sort of weaponry emerges in Leone's films—blunt instruments of death that require force, not skill, to implement them, instruments that enable men to kill each other without looking their victims in the eye—indeed, without seeing them at all. Sean's coat-lining arsenal in *Duck, You Sucker!* is the post-mythic world's crude variation on Mortimer's mobile armory. The dynamite of that film is prepared for by the purely pyrotechnic use of explosives in *A Fistful of Dollars*, also by its utilitarian role as a tool of theft in *For a Few Dollars More*. A more serious foreshadowing of the coming of dynamite, however, is the heavy use of cannon fire in *The Good, the Bad and the Ugly*, which provides another razor with which to separate men like Blondie, Tuco, and Angeleyes from lesser spirits. But Angeleyes, however one-sided and unfair his killings may be, at least looks right at his victims. The ignorant armies that counterpoint the film don't; they use methods of wholesale, impersonal slaughter.

Violence isn't a pat issue, however. Even the "good" protagonist is corrupted by this new weapon system that substitutes blunt force for skill, quantity for quality, safety for the inherent danger of moving in for the kill: Blondie takes a cannon shot at Tuco. Although the moment is funny and powerfully rhythmic, it also marks the beginning of the end for the Leone gunman as self-respecting man of integrity. The introduction of the pistol over the sword in *Yojimbo* has impact in that it presents a way in which a man might kill his enemies without exposing himself to danger. The message is the same in the analogous superseding of pistols by rifles and of rifles by explosives in Leone's films; it announces the end of any meaningful manhood. In *Once Upon a Time in America*, Noodles's use of a knife against pistol-carrying Bugsy is an act of courage as well as of craziness. The profusion of pistols and machine guns appearing later in the film make men seem to lack all character.

Despite the detail with which Leone depicts them, the pistols and rifles in his Westerns seem no more realistic than those of the Republic Westerns and other puff-of-smoke programmers. When people get shot, they just fall over—sometimes clutching a wound, but not always. The infliction of a gunshot wound is never as graphically realistic in Leone as it is in Peckinpah, or even in Mann, Boetticher, or Sturges. That's because, when all is said and done, the essential Leone weapon is not the gun at all but the fist. Oh, guns are handy for getting rid of a lot of people in a hurry, for matching skills, for speeding a plot along. But the emotional dynamics of Leone's films are predicated upon the use of the most personal and brutal of weapons, the human fist. The violence we really feel in these films is not the bang-you're-dead gunfire but the physical beating of one human being by another: Rojo's men kick a little boy; Consuelo Baxter slaps her errant son; No Name, Silvanito, Manco, Mortimer, and Tuco are beaten savagely, almost ritualistically; Tuco kicks Blondie in the desert; Harmonica beats Wobbles; a savage beating of Harmonica by the sheriff's men was cut from the film before release, but leaves its mark on Harmonica's face in ensuing scenes nevertheless; Syndicate thugs torture Fat Moe; Max pistol-whips Noodles. In contrast to the almost bloodless gunplay, these beatings, and the wounds they inflict, are always hideously graphic. After the gundown, what Harmonica does to Frank with his hand (and harmonica) is infinitely more powerful than his shooting of Frank. As may be expected, the fist disappears completely from Leone's world in *Duck, You Sucker!*; so, it seems, does everything of value.

"He Not Only Plays—He Can Shoot, Too"

Morricone Encomium

Leone has worked regularly with certain actors, technicians, and creative talents, but only one name other than his own appears on all six Leone films: Ennio Morricone. Next to Leone himself, Morricone is the man most responsible for the atmosphere, the impact, and, in large part, the popularity of Leone's films.

When *A Fistful of Dollars* was first released in the United States, viewers were baffled: What is music like that doing in a movie like this? The *Titoli* (a romantic-sounding name that means simply "titles," denoting the tune's initial use in the film) became at least as popular as the film itself, has subsequently provided arresting ambience for television and radio commercials advertising products as diverse as real estate and automobiles, and is still widely imitated and parodied. The simple melody for whistler and guitars, with percussive comment from bells, whip cracks, penny whistles, and male chorus, echoed "Ghost Riders in the Sky" for Bosley Crowther, but the melody's true roots lie in Woody Guthrie's "Pastures of Plenty," specifically an arrangement that Morricone created for the expatriate American ballad singer Peter Tevis.

In Peter Tevis's own words:

> I was working at the Teatro De Opera as a stereo stage manager at about twenty-four years of age in 1961, when I was introduced to an Italian lady who had established herself by helping singers get started. She made an appointment for me to go to RCA, to meet Pierrot Ricordi. I remember putting my foot on his desk and singing my own rendition of "Pastures of Plenty." He offered me a contract of two singles. He also made an appointment for me to see Morricone. We cut the record and I was lost for a while.
>
> At this time, Sergio Leone needed a score for his film *Per un Pugno di Dollari* better known to us as *A Fistful of Dollars*, and he didn't like any of the ones Morricone had written so far. While trying to find something that was "different" and could work for Leone's film, my single "Pastures of Plenty" happened to get played. At this point I had developed a bombastic way of playing guitar. From what I've heard, when Leone heard the single he cried out, "That's it!" and thus was the score to *A Fistful of Dollars* born. At about this time, I went to the movies in Italy and heard my song played as the background music for the opening sequence. Except, they had removed my voice and the lyrics to the song, and replaced them with the whistling we hear when we see the film today. I went to RCA claiming that I was going to file a suit, but according to them there's an Italian clause that says "The injured party must gain something from the other party" and so they asked me what I wanted. I said I'd like to make an album with Morricone, and so I got

my wish and he and I made the "Fistful" LP record. My original "Pastures of Plenty" was suppressed, otherwise that first single would have appeared on the LP. As naive as I was, I had no idea that it would become one of the biggest films in cinema history. I felt that Ennio was under pressure to produce a cheap soundtrack as he had no idea how the movie would do either. I often wonder what happened to all those 45s containing my "Pastures of Plenty."

With the appearance of *For a Few Dollars More* and *The Good, the Bad and the Ugly*, critics' hasty dismissal of Leone entered a period of revision. Morricone's scores became more integral, and a recognizable (though never formulaic) pattern developed. To scenes of primal violence, Leone and Morricone were lending not only music but, astonishingly, melody, haunting and lovely, a kind of melody worlds away from the neo-Wagnerian "mood music" and Coplandesque American folksong variations that even in its best incarnations (in the hands of Dmitri Tiomkin and Elmer Bernstein) had, until then, typified the Hollywood Western score.

Given Leone's spare use of dialogue, it's easy to see how the music comes to dominate the soundtrack. "Background" it isn't. Score combines with cinematic image to create a single composite foreground effect. Never merely accompanying or commenting on the shots or on the action, the music assumes equal proportion to what is taking place on screen. Often, Leone designed montages and even shot scenes to fit Morricone's already-composed music, this being a marked reversal of the traditional approach to film scoring. Like Hitchcock and Bernard Herrmann, or Fellini and Nino Rota, or John Milius and Basil Poledouris, Leone and Morricone represented that perfect marriage of director and composer that turns even the most audaciously assertive and ear-catching music unerringly to the service of a wholly integrated film. So much a part of that ineffable atmosphere is Morricone's music, in fact, that a score by him or imitative of his style became a sine qua non of the Spaghetti Western and its American progeny.

Nevertheless, Morricone was far from solely responsible for the sound that became associated with the "Spaghetti Western" and played such a key part in building its cult popularity. A whole school of composers—many of whom had already worked in peplum films—built a new compositional style around the phenomenon of the Italian Western. Morricone was certainly the leading practitioner of the art, and the one who went on to the most spectacular international success. But the development of the sound and the continual inventiveness that kept giving it new life was the work of so many: choral arranger (and whistler) Alessandro Alessandroni, harmonicist Franco de Gemini, and such composers as Luis Enriquez Bacalov (later to win an Academy Award for his score for *Il Postino*), Francesco De Masi, Stelvio Cipriani, Bruno Nicolai, Carlo Savina, Santemaria Romitelli, Carlo Rustichelli, Franco Micalizzi, A. F. Lavagnino, Riz Ortolani, Nora Orlandi, Piero Piccione, Armando Trovajoli, Marcello Giombini, and oh, so many more.

One reason Morricone's scores for Leone are so strikingly different from the kind of music generally associated with the B-Western up till that time is that their rhythms are not usually the rhythms of montage but of camera movement or character movement (and unless they're shooting guns, Leone's characters don't move much faster than his camera does). Even when Leone uses accelerating montage, cross-cutting faces, hands, eyes, closeups and long shots, Morricone delivers a slow, majestic mariachi tune (he began his musical career as a trumpeter), underscoring not the mounting suspense but the elemental triumph of that frozen moment of reckoning occurring just before explosive action.

When the camera moves, the tempos of the music are those of tracking shots, pans, and Leone's long, brooding crane shots. The slow-tracking, long-take pace of *Once Upon a Time in the West* is reinforced in the score, whose principal themes are all slower than any of Morricone's music for Leone's first three films. Even the rattly dance tune ("Bad Orchestra") that colors Jill's arrival in Flagstone is slow for its genre. The very concept of tempo is virtually obliterated in the atonal percussion ensembles of the wary, stalking sequences (Cheyenne freeing Harmonica from Morton's train, Harmonica helping Frank pick off Morton's assassins in Flagstone)—an idea first developed in the El Paso sequences of *For a Few Dollars More*, when Manco and Mortimer watch the comings and goings of Indio's gang.

To be sure, montage-paced music is not absent from Morricone's Leone scores; it's just used sparingly and, in *A Fistful of Dollars*, evident only at the point when the blustering batucada and rising agitato ("The Chase") of the fast-cut, night-time riding sequence segues into a down-tempo version of the Titoli during No Name's rescue of Marisol and her family. In *For a Few Dollars More*, the music occasionally (and deliberately) punctuates the cutting. In "Il Colpo," for example, an almost exclusively percussive scoring of the set-up to Indio's explosive snatching of the safe (scattered piano chords and shuffles from bass and side drums) emphasizes the fragmentary nature of Mortimer's and Manco's isolated, wrong point-of-view glimpses of the gang's creeping around. At one point, a single trombone blare is held for what seems like an eternity as Indio and four of his men pass all the way across that widest of screens. The trumpet then gives way to an abrupt, heavy bell and piano chord as Leone cuts to a static shot of the fake cabinet inside the bank.

To the often repeated dictum that the best film editing is "invisible," there must be a corollary that the best film music is inaudible, or at least unnoticeable. But Leone and Morricone fly in the face of both notions. In all cinema, one of the most remarkable examples of an eminently visible and audible montage is the "Ecstasy of Gold" sequence from *The Good, the Bad and the Ugly*: On the piano's rolling repetition of a four-note figure, Morricone builds a simple but rapturous reed theme that, carried by female voice and strings, accelerates in tempo with the speed of Leone's montage and his swish pans. Feeling increasing excitement, Tuco explores the cemetery; the music rises through several octaves until, finally, at fever-pitch, graves flash by in a blur. Greedy anticipation—Tuco's and ours—becomes unbearable as bells go crazy and fragments of discord ring out from the brass; then, as the right grave is reached, Tuco, camera, montage, and music—all triumphant and exhausted—stop dead.

Morricone's scores for Leone work against conventional expectation, but they do not always defy convention. Many of the composer's best musical conceits are whimsical parodies or powerful transformations of generic Western clichés—as, indeed, are many of Leone's own best moments as director. Like Puccini's use of rag rhythms in *Girl of the Golden West*, Morricone taps and overhauls period music.

A "Square Dance," in the tonality and structure of folk dances unchanged since the Renaissance bourée, scores the arrival of the gold shipment and its escort in San Miguel. Morricone gives the form a new twist by winding the dance wheezily down through ever-slower tempos until the fiddles finally saw to a weary stop. In *For a Few Dollars More*, a tinkly dimestore piano plays another dance tune, "Aces High," as Manco engages in his deadly poker game with Baby Red Cavanaugh: A sprightly theme and variations dart among the upper registers, while the lower keys lay down an oom-pah rhythm that threatens to become a second melody and turn the score into a medieval polyphony. A similar tinny piano stomp ("Bad Orchestra"), accompanied by tuba, slide whistle, banjo, and fiddle, creates the mood of a thriving but not very organized country town as Jill arrives in Flagstone early in *Once Upon a Time in the West*. The tune, like the scene, is whimsical and capricious, carefully structured but unsure of its destination. All three of these bouncy combo pieces point toward the use of jazz in *Once Upon a Time in America*.

The score to *The Good, the Bad and the Ugly* taps Civil War movie convention in its use of a lilting sentimental ballad played off against a recurring march tune. The ballad, "Story of a Soldier," is derivative of the Confederate standard "Lorena" (a leading motif in Max Steiner's score to *The Searchers*, where it seeps into the opening scene to characterize Ethan for us before we even see him clearly, and in David Buttolph's music for *The Horse Soldiers*, for which it is the main theme). Sung phonetically by an Italian chorus, the lyrics of the song are only sporadically intelligible, but they reflect an antiwar tone consistent with both the film's treatment of war and the prevailing mood of ballads appearing during the period. The supporting instruments—guitar, harmonica, and fiddle—don't fully match those of the tatty prison band that "plays" the tune in the film. This irony extends the already existing ironic use of music to cover Wallace's savage beating of Tuco.

Interestingly, no other Leone film features an original song, despite the fact that sung ballads are staples of Morricone's Western scores for other directors: "Lonesome Billy" from *Pistols Don't Argue*, "Angel Face" from *A Pistol for Ringo*, the title tune from *The Return of Ringo*, "Run, Man, Run" from *The Big Gundown* (a sly inversion of the "Ecstasy of Gold" music from *The Good, the Bad and the Ugly*), "Al Messico chi vorrei" from *Tepepa*. Lyrics were written and recorded in English for both the trumpet title tune from *A Fistful of Dollars* and Indio's "gundown" music in *For a Few Dollars More*, and the recordings are available, but they were never used in American release versions of either film.

"Story of a Soldier" has a definite onscreen "source," as well as a direct relation to the action of *The Good, the Bad and the Ugly*. Knowing this, the Leone student may surmise that Leone wants only songs that are integral; if he can't have those, he wants no songs at all.

The march ("Marcetta") is at first lighthearted and jaunty, its harmonica and whistling chorus accompanying the semicomic marching of Tuco and Blondie into the Union prison camp after their masquerade has tripped them up. Retitled "Marcetta senza speranza" ("March without Hope"), the march recurs at dirge-like tempo, no longer whistled, and more moaned than hummed by a lugubrious male chorus, side drums and piano unevenly punctuating ragged footsteps: The soldiers in the town and along both sides of that "crucial" river are—unlike the prisoners—"without hope." Cockeye's pan-pipe tune ("Friends") in *Once Upon a Time in America* evolves from a pipe solo to a similarly jaunty orchestral march when the boys cross town to set up the cache that seals their partnership, and is later transformed into a dirge-like theme of regret.

The mariachi trumpet air is another convention to which Morricone gave new life. The main theme of *A Fistful of Dollars* consists of long, fateful rising notes, interrupted by short ones tripping downward: The pattern betrays the tune's roots in the Mexican trumpet air "Deguello" ("Massacre"), played at the Alamo on Santa Ana's order, to signal that no quarter would be given the defenders of the besieged mission. The same tune was played throughout the long nights of *Rio Bravo* by a lone trumpeter hired to strike terror into the hearts of Sheriff John T. Chance and his handful of misfits guarding the jail. Later Dmitri Tiomkin—who scored *Rio Bravo* partly from his *Red River* music—built an entire score out of "Deguello" and variations for John Wayne's *The Alamo*. This must surely have captured the imagination of trumpeter Morricone, then on the threshold of his first work in films. What he made of it became a staple of the Italian Western score. Rare is the "Spaghetti Western" that doesn't have its "deguello."

When the ending of "The Chase" in *A Fistful of Dollars* segues into a falling motif that quotes the last few measures of Tiomkin's *Alamo* ballad "The Green Leaves of Summer," it's like an acknowledgment of a debt. Of all Hollywood composers, Tiomkin clearly had the strongest influence on Morricone—one needs only ears to recognize that. Tiomkin's award-winning *High Noon* and his scores to *Red River*, *Rio Bravo*, and *The Gunfight at the O.K. Corral* are definitive Western movie scores (with sung ballads, by the way). His Oscar-winning *The High and the Mighty*, not a Western, pioneered the use of a main title song that was whistled rather than sung (backed by soprano and full chorus), and, featuring choral understatement, his *Alamo* score made ample use of overhauled folk themes.

Morricone's mariachi theme in *A Fistful of Dollars* recurs throughout the film. But it is most evocative accompanying the Baxters during their resolute walk through the streets of San Miguel when they are on their way to keep their dinner engagement with the Rojos: The trumpet solo wraps virtuoso improvisation around a central slow march rhythm on guitar and bass strings; female chorus join in on the rise to crescendo. (The fatalism is profound: the Baxters may as well be going to dinner at the Borgias'.) The same arrangement is used for the tense prisoner exchange and for No Name's climactic "resurrection" from the smoke to face an unnerved Ramón.

A trumpet solo is the key device used for the climactic triangular face-offs in *For a Few Dollars More* ("Sixty Seconds to What?" built on the chime tune from the locket-watch) and *The Good, the Bad and the Ugly* ("The Trio"). In the latter instance, a guitar introduction (with rattling castanets and tinkling chimes à la the lockets of the earlier film) sets an ominous mood into which the mariachi trumpet slips easily as the guitar underbeat becomes a stately bolero, recalling Puccini's use of the Cuban bolero in *Girl of the Golden West*. Strings and chorus echo the trumpet, side drums shiver; the entire ensemble builds to a crescendo, starts to ebb, then ends abruptly a note or two away from home. The sense of incompleteness creates a slightly off-balance feeling, anticipating the shoot-out; it implies, in fact, that someone (Angeleyes) has jumped the gun. You don't draw until the music is over.

The fatalistic trumpet tune is reorchestrated in *Once Upon a Time in the West* and becomes an ominous theme whose title—"As a Judgment"—carries a sense of inescapable fate. Introduced with twanging strings that resemble electronically amplified harpsichord sounds, the theme recurs throughout the film, but appears most notably during the first appearance of the Man with the Harmonica, the shooting of the McBains by Frank and his men, Cheyenne's first confrontation with Harmonica at the roadside tavern, and the final reckoning between Harmonica and Frank.

The harsh first note of "As a Judgment" heightens our reaction to our first good look at Harmonica's face (occurring after the camera crawls up Harmonica's body to the wail of his harmonica); it links that portrait with the closeup of Timmy McBain as he comes out of the barn to find the rest of his family dead and his own murderers approaching—it climactically relates both faces to the face of the boy that Harmonica was, when the final flashback reveals all. In between, the tune accompanies another shot of Harmonica's face when, during the first tavern scene, Cheyenne sends a suspended lantern along its wire to light up the corner where the Man sits sawing on his harmonica; both lantern and music hang there, swinging, playing on that face.

Once Upon a Tine in the West also features one of Morricone's most daring uses of generic cliché. The theme associated with Cheyenne has as its basic rhythm, of all things, the clip-clop of a plodding horse! A banjo takes up the motif and builds it into a tune of sorts, an ambling one-note fantasy for a lazy male whistler, which is further delayed by long rests and—at the moment of Cheyenne's death—an exasperatingly but reverently extended silence between the penultimate and the final notes. All this is just right for a death and for summing up the sardonic manner and casual style of the solitary, doomed Cheyenne.

Another influence on Morricone was the popular guitar instrumentals of the early '60s. When Danny Peary mentioned to me, once, the similarity between Morricone's lilting/galloping Western themes and an old tune by the Tornados (circa 1962), the comparison set in motion a train of thought. The surf sound—developed from Hawaiian slack-key, the country twang of Link Wray and Duane Eddy, and Dick Dale's speed-guitar enhancement of Les Paul's double-chording—created a vogue for guitar instrumentals in the '60s. The British permutation of this sound, godfathered by Joe Meek and embodied best in the work of the Shadows and of Meek's own Blue Men, Tornados, and Fabulous Flee-Rakkers, formed a crucial part of the pop-consciousness of the Italian Western composers. The twangy lead speed-guitar with a galloping underbeat in rhythm guitar and percussion is the Italian Western main theme at its most fundamental, and its roots may be heard in the numerous "surf" guitar instrumentals, both American and British, that were popular in Europe at the time of Morricone's apprenticeship, and were widely imitated by European pop groups: "Walk, Don't Run" (The Ventures, August 1960); "Apache" (Jorgen Ingman, March 1961); "Ridin' the Wind," "Love and Fury," and "Telstar," from the Tornados' album *Telstar* (December 1962); "Pipeline" (The Chantays, April 1963); and "Moon Child" and other cuts on the Ventures' *Out of Limits* album (1964). All predate or are contemporary with the first Western scores of Morricone and his Italian contemporaries, and the similarity is readily apparent. Indeed, Quentin Tarantino, when asked why he so frequently uses surfing music in his films, commented that he never understood why it was referred to as "surfing music," since it all sounded like Spaghetti Western music to him. Of course it did—the Spaghetti Western composers got many of their musical ideas from "surf" guitar instrumentals.

Morricone doesn't generally write leitmotif music in the "So-and-So's Theme" sense, as Rózsa, Williams, Bernstein, and other Wagnerians of film music tended to do. His music is more *arioso* than *recitativo*—tapping, not surprisingly, the Italian (not the German) operatic tradition and running to the repetition of melodic set-pieces rather than the commingling of themes or the purely atmospheric commentary of most film scores. So when Morricone's themes do associate themselves with specific characters, as the Cheyenne piece does, it's to a purpose. The female voice in the title theme to *Once Upon a Time in the West*, belonging to the magnificent Edda dell'Orso, inevitably associates that music with Jill, Leone's only female protagonist, and to her building of her corner of America. But the theme is more than a signature tune; this is evident from its expansive use in the finale: The music swells and takes over, even as Jill shrinks into the milling bodies during the ever-widening final crane shot.

Another orchestration of this theme ("A Dimly Lit Room") serves quite a different purpose by shading Jill's first night in the McBain house. The glockenspiel used in the introductory passage sounds like a child's musical toy. This effect not only underscores Jill's discovery of what she takes to be toys in McBain's trunk but also gives us a momentary sense of her own lost innocence. Similarly, the droning harmonica motif does more than simply signal the (not always visible) presence of the Man with the Harmonica. Its wails are sometimes phantom cries in the night, cautionary warnings, or the cries of a wounded animal (or boy). In a harmonica tour de force called "Death Rattle," the figure is reduced to a series of ever-shortening throaty bursts—intermittent, dying croaks.

"As a Judgment" is not tied to a single character; Harmonica and Frank more or less share it. The segment represents not a character but a collision—not only the debt between the two men but also the one means of final resolution to which they have recourse. (Morricone composed an explicit parody of this theme for the confrontations between Nobody and Beauregard in his whimsical

My Name Is Nobody score.) In the roadside tavern scene, the tootling harmonica of Harmonica and the plucked banjo of Cheyenne wind themselves around "As a Judgment." This arrangement signals potentially violent confrontation between Harmonica and Cheyenne and reminds us, at this point in the story, that Harmonica is disposed to suspect Cheyenne of the ambush set for him in the film's opening.

Similar theme-sharing is found again in *Duck, You Sucker!*, when a theme initially accompanying Juan acquires the choral refrain "Sean-Sean." Just as the two Johnnys become facets of a single force and cross in viewpoint during the course of the film, so each man's musical motif links with the other's, till we can no longer keep them straight. When Juan faces the firing squad, he hears, just as the rifles are raised, a familiar whistled tune. Sean is never seen whistling the tune (and it is the first time a character in the film acknowledges any of the soundtrack music), but Juan smiles as a low voice expectedly says, "Duck, you sucker." It is almost as if Juan has become privy to the nuances of Morricone's score and, thereby, knows rescue is at hand.

Morricone made his earliest exploration of the complex interweaving of shared character-related themes in *For a Few Dollars More*. The film is worth examining in some detail because of the remarkable integration of its music into the film's story, characterization, and atmosphere. The title tune is introduced and punctuated by the gunshots that knock a lazily whistling rider off his horse and then run the horse away in the opening shot. It is an energetic melody for whistler (in the same vein as the "Titoli" from *A Fistful of Dollars*), and built on a jew's-harp beat that is syncopated with a six-note flute motif, which becomes a counter-theme. The sproing! of the jew's-harp recurs as a logo for Colonel Mortimer, and the staccato flute burst becomes a signature for Manco (as a similar five-note motif did for No Name in *A Fistful of Dollars*).

Indio, too, has an associated theme: A simple, percussive chime figure underscores his gang's infiltration of the prison; only later do we identify this chime as the tinkling carillon of the locket-watch. In the abandoned church, when Indio faces off against the man who betrayed him, castanets, guitar, and strings join the locket-watch sounds. There's a rising choral bridge; a full pipe organ enters with the "Sixty Seconds to What?" theme. (That English title, by the way, fails to capture the Leonean sense of justice implicit in the Italian name of the piece: "*La Resa dei Conti*," which means "the settling of accounts," the final reckoning. The same phrase is the Italian title of the Sergio Sollima film known in English as *The Big Gundown*, also scored by Morricone.) The presence of an organ enriches the scene's church setting. The organ then gives way to the mariachi trumpet, which repeats the theme in rising octaves and is supported by richer orchestrations. Gradually, the instruments begin to drop back out, at last leaving the watch chimes to finish the tune alone and to measure with a decelerating, dying fall the last breathless moment during which the desperate, doomed little man goes for his gun.

The tinkly bell motif of the watch is never quite a full-blown melody, though the subtle string accompaniment treats it as one. The motif is heard whenever the locket-watch is opened; it becomes the emblem of Indio's fixation on both the watch and the woman inside it. The carillon introduces each of the film's flashbacks (they are presented as Indio's reveries); it accompanies them in increasingly eerie, discordantly overlapping distortions and is the music of Indio's disordered mind as well as of his distorted perception while smoking marijuana. And, of course, in a device used even more intensely in *Once Upon a Time in the West*, the locket-watch itself is not only the source of the music but the key image in the flashback.

Relatively late in the film, when Indio and Mortimer finally meet for the first time in the cantina in Agua Caliente, the chime tune recurs to underscore Indio's ominous "Who are you?" (the tune is whisked away then as Mortimer cuts the tension with his lighthearted, evasive answer).

The locket-watch is, of course, the crucial image, present during the final reckoning of the two antagonists. At this time, the chimes slow to a near-finish, only to be drowned out by the faster chimes issuing from the duplicate locket-watch in Manco's hand. The theme repeats from the beginning, and during this scene a mounting mariachi trumpet version of "Sixty Seconds to What?" builds, then dies to allow the last few notes to sound from the locket-watch before the men became engaged in the fury of the draw.

In the denouement, while Manco totals up his bounty, Colonel Mortimer begins his weary ride out of town, accompanied by a dirge-like restatement of "Sixty Seconds to What?" played on strings, reeds, and bells. This deeply nostalgic variation, "Farewell to the Colonel," conveys a strong sense of loss and thus undercuts Mortimer's victory. Indio's chime theme, along with the dead bandit's burden of obsession and guilt, is subtly transferred to Mortimer.

This integration of a musical instrument points, of course, to the use of the harmonica in *Once Upon a Time in the West*. In this film, Leone's creative use of flashback delicately, gradually reveals how and why the Man with the Harmonica's grudge against Frank is tied specifically to the instrument he plays and to the way he plays it. Beyond relating plot and character to music, the harmonica links all three to the folk convention of the singing cowboy and fills the cliché with a depth and richness Gene Autry and Roy Rogers never dreamed of.

Much of what is astounding about Morricone's scores for Leone derives from the composer's eccentric approach to the orchestration. His association of a whistling voice with a wandering loner (in the five Westerns) is the most melodic of a bizarre library of devices he uses to create a non-orchestral music: The sproing of the jew's-harp, the wah-wah of an amplified harmonica, whip cracks, gunshots, and an exotic arsenal of less identifiable twangs, bangs, clicks, and clangs, characterize his orchestration of the savage.

The most remarkable instance of this nonmusical music occurs during the opening sequence of *Once Upon a Time in the West*, the scene sets the tone for a film that is as much about its music as it is about anything else. The three killers await the train amid a symphony of natural and mechanical sounds that include a creaking windmill, a clicking telegraph key, chalk scraping on slate, dripping water, the deafening crunch of knuckles being cracked one at a loving time, and the piercing hum of a persistent fly.

The fly is trapped inside the pistol barrel. Then the tip of the gun is pressed against the clapboard walls of the station, capped with a fingertip, and held to the captor's ear, the humming becoming a high-pitched whine that segues neatly into the distant whistle of the approaching train. This whistle is a tonal harbinger of the first conventional—if that's the word—music of the film: the harmonica wail that announces the presence of the anonymous protagonist as the train pulls away.

Though Morricone has denied having any involvement in the creation of this symphony in sound beyond simply discussing it with Leone, who originated the idea, the sequence nevertheless stands as the best example of how Leone's films, at their best, completely integrate both music and nonmusical sound with image and theme.

In *The Good, the Bad and the Ugly*, the human voice is an essential element in Morricone's offbeat orchestration: That cry (war whoop? scream of terror?), initially associated with Tuco's crash through the window, evolves into a five-note staccato flute motif (rooted, interestingly, in the "Almost Dead" music from *A Fistful of Dollars*). In turn, the flute motif forms the basis for every thematic development in the film's score. Morricone always treats the voice as an instrument—often of percussion rather than melody—and even when he employs it as a carrier of words, the sound is always more important than the meaning (which helps account for, and excuse, the decidedly strange lyrics of the ballads in *The Good, the Bad and the Ugly* as well as in the Westerns not directed by Leone). The main title themes to each of the Eastwood films feature guttural male chorus monosyllabics. These occur to the insistent throb of a tomtom, which stresses the downbeat and emphasizes the primitive aura of Leone's world by recalling the generic "Indian music" of many a Hollywood Western.

Indians, at least as specifically tribal peoples, never appear in Leone's films, though Indio has his name for a reason, and there is an Indian woman at the train station at the beginning of *Once Upon a Time in the West*. But Morricone taps heavily the kind of music traditionally associated with aboriginal natives in American Western film scores. Particularly noticeable is the romanticized "Indian music" of the "Vice of Killing" theme in *For a Few Dollars More*. The theme is an enlargement of the piano stamp "Aces High," which is reorchestrated for a majestic chorus with female solo. It makes its first appearance when the film shifts into high gear at the blowing away of the back wall of the Bank of El Paso. Edda's voice intones something that sounds a little like the "Indian Love Call." This, perhaps, is a reference—direct as well as ironic—to the character "El Indio" (the piece's title is, in its Italian sense, not a general comment on the moral quality of murder but a reference to obsession or addiction). The male chorus syncopates with the guttural under-beat from the main title theme—a composition that has become Manco's logo. At this point, it is almost as if the female voice is associated with Indio and the male with Manco—a pairing that exactly reflects the film's psychodramatic sexual dynamics.

If the soprano air of "Vice of Killing" is reminiscent of "Indian Love Call," I suppose there's nothing wrong with Richard Corliss's asserting that the main theme to *Once Upon a Time in the West* reminds him of "Sweet Mystery of Life." The overpowering reverence of this theme is as important in delineating Leone's West, his characters, and his emotional attitude toward this fairy-tale world, as anything else in the film.

The handling of the *Once Upon a Time in the West* score—though with less thematic variation, slower tempos, a longer, lusher score for a longer, more lavish film—looks ahead to *Duck, You Sucker!*, which has even fewer melodic variations than *Once Upon a Time in the West*, and which uses the female voice more than other Leone films have. In addition, the score prefigures the more meditative beauty of later Morricone main themes, especially those of *Days of Heaven*, *Exorcist II: The Heretic*, *Once Upon a Time in America*, and his last work with Edda dell'Orso, the beautiful score for Alastair Reid's television miniseries of Joseph Conrad's *Nostromo*.

The main theme of *Duck, You Sucker!*, a Bachian air for soprano, is associated specifically with Sean Mallory, and is heard—like the chimes in *For a Few Dollars More*—each time the character enters one of his daydream flashbacks. A chorus counterpoints the solo aria using the lilting refrain of "Sean-Sean, Sean-Sean!" The sequence is slower, more reverent (almost holy!) than the jaunty, walking-rhythm tune associated first with Juan and later, in a whistled version, with the lighter side of Sean. Curiously, the choral comment "Juan-Juan," heard in the main title rendition of this theme, never recurs. It is quickly and permanently replaced with "Sean-Sean," just as the theme initially associated with Juan—reorchestrated as something like a penny whistle—becomes Sean's.

At the end of the film ("After the Explosion"), the soprano air associated with Sean vanishes (like Sean himself). The two introductory themes that normally led into it appear by themselves, and, in doing so, emphasize the finality of Sean's departure. Gone, too, is the "Sean-Sean" of the chorus that, earlier in the film, stressed Sean's almost spiritual ubiquity. It's not without its whimsy: at one point a theme associated with Juan segues cutely into Mozart's *Eine Kleine Nachtmusik*. Morricone also employed classical quotes for comic effect in *My Name Is Nobody* (Wagner's Valkyries for the Wild Bunch) and *Once Upon a Time in America* (Rossini's Thieving Magpie for the baby-switching scene); and to darker purpose in *The Big Gundown* (Beethoven's "*Für Elise*") and *Days of Heaven* (Saint-Saëns' "Aquarium"). But on the whole the score for *Duck, You Sucker!* was the most serious and somber for a Leone film up to that time, adding an extra layer of irony to what was at once Leone's most comic and his most serious film.

In both *Once Upon a Time in the West* and *Duck, You Sucker!*, Morricone gives the chorus more hymn-like melodies; indeed, through all six films, echoes of chant and liturgical music ironically underscore the moral fatalism and terrible beauty/violence of Leone's world. Such usage suggests, perhaps, the sacredness of the material, and reaffirms the elemental nature of theme, character, and confrontation in Leone's vision. Certainly the religious tone of much of the music serves to amplify the omnipresence of Leone's "joking Jesus" religious imagery. So thoroughly ingrained in Morricone's music is this liturgical strain that the composer parodies it himself (with a farcically upbeat extension of Gregorian chant in his main theme for the latter-day Italian Western *La Vita a volta è molto dura, vero Provvidenza?*).

Once Upon a Time in America is, of necessity, Morricone's most eclectic Leone score, tied as it is to the popular music of three distinct periods in modern American history. Morricone grounds his score in the hot jazz of the Prohibition era, but taps three popular songs to earmark the film's three times. J. M. La Calle's "Amapola," perhaps the biggest hit of 1924, is Deborah's favorite tune for eurhythmic dancing, and becomes, tacitly, "our song" for her ill-fated relationship with Noodles. The Beatles' "Yesterday" (1966) bridges the film's first time-jump, from 1933 to 1968; Morricone places it evocatively behind Noodles's last talk with Max at the end of the film. Bracketing the film—and associated with the December 1933 scenes—is Kate Smith's famous rendition of Irving Berlin's "God Bless America." The song, having been composed in 1918 but not performed publicly until Miss Smith introduced it on Armistice Day, 1938, is the only anachronistic use of music in the score. Chronology be damned, though: Leone wanted the song at the beginning and end of the film because it keys us to the intended irony in his ambitious approach to his subject.

Period music notwithstanding, however, the near-religious theme of Morricone's later scores is pervasive in the original music for *Once Upon a Time in America*. The primitive sound of the pan-pipe melds with Hebraic themes to evoke a sense of the community of Jewish immigrants. And, as in every Leone score since Indio's mob hauled that safe out of El Paso in *For a Few Dollars More*, the female voice is used in crucial passages. Particularly evocative is Morricone's use of soprano harmony. He includes it in his reprise of the title theme when—at the end of the film—Noodles draws on the opium pipe—a suggestion, perhaps, of the unattained ideal that provokes that final, haunting grin.

Beyond merely extending Leone's quasi-religious style and imagery, the music is at its most reverential when it achieves the delicate timelessness (I've already borrowed Mircea Eliade's phrase "sacred time" for it) that informs Leone's strangest moments. The pre-gundown montages, of course, are examples that immediately come to mind—the audacious "Ecstasy of Gold" sequence at Sad Hill Cemetery is an excellent illustration, too. But so is "Sundown," from earlier in *The Good, the Bad and the Ugly*—a strangely holy-sounding music to accompany our first glimpse of the heinous villain with the strangely holy name. Before guitar ripplings send the tonality scurrying in all directions, acoustic guitar and a pedal chord in the strings create a movingly beautiful figure as Angeleyes rides ominously toward Stevens's farmhouse (a musical moment so powerful that Quentin Tarantino reused it to score his visual evocation of Ford's *The Searchers* in *Kill Bill Volume 2*). And then there's "The Strong," a slow trumpet tune supported by mixed chorus. The melody is embattled by fragmentary major-key bugle calls and overpowered by the basically mournful quality of the lead theme, which, accompanying a military advance, creates the ironic sense of an army already defeated (a variation of the same music is used for the entry of the "Carriage of the Spirits" into Tuco's and Blondie's destiny in the desert). The "Mesa Verde" passage in *Duck, You Sucker!* (whose title, on the album, is mistakenly translated into English as "Green Table") underscores the quasi-religious nature of Juan's devotion to his bank-robbing dream and to the shattering of his illusions about the town (which he finds filled with firing squads, madness, and death). The title theme of *Once Upon a Time in America* and the score's slower version of "Friends" achieve the same kind of ironic majesty.

At last, and forever, there are the final moments of *Once Upon a Time in the West*: The main title theme broods quietly, then begins to grow slowly to an overpowering crescendo as the camera cranes up and away from Jill and the workers to catch that last glimpse of Harmonica with the body of Cheyenne. The camera-work and music broaden our vision of the little station destined to become a city and of the glorious never-was West that Leone and Morricone continually conspire to create and celebrate. If ever there was a musical crane shot, this is it—a cinematic and musical apotheosis that is surely the most masterful moment of two masterful, and inexorably intertwined, careers.

"You Know Music—and You Can Count"

Bob Robertson and Joe Green

> Opera is not a theater of action. It is a theater of contemplation. What interests us in opera is not what happens, it is what people think about before something happens or after it happens.
>
> —Gian-Carlo Menotti

> It took a long time to understand why I like *Once Upon a Time in the West.* It's an extension of opera, the Italian theatrical tradition. The music, the framing, the camera movement, the bigger-than-myth epic characters and story are opera. The Italians are not making Westerns; they're making opera for today. That's why the music is so important in all of his films.
>
> —Martin Scorsese

> One critic called *Once Upon a Time in the West* "an opera in which arias are not sung but stared."
>
> —Christopher Frayling

> The intent is operatic, but the effect is soporific.
>
> —*Time* review of *Once Upon a Time in the West*

> Like Visconti, Leone's style is operatic, and fortunately it also is very sturdy.
>
> —Kevin Thomas,
> *Los Angeles Times*

Sooner or later, everyone who writes about Leone calls him "operatic." But what does that mean? In what sense are his films like operas (if they are)?

Certainly music is integral to the Leone films; Leone's heavy reliance on music to convey mood and build suspense reflects his awareness of that. The most important events in Leone's films are always prepared for—and held back—by long, *arioso* musical passages, calling to mind that operatic cliché, the interminable singing death scene.

The integrality of music—indeed, the essential musicality of the whole narrative process in Leone's films—is clear from this description of the making of *Once Upon a Time in the West,* from an interview with Leone:

> I shot *Once Upon a Time in the West* (contrary to the practice of my previous films) when Morricone had already completed his music. Throughout the shooting schedule we listened to the recordings. Everyone acted with the music, followed its rhythm, and suffered with its "aggravating" qualities, which grind the nerves.

This is music in service of a greater totality, music as a means not an end—the very attitude for which Nietzsche took Wagner to task: "'Music is always a mere means': That was his theory, that above all the only practice open to him. But no musician would think that way." Leone certainly approaches Wagner, in his mythic sensibility, his thirst for grandeur, his audacity, and his unshakable confidence in the importance of his own work. But Wagner, if anything, was anti-operatic, insisting on his works as "music drama," declaring himself as having gone beyond opera, much as Brecht later went beyond theatre. Leone, on the other hand, evidenced no desire to transcend or even transform the movies, but seemed only to pursue the perfection of his own style and vision. Despite his Wagnerian aspects, Sergio Leone was inescapably the child of the Italian operatic tradition.

His stories, for example, are not the transcendent tales of love and redemption that characterize the Romantic tradition, and they are not the emotional depictions of human relationships around which German and French opera and literature were built. They are the classically based tales of destiny, revenge, betrayal, obsession, and madness that sprang from the Attic stage to form the basis first of Italian Renaissance poetry and eventually of Italian opera. Beneath the surface, Leone's stories are all twice-told tales; hence their overhanging sense of fate, of a predestined outcome.

Structurally, too, Leone's films show operatic roots: The Italian grand opera form, against which Wagner and his disciples rebelled, developed from a marriage of the oratorio and the stage drama, and was built around a succession of individual exchanges among relatively few major characters: duets, trios, quartets, and—rarely—quintets and sextets. Choral scenes are the establishing shots and end-title flourishes of Italian opera. From the *bel canto* era onward, Italian opera emphasized the moment rather than the flow, the scene rather than the story. This was due partly to the limitations of the stage, but more to a classical view of time as a succession of isolated compartments or moments. No longer is time a continuous, never-freezing movement, as Romantic apologists like Wagner, and later Bergson, insisted. If ever a film-maker compartmentalized time, that person is Sergio Leone.

The opera, first and foremost, of course, is spectacle. Until the movies came along, opera was the great synthetic art form, the hybrid that combined all other art forms: acting, mime, dance, song, orchestral music, architecture, painting, sculpture, costume, masks, makeup, lighting, and poetry. Verdi and Boito recognized that with the sheer width and depth of stage spectacle must come a simplification of story and character: Opera could not treat character psychologically as literature and drama could; and, without a Wagnerian revision, the form could not admit the leisurely exposition of character, motivation, and philosophy found on the German stage.

That simplifying process created genres of great diversity. Mostly, grand opera was tragedy of the most morbid sort, emphasizing violence, treachery, madness, and death. When it was comic it was *buffa*, farcical, earthy. And certainly Leone's own stark mixture of the broadest comedy with the most intimate violence exemplified an effort to resynthesize that same simplistic dichotomy. In the same way, one can detect in Leone's work traces of the influence of other Italian masters.

His emphasis on details of costume, property, and decor recall the *verismo* of Leoncavallo and Mascagni, who joined the simplistic love-and-treachery tragedy to "realistic" contemporary characters and situations, thereby stressing internal as well as external motivation. His tendency to overstate the importance of moments of emotion, conviction, or decision recalls the sentimentality of Puccini—with whom Leone shares a rabid interest in American themes, and whose opera *La Fanciulla del West* has often been cited as an influence on Western movies, both American and Italian. Its plot, adapted from David Belasco's play, contains a number of themes and images reiterated in Leone's work: the outlaw-hero; the bad-guy lawman; the good-hearted saloon-keeper; the romantic "Eternal Feminine" manifest in a woman who is a ministering angel to lonely, hardworking men; the cigar as an emblem of character; a bandit named Ramerrez who goes by the pseudonym Johnson and is called "Mr. Sacramento" by the sheriff; a game of poker on which a life depends; a rescue from the noose. Morricone's work for Leone—and for other Italian Westerns—was profoundly influenced by Puccini's liberal incorporation of folksongs, rags, and the Cuban bolero into the score.

But, unquestionably, the one who had it all was Giuseppe Verdi. This operatic genius was a master of music, of spectacle, of characterization, of drama, of both tragedy and comedy. Advocating neither Wagnerism nor *verismo*, he was able to treat his characters intelligently and sensitively through music alone, and his naive characters, primitive plots, and simple themes are only deceptively so. Like Leone's.

Of course Leone himself would have had little patience with all this. When Noel Simsolo prefaced an interview question with the remark "Music is important to Italians," Leone cut him off:

> Italians hate music! People talk about Italy as if it were a country of people who are music-mad; that's entirely false! We are one of the most underdeveloped countries in that area.

This iconoclastic comment may have been intended more as shock value than cultural analysis. Few are the Italians who have not heard of Verdi—an artist with political ideals, a patriotic democrat who fused passion with values and whose artistic vision espoused a morality of emotion, not of law. Leone, though he hardly enjoyed in his time the hero worship his countrymen gave Verdi, nevertheless exemplified a twentieth-century version of the Verdi vision by including in his movies spectacle, virtuoso artistry, deceptive simplicity, mythic power, the replacement of decadent structures of authority with a code of

ethics based on raw will and gut response, and the willingness to be political—
or anti-political—as the situation demanded.

If Leone had lived a hundred years earlier, he'd have written, or at least
staged, operas. If Verdi had lived a hundred years later, he'd have been making
movies. Maybe even Westerns. Maybe he'd have signed his first one "Joe
Green."

"There's a Hole in the Roof"

Sergio Leone—Catholic Filmmaker

Fairy tales also abound in religious motifs; many Biblical stories are of the same nature as fairy tales.

—Bruno Bettelheim
The Uses of Enchantment

We profit from evil: Let us at least know that it is evil from which we profit. Or—what comes to the same thing—let us expel evil, but at the same time acknowledge that its expulsion does not leave us with clean hands.

—Eric Rohmer and Claude Chabrol
Hitchcock

I've related Sergio Leone's Western vision to the Hollywood cowboy mythos, to the Graeco-Roman tradition of Titans and Olympians, and to the Norse myth of the fall of the gods. But so far I've only hinted at the most pervasive mythic context of Leone's films: the Christian—and specifically Roman Catholic—mythos. Is Sergio Leone a "Catholic director" in the sense in which, for example, Rohmer and Chabrol found Hitchcock to be one?

Certainly the most immediate evidence of Leone's own acknowledgment of the Catholic milieu is the proliferation of Christian iconography in his films. Even the nominally Judaic atmosphere of *Once Upon a Time in America* abounds with it. What follows is a representative—and by no means exhaustive—catalogue of key examples.

A Fistful of Dollars
> A loner rides into town on a mule
> A "Holy Family" with a child named Jesus
> A bell ringer named Juan de Dios
> A mock resurrection in No Name's cemetery ruse
> A symbolic Passion of the Christ in No Name's torture and apparent resurrection

For a Few Dollars More
> The opening shot of a Bible
> An emphasis on bells
> Indio's hideaway in a church, a pseudo-monastery
> Indio explains his plan in a sermon from the pulpit

Manco and Mortimer shoot apples off a tree
The spirit of a woman (Virgin?) haunts the film

The Good, the Bad and the Ugly
The Last Supper: I: Stevens killed at meal table by Angeleyes
"A golden-haired angel watches over that boy"
Ordeals in the desert: Tuco's, then Blondie's
Tuco's frequent and emphatic sign of the cross
Tuco casts himself as Christ to Blondie's Judas
The "confession" of the dying Bill Carson
The monastery
The "resurrection" of Blondie
The Last Supper: II: Tuco treated to a meal before being savaged by
    Corporal Wallace
The shared "confession" of Tuco and Blondie under the bridge
The gold in the grave: symbol of a triumph over death
The triangular gunfight and the one unloaded gun: Free Will vs. Pre-
    destination
Tuco's predicament at the end: a neat linking of Christ's cross with
    Adam's tree

Once Upon a Time in the West
Harmonica's "resurrection" after the opening gundown
The Last Supper: III: the McBain wedding feast
Harmonica as Christ to Jill's Magdalene
Cheyenne casts himself as Christ to Harmonica's Judas
The symbolic crucifixion of Harmonica as a boy

Duck, You Sucker!
Sean and Juan: two Catholics named John
Sean: Christ as revolutionary
Juan and his niños: disciples
Massacre of Juan's niños: the slaughter of the innocents

My Name Is Nobody
Nobody in the water, catching a fish with his hands
Nobody's godlike manipulation of Beauregard's actions
Recurring patterns of three
Beauregard's faked death and "resurrection"
Crosses in the cemetery

Once Upon a Time in America
Emphasis on a community of men
The Eve/Mary ambivalence toward women
The assertion of free will over predestination
Immersion in water as a renewal ritual

Max, Judas to Noodles's Christ, lets Noodles think it was the other way
around
Max's "resurrection"—and Noodles's, too
Life-in-death: the woman in the coffin
Max's "confession" and search for penance

All this Christian imagery is not incidental, but the inevitable correlative of
a Christian dialogue. Leone's characters, like Jesus Christ, spend a lot of time
talking in parables and sayings. In *The Good, the Bad and the Ugly*, where the
Christian imagery seems most insistent, "There are two kinds of people in the
world" is scarcely different from "The Kingdom of Heaven is like a man who
had two sons." In fact, to stay with that particular example for just a moment,
the tale of Tuco and his brother, the monastery priest, is a twisted retelling of the
Parable of the Prodigal Son: here the two brothers compete for the position of
greatest credit with respect to their now-dead parents. Like the Good Son and
the Prodigal Son, Tuco and Padre Ramirez are "two kinds of people," their opposition epitomizing the balanced opposition of character types that obtains
throughout Leone's work. Bettelheim's comment on this phenomenon in fairy
tales is relevant:

> In other fairy tales in which two protagonists—usually brothers—stand for
> seemingly incompatible aspects of the human personality, the two usually
> separate after an original period of having been united, and have different
> fates. The two figures symbolize opposite aspects of our nature, impelling us
> to act in contrary ways.

In the context of the Christian mythos, this tendency to divide personality
into two divergent characters, then chart their oppositions, reconciliations, and
eventual fates, reflects the eternal dualism of body and soul, right and wrong,
good and bad, Heaven and Hell, absolute freedom and absolute determinism. It
also suggests the importance of seeing *The Good, the Bad and the Ugly* as a
parable about Tuco, who, as "Ugly," steers a middle course through the dualistic
extremes. Tuco is for part of the film an ironic inversion of the Good Samaritan,
trying to keep Blondie alive after having tried to kill him—combining bad and
good in one. Just as *For a Few Dollars More*, touted as the "sequel" to *A Fistful
of Dollars*, turned out to be about Colonel Mortimer, not about the Man with No
Name, so *The Good, the Bad and the Ugly* turns out not to be about the Good
Blondie or the Bad Angeleyes, but about Tuco.

The Catholic dichotomy between the material world of death and the spiritual world of life everlasting is grounded in the notion that the material world is
inherently defective. The doctrine of Original Sin locates this flaw not in the
nature of mutability—where Buddhism and Hinduism find it—but in the nature
of human beings. The sin of Eden did not create this flaw. There must have been
an inherent defect that made the sin possible in the first place, an inherent defect
the same as the one that made the sin of Lucifer possible: a tendency to pride, a
will to be godlike, even to be God—and, failing that, to play at being God. This
is the original flaw in the fabric, from which proceeds the notion of depravity—

man's propensity toward evil—as well as the perception of his life as a "vale of tears" in which misfortune and misery win out and only those who endure the sufferings and surmount the tendency toward evil with a willful commitment to good, will achieve eternal happiness.

The inevitable conclusion drawn from the perception of material reality as "fallen man in a fallen world" is one of universal guilt, guilt that is (as Rohmer and Chabrol observed in the films of Hitchcock) readily transferable from one human being to another merely by virtue of everyone's being human. "It's a small world," Mortimer tells Wild in Agua Caliente, and the hunchback replies, definitively, "Yes—and very, very bad." But the badness is undeniably attractive. In literature and film, evil has always been more interesting than good—something that has more to do with the nature and purpose of art than with any universal truth about evil or human nature. The bad guys always get the meatiest roles; one of the basic attractions of Leone's films is not that his heroes are, in a relative way, good, but that *all* his characters are in some way bad. The bare-bones moral order of Leone's world is, after all, amorality, and that is one of the chief reasons these films convey such a sense of fancy. Reacting as he does against the guilt-centered ethos of Catholicism, Leone fantasizes a world in which one may sin without guilt or accountability. In such a world, of course, one takes one's chances and runs the risk of being more sinned against than sinning. Leone's characters are, in one sense, metaphoric gods but in another sense are human beings playing God—with varying degrees of success.

Of course, the prerequisite to playing this game is free will. Leone's characters actively choose their deeds. Only very rarely is fate thrust upon them (as, for example, when the carriage of the dead miraculously appears with its message of hope at just the moment Tuco is about to finish Blondie off). These men—good and bad—are no shilly-shallying hand washers. There is no room in their world for the likes of Wobbles, no messing with Mr. In-Between. The emphasis on a commitment to a position, however extreme, is reflected in Leone's penchant for intercutting long shots with closeups, avoiding the comparatively dull middle distance. What Rohmer and Chabrol wrote about Hitchcock's vision is true here, too:

> Evil hides not only under the appearance of Good, but in our most casual and innocent acts, those we think have no ethical significance, those which in principle involve no responsibility. The criminals in this universe are attractively portrayed only so that they can better denounce the Pilates, which in one way or another we all are.

At times, Leone has stood this world on its head, choosing to conceal good under the appearance of evil, rather than doing the reverse. For example, the conscienceless wholesale bounty killer of the Eastwood films emerges as "good" in spite of himself, and a certain sympathy is felt even for heinous child-murderers like Indio and Frank.

The exercise of free will is necessary to the Catholic view of man, for if man is inexorably fated by his very nature, what meaning is there to the rewards of Heaven and the punishments of Hell? One cannot choose good if one cannot choose at all; so, though the outcome is foreknown by God, choice and action are free, determined only by the individual's will.

This is a crucial bone of contention between Deborah and Noodles in *Once Upon a Time in America*. Deborah's editorialized parodying of the "Song of Solomon" concludes, "He is altogether lovable, but he'll always be a two-bit punk, so he'll never be my beloved—what a shame." But she is really criticizing Noodles's own sense of predetermined self-damnation, which she sees as something he freely chooses and could escape if he wanted to. In Fat Moe's speakeasy, Noodles, just returned from prison, is mildly disappointed to learn that it was Moe, not Deborah, who counted the days and remembered when Noodles was getting out. As Deborah dwells on the length of his sentence, Noodles interjects, "It wasn't my choice," to which she counters, "Yes, it was. It still is." (Modern psychology, of course, argues that the individual's will is illusory, itself determined by the sense of guilt and conscience imposed by moral frameworks like the Catholic Church. But it is precisely this kind of imposed moral order that Leone is escaping in the fairy-tale world of his films.) Blondie's adjustment of the odds in the final shootout at the cemetery in *The Good, the Bad and the Ugly* is a perfect metaphor for that eternal conflict between free will and determinism. No one can deny that Tuco acts freely and deliberately, even though the effects of his action are limited by Blondie's having unloaded his gun. Blondie has played God here (as throughout the film he is the "rope-cutter" who has power over Tuco's life and death). But his unloading of the gun has in no way limited Tuco's freedom to draw when he wants to and to fire at whomever he wishes. The importance of this scene rests in Tuco's *not knowing* his gun is empty. His lack of foreknowledge (also imposed on the viewer) makes him capable of acting freely, no matter how illusory that freedom may be.

No one knows whether God throws us all, or some of us, into the arena with unloaded guns. But as long as we perceive our actions to be free, they are free. Divine foreknowledge does not constitute predestination. And who should be in a better position to propound that most Catholic of notions than a film director, whose very stock-in-trade is the manipulation of equal parts determination, foreknowledge, free will, and accident?

Of course the great metaphor for human guilt and fallibility in this fallen world is sexuality. It is the most obvious example of man's tendency to embrace the flesh for its own sake, and it places us at our most vulnerable. Is it an accident that the Original Sin of Adam and Eve has been so frequently represented as a sin of sexuality? Woman's temptation of man and the resulting sexual congress has long been the popular image for that too-abstract notion of "eating the fruit of the Tree of Knowledge of Good and Evil"—a notion that implies, as the anti-Christian Nietzsche did much later, that morality is its own punishment. The penalty for the godlike discovery of good and evil is to have to live under a moral code—to live, in other words, with guilt.

This mythos and ethos are first represented by Leone in *For a Few Dollars More*, during which a transgression of a sexual nature, lost now in the dim-remembered past, has created a world of guilt and obsession for both Indio and Mortimer. The young woman's suicide is for Indio a psychological castration that perverts his already gross sexuality into the sadism of an Estéban Rojo. Indio's fetish with the locket combines death (both the dead woman and his "vice of killing" other innocents as well) with his own failed sexuality and with the characteristically Catholic idealization of woman.

This idealization, as well as the condemnation of those who would violate womanhood, is seen often in Leone's films, from Ramón Rojo's violation of Marisol and disruption of her holy family, through Indio's unspeakable crime and Angeleyes' abuse of Bill Carson's abandoned sweetheart, to the canonization of the Magdalene-like Jill and the flashback depiction of Sean Mallory's lost Irish girlfriend as a kind of Eve before the Fall. Whatever Leone may say about his contempt for the "world without balls" created at the end of *Once Upon a Time in the West*, his respect—even reverence—for womanhood is apparent.

Produced in an era of unprecedented sexual freedom on the screen, his films before *Once Upon a Time in America* worked against the tide by scrupulously avoiding the depiction of any kind of sexual activity. What little sexual interest there is, Leone renders with an almost prudish reserve: Ramón's relationship with Marisol is demonstrated only in public terms; the impassive masculinity of Manco is expressed in a deliberately comic sequence (again public) with the hotel's oversexed landlady; the flashbacks revealing Indio's rape of Mortimer's sister are so tastefully done that many first-time viewers don't understand what's going on in the scene; the apparent sexual aggression of Harmonica's tearing away the bodice of Jill's dress is immediately excused as utility; Frank and Jill are more involved in talking than in having sex during their bed scene, where Leone's staging and camera—not the characters' sexual activity—determine who dominates and who submits; Jill's past as a prostitute is soft-pedaled and vindicated by Cheyenne's association of her with his revered (though not inviolate) mother; Juan Miranda's masculine sexual aggression is conveyed comically in his taurine stalking and mounting of a shocked and squealing aristocratic dame.

All this changes in *Once Upon a Time in America*, where sexual activity is blunt, direct, and brutal, a mirror of the violence Leone sees inherent in twentieth-century American life. But Deborah and Carol, unwilling and willing victims, respectively, of Noodles's violent sexuality, are given their dignity; Noodles remains more pathetic than tragic, the one Leone protagonist who commands virtually no respect on or offscreen. His violent approach to women ultimately excludes them—and, with them, the chance for family—from his world, solidifying his dependency on the pseudo-monastic community of male friends.

Even when Leone's heroes and antiheroes talk about sex, which is rare, they employ low humor of an anal-scatological bent, seldom genital—and, more often, they eschew both for a kind of high wit, an intellectual flirting with one another. Leone's Western characters are celibate ascetics, priests of violence residing in almost monastic communities: the house of the Rojos; Indio's abandoned church; a mission-turned-hospital; a Union prison camp. Pointedly, the loner-hero always absents himself from the community, particularly at bedtime. Even in the casualty-filled mission, Blondie somehow gets a private room, and his shaky partnership with Angeleyes is his ticket out of the concentration camp. Shortly afterward, Blondie deserts the company of Angeleyes' men to reunite with Tuco. And recall the resentment of Noodles's friends when he returns from his failed tryst with Deborah and his several days in the opium den.

The image of the male community weaves itself throughout Leone's films: The Rojos and their gang, the Baxters (with one matriarchal exception), Indio's gang, the Confederate and Union armies, Angeleyes' gang, the prisoners of war, the gang of men who work for Frank and Morton, Cheyenne's men, various gatherings in saloons and taverns, Juan's niños, the band of revolutionaries, the four horsemen of *Once Upon a Time in America*. It's a distinctly monastic brand of Catholicism that substitutes a community of male strangers for the traditional family circle (which is consistently disrupted in Leone's films): The image is crystallized in the mission scenes, during which Tuco argues with his monk-brother about familial responsibility and offers (however insincerely) to be Blondie's "family." In *Once Upon a Time in America*, Max's identification of Noodles as his uncle becomes a running gag and a mainstay of their relationship.

Though the preeminence of family is negatively expressed in Leone's films (which depict the disruption and restoration or replacement of the traditional family), family as an ideal is nonetheless integral to the films' vision—the logical extension of the Catholic insistence that sexuality is for procreative purposes only. Family is the goal. Those who express their sexuality in anti-familial ways are identifiable villains. Police Chief Aiello, in *Once Upon a Time in America*, for all his shortcomings, epitomizes male-dominant, family-centered Catholicism. He is outraged by the way Max's gang arbitrarily shifts children around, so much so perhaps, they are never to be reunited with their true parents. Noodles's sexuality never has anything to do with family, and Max's fathering of a son seems to have been accomplished in spite of himself—more as an extension of his usurpation of Noodles's life than as the result of any domestic motivations of his own.

The worst outrage against family is, of course, child-murder: Cheyenne, in *Once Upon a Time in the West*, declares that killing a child is as bad as killing a priest. Frank's slaughter of the McBains—an Irish Catholic family—is a contemporary echo of his earlier violation of Harmonica's family by using the boy as instrument of his brother's execution. This propensity toward family-destroying murder is but the flip side of Frank's sexuality, which he uses as a weapon in the power struggle with Jill for control of the McBain land—another violation of the privilege of family.

In *Duck, You Sucker!*, Juan rapes the coach passenger only after establishing that her husband cannot "make a baby." Both husband and victim are objects of comic contempt, emblems of the sterile aristocracy who would set themselves above the simple religion and familial ways of the peasantry. Juan is a buffoon-bandit, nothing more, so at this point in the evolution of Leone's "world without balls" a lighthearted view of psychotic, sexual violence becomes the norm. *Once Upon a Time in America*, even though it opposes the Catholic reverence for woman in the ideal, reiterates the Mary-vs.-Eve syndrome: Real women are at least ridiculed—and often condemned and "punished"—for being less than the perfect objects of worship envisioned in Catholic literature and art, as well as for carrying with them the guilt of having tempted Adam into Original Sin.

All this, of course, results from confusing symbol with reality. For Original Sin is rooted not in carnality but in the more serious of the two great theological sins, presumption. Presumption is the conviction that one is saved, and will prevail, regardless of one's actions. Of this great sin, Ramón Rojo, Angeleyes, Frank, and Max are clearly guilty, and each is distinctly and emphatically surprised at the end he comes to. The other theological sin, despair, is the hallmark of that obverse Catholicism known as Jansenism—an austere Catholicism considered by orthodox theologians to be Calvinist in nature. Jansenism stresses the necessity of the Church for salvation; it preaches a kind of predestination that limits human freedom in a way that divine foreknowledge does not, by scrupulously discouraging frequent participation in the Sacraments. Despair is the notion that one's fate—good or ill—is sealed, regardless of one's actions; in the Catholic context it takes the extreme form of feeling irredeemably unworthy. Indio and Noodles are the principal proponents of despair in Leone's world, though John Baxter and a number of other minor characters are similarly tainted.

Both of these sins are, of course, variations on the one self-centered primordial sin of pride. It is through pride—or lack of it—that the good and the bad among Leone's characters are distinguished. The good characters have—or learn—a kind of humility: No Name rides a mule, and he's soft-spoken, even self-effacing; Manco acknowledges Mortimer's righteousness and bows to his moment of justification; Blondie ministers to the dying Union officer and to the dying Confederate soldier-boy; Harmonica keeps to himself, helps Jill as it serves his purpose to do so, acts in his own behalf when the time is right, and graciously bows out of human affairs when his hour is past; Jill learns to carry water and tolerate the fleeting touches of the railroad men; Juan carries on his continual dialogue with God; Sean learns from his own flashbacks to "judge not, lest ye be judged." It's hard to find a "good" character in *Once Upon a Time in America*, but after thirty-five years of anonymity, Max and Noodles do acquire a certain mildness. Anonymity is a kind of built-in humility, a disclaimer of self-interest, a disclaimer, in fact, of self. The Eastwood characters are, of course, interested in money; but money is usually seen as a metaphoric goal, an easy excuse for actions that might otherwise be viewed as too plainly and embarrassingly Messianic, or too simply and obviously devoted to the elimination of the bad guys.

Other safeguards against overweening pride are such exercises in humility as confession and participation in the other Sacraments of the Church. Rohmer and Chabrol quote Jacques Rivette apropos Hitchcock's *Under Capricorn*:

> The secret subject of this drama is confession, the liberation from a secret, liberation in its double meaning: in the psychoanalytical sense, because it frees us from memory by giving memory a verbal form, and in the religious sense; in this case the confession of sins is the same as their redemption.

Certainly there is no end to secret-sharing in Leone's films: In *A Fistful of Dollars*, No Name and Silvanito know about Ramón's massacre of the *federales* and about No Name's subsequent graveyard ruse; Silvanito and the coffinmaker know the secret of No Name's hiding place; during the final reels of *For a Few Dollars More*, Manco and Mortimer know where the money is hidden; in *The Good, the Bad and the Ugly*, the dying Bill Carson confesses half his secret about the gold to Tuco and half to Blondie; Jill and Brett McBain keep their marriage (and Jill's past) a secret in *Once Upon a Time in the West*; Cheyenne and Harmonica are a secret alliance in that film, as are Sean and Juan in *Duck, You Sucker!*; Max makes a final confession to Noodles in their last reunion in *Once Upon a Time in America*.

In Leone's films, a confessional atmosphere always accompanies the sharing of secrets. Witness, for example, the embarrassment and difficulty with which Tuco blurts out his half of the secret after he and Blondie, before dynamiting the bridge, agree to tell what they know; or the last-rites desperation of Bill Carson that makes him live long enough to tell all about the gold, even though doing so can no longer profit him. And witness especially Leone's use of flashbacks in three of the films; the technique allows the secret of a long-buried guilt to be confessed to us, the viewers, but not to the characters in the film. The flashbacks in *For a Few Dollars More* and *Once Upon a Time in the West* are implicitly shared between two characters. Sean's secret in *Duck, You Sucker!*, however, is purely between him and us. Confessions are so in evidence in Leone's films, and so frequently unmotivated, that the act of confessing becomes not a means but an end in itself—perhaps its own redemption, as Rivette wrote of Henrietta's confession in *Under Capricorn*. There is doubtless some truth to the old adage, for it seems confession is good for the soul.

Similarly, Leone reserves special time and space for the taking of sustenance, an emphasis that can be related to the importance of the "bread of life" in Christian symbolism. Last Suppers are everywhere: The association of wining and dining in the face of subsequent violence and death occurs at least incidentally in every film, and integrally in most; this association mirrors precisely the Roman Catholic Mass and its linkage of sacramental banquet with sacrificial slaying.

To the Jansenist insistence that the Church is necessary for salvation, Leone reacts with another negative emphasis. The importance of the Church as order is expressed offhandedly by his creation of a world in which there is no established order, and in which—not coincidentally—there are no churches. Empty churches, ruins of churches, bell towers without churches, yes—all reminders of the *absence* of moral order. In the modern-world setting of *Once Upon a Time in America*, business is allied with crime, authorities are corrupt, and religious worship remains an offscreen activity attended by extras. When churches appear in Leone's films, they do so with heavy irony: Tuco's brother's mission is filled with dead and dying soldiers—a stinging vision of the failure of church-based ethical structure. Leone's vision of the absence of organized religion and its attendant lack of moral discipline embraces a two-edged sword: on the one hand the absence of organized religion means the absence, too, of inhibition and guilt, and the restoration of absolute freedom; on the other hand, the absence means lack of grace.

But where God no longer acts, the film director still does. Leone himself has conferred grace on certain of his characters; and by doing that he has brought back a kind of moral order to the stripped-down world of his own imagining. "Salvation," Rohmer and Chabrol note in passing, "can be obtained only through the combined interplay of ... Providence and free will." In other words, grace may be bestowed deus ex machina (as evidenced by the critically timed arrival of the carriage of the dead in *The Good, the Bad and the Ugly*, for example) or it may be earned (the honor accorded Frank in his final moments in *Once Upon a Time in the West* and even, perhaps, Noodles in the more hopeless world of *Once Upon a Time in America*). In either case, it is the central and necessary miracle upon which the whole Roman Catholic doctrine of salvation depends.

The miracle making grace possible is that God became man, walked among men as a superior example, took upon himself the universal guilt of mankind, suffered the tortures and death necessitated by the condition of Original Sin, and then rose from the dead and ascended into Heaven, leaving mankind the promise of deliverance, release from guilt, and life everlasting. Resurrection images are ubiquitous in Leone's films; the high-angle shots with which most of them end and the rising motion as the hero departs toward the top of the frame in the first four movies are nothing if not symbolic ascensions.

Unlikely? Leone's pistol-packing Christ-figures (No Name in *A Fistful of Dollars*, Tuco and Blondie at different times in *The Good, the Bad and the Ugly*, Cheyenne and Harmonica at different times in *Once Upon a Time in the West*, Sean in *Duck, You Sucker!*) are not so much far-fetched as they are too literal depictions of the Jesus who said, "I bring not peace but a sword"—the revolutionary Ur-Communist of Pasolini's *The Gospel According to Saint Matthew*, and of much other Italian film and literature. Consider: Into a fallen world comes a presence—imposing yet soft-spoken, provocative yet enigmatic in act and word, humble yet possessing supernormal skill and endurance. This one comments and teaches, fights and resists, is tortured and suffers, is lost but returns to destroy the forces of evil, and finally, having restored the world to its rightful inheritors, the meek, departs in a symbolic ascension. This is the redemption in abstract, and it more or less fits the storyline of every Leone film. *For a Few Dollars More* and *Once Upon a Time in America* are perhaps exceptions, having a consciousness more of the Old Testament than the New.

Mortimer is an avenging God of wrath, and only at the end of the film is there a suggestion that, Christ-like, he takes the burden of human guilt onto his own weary shoulders. The Jewish gangsters of *Once Upon a Time in America* understand only the power of violence, which they practice with the avidity of an inverted "chosen people." In the Old Testament moral order, salvation is the result of humility, self-denial, Job-like recognition of the futility of resistance, Abraham's commitment to absolute faith in an all-powerful God. Only in the New Testament do love of neighbor and good works enter the picture—in *For a Few Dollars More* and *Once Upon a Time in America*, there are no immediately recognizable acts of kindness or charity to a stranger.

Tuco is certainly Leone's most unlikely Christ-figure, but there he is: He shares with Christ the quality of being a member of a Trinity (the middle member, in fact, if the Italian title is borne in mind). Tuco undergoes an ordeal in the desert, has a Last Supper, suffers torture, is resurrected from imminent death several times, is judged and symbolically crucified, and at last is delivered, to enjoy a rich reward. Blondie, of course, is the more active and typical Christ-figure in the film; so in a sense the dynamics of the film involve two possible Christs. In *Once Upon a Time in the West*, we once again see an interplay of two Christ-figures: Harmonica has a resurrection, a crucifixion (in flashback), and an ascension; Cheyenne literally compares himself with Christ after the auction, casting Harmonica in the role of Judas.

A critical feature of redemption is, of course, recognition of the redeemer: it is through recognition that Leone, film director, confers a kind of redemption on even his most reprehensible characters. The sympathy Leone bestows on the tormented Indio and the strong but ultimately self-betraying Frank has already been pointed out, as has the dignity accorded Villega and even Angeleyes in their final moments. But for the definitive redemption it's best to return to the source, the seminal Leone Christ-film, *A Fistful of Dollars*.

The shield that No Name wears as he faces Ramón Rojo helps him—metaphorically—hedge the bet. The shield is No Name's "divinity," and in that divinity lies the power of foreknowledge as well as No Name's assurance that he can't be killed. The certainty doesn't prevent Ramón from freely trying—and try he must—to kill No Name, just as the unloaded gun did not prevent Tuco from trying to fire. Leone places great emphasis both on the moment of No Name's revelation and on his removal of the shield where Ramón's seven shots—any one of which could have been fatal—are implanted perfectly around the spot that covered the heart. Once the shield is dropped, Ramón could fire again and have done with all this—but he doesn't: The recognition. There is something in his eyes as he looks at the man who walks toward him now. No Name kills Ramón's two henchmen. Ramón cringes, then straightens again. He's been left alive. Recognition returned: the moment of grace. No Name shoots the rope that binds Silvanito, liberating the victim of evil. Now he turns his attention to the agent of evil, who is not, himself, beyond redemption. As Ramón dies, Leone goes to an intimate subjective point-of-view, Ramón's look at his slayer/deliverer, his last look at the world and at the sky above. We share that death, from Ramón's angle, because we are Ramóns, and stand in the same relationship to the all-powerful—and merciful—God as Ramón does to the Man with No Name.

The coffinmaker has something he wants to say: "Joe, I want to …" But he only looks at the impassive hero and walks off, shaking his head: "Joe, Joe … " Gratitude—if that's what he had in mind—is not enough; is, in any case, unnecessary. The bell rings.

After telling Silvanito that it would be "too dangerous" to play man-in-the-middle between the Mexican and American armies, the Man with No Name rides out of San Miguel, headed for somewhere above the top of the frame.

No Name, Manco, Harmonica, and Sean—all these mesa messiahs and sagebrush saviors are the sons of one heavenly father only: One who redeemed his characters and his audiences, who redeemed an entire genre and a nearly lost mythos. Once upon a time, he called himself Bob Robertson.

APPENDICES

Chronology

Selected Highlights in the Career of Sergio Leone
January 3, 1929–April 30, 1989

1947   Begins work in films as crewman and bit actor

1958   *Nel signo di Roma* (*Sign of the Gladiator*): Co-scenarist and directorial assistant

1959   *Gli ultimi giorni di Pompei* (*The Last Days of Pompeii*): Co-scenarist, directorial assistant. Uncredited, finishes direction of the film as substitute for bedridden director Mario Bonnard

1961   *Il Colosso di Rodi* (*The Colossus of Rhodes*): Co-scenarist and director
Sodoma e Gomorra (*Sodom and Gomorrah*): Second-unit director to Robert Aldrich

1964   *Per un pugno di dollari* (*A Fistful of Dollars*): Co-scenarist and, as "Bob Robertson," director. The film is an overnight success, and American critics make "Spaghetti Western" a household word

1965   *Per qualche dollaro in più* (*For a Few Dollars More*): Co-scenarist and director

1966   *Il buono, il brutto, il cattivo* (*The Good, the Bad and the Ugly*): Co-scenarist and director

1968   *C'era una volta il West* (*Once Upon a Time in the West*): Co-scenarist and director

1971   *Giu' la testa* (*Duck, You Sucker!*; *Once Upon a Time the Revolution*): Co-scenarist and director. Leone was to produce only, for his newly founded company Rafran Cinematografica, and Peter Bogdanovich was to direct. When the collaboration failed, Leone stepped in once again to direct

1973   *Il mio nome e nessuno* (*My Name Is Nobody*): Story author and production supervisor (for Rafran)

1975   *Un genio, due compari e un pollo* (*A Genius*): Production supervisor (for Rafran)

1978   *Il Gatto* (*The Cat*): Production supervisor (for Rafran)

1979-81 Several false starts on *Once Upon a Time in America*, sporadic production efforts at Rafran

1982   *Once Upon a Time in America* begins filming in New York City

1984   *Once Upon a Time in America* released in three versions
Negotiations on *Leningrad* begin

1989   After many rumors and false starts, *Leningrad* is officially announced (February) as Sergio Leone's next film

Filmography

A FISTFUL OF DOLLARS (*Per un pugno di dollari*)

A Co-production of Jolly Films (Rome), Constantin Films (Munich), and Ocean Films (Madrid). American release: United Artists. 1964.

Direction: "Bob Robertson" (**Sergio Leone**). *Screenplay*: **Sergio Leone**, Duccio Tessari, Victor A. Catena, G. Schock, after a story by Toni Palombi; uncredited adaptation of Akira Kurosawa and Ryuzo Kikushima's story and screenplay for *Yojimbo* (1962). *Production Design*: "Charles Simons" (Carlo Simi). *Cinematography*: "Jack Dalmas" (Massimo Dallamano). *Editing*: "Bob Quintle" (Robert Cinquini). *Music*: "Dan Savio" (Ennio Morricone). *Production*: "Harry Colombo" (Arrigo Colombo) and "George Papi" (Giorgio Papi). Technicolor, Techniscope. Running time varies from 96 to 100 minutes, depending on the print.

Players

The Man with No Name ("Joe")	Clint Eastwood
Ramón Rojo	"John Wels" (Gian Maria Volontè)
Marisol	Marianne Koch
Silvanito, the innkeeper	José Calvo
John Baxter	Wolfgang Lukschy
Estéban Rojo	"S. Rupp" (Sieghardt Rupp)
Don Miguel Rojo	Antonio Prieto
Consuelo Baxter	Margherita Lozano
Julián, husband of Marisol	Daniel Martín
Rubio, a Rojo henchman	"Benny Reeves" (Benito Stefanelli)
Chico, a Rojo henchman	"Richard Stuyvesant" (Mario Brega)
Antonio Baxter	"Carol Brown" (Bruno Carotenuto)
Piripero	Josef Egger
Juan de Dios	Raf Baldassare
Rojo gang member	Aldo Sambrell

The Story

*In an introductory scene included in some American television prints and di-
rected by Monte Hellman, a convict is released from prison, with instructions
from a sheriff (Harry Dean Stanton) to "clean up" the town of San Miguel.*

A lone gunman rides into the town of San Miguel, which is near the American-
Mexican border. He sees a little boy crying "Mama" and trying to gain entry to a
hut. Brutish guards roughly drive the boy away. In town, the Man with No
Name meets Silvanito, operator of the cantina, who tells him that San Miguel is
a town torn by violence. Two families—the gun-running Baxters and the liquor-
dealing Rojos—are locked in a death struggle for control of the territory. Seeing
an opportunity to fill his purse, No Name "auditions" for Don Miguel Rojo by
picking a fight with four of Baxter's henchmen and shooting them all dead.
Rojo, impressed with No Name's skill and speed, hires him on. In the Rojo
house, No Name catches a fleeting glimpse of a woman, Marisol, who, No
Name learns, is being kept by Miguel's younger brother, Ramón Rojo, who has
forcibly separated her from her husband, Julián, and their small son, Jesus.

A detachment of Mexican soldiers is escorting a wagon which holds a mysterious cargo; the soldiers pass through town on their way to a rendezvous near the
border. No Name and Silvanito follow the soldiers to see what will happen. The
soldiers are massacred. Their wagonload of gold is stolen by a band of men led
by a ferocious sharpshooter whom Silvanito identifies as Ramón Rojo. Back in
town, Ramón is introduced to No Name by his brothers Miguel and Estéban.
Ramón announces his plan to settle a truce with the Baxter clan—ostensibly
because he wants peace, but really because he wants to avoid a federal investigation that might uncover his role in the slaughter of the soldiers and the theft of
the gold. Seeing his fortune slip away, No Name stirs the hornets' nest. He
moves two of the dead soldiers from the scene of the massacre to the nearby
cemetery, posing them as if they were alive. He then spreads word to both the
Baxters and the Rojos that at least two men survived the massacre and are hiding
in the cemetery. The Rojos make for the cemetery in order to silence the "survivors," while the Baxters head for the cemetery to try to get the goods on the Rojos. In the meantime, No Name raids the Rojos' stronghold, where he finds
Marisol and delivers the woman to the very interested Consuelo Baxter. Consuelo's son, Antonio, gets himself captured in the gun battle at the cemetery.
The next day a prisoner exchange is set up, the Baxters returning Marisol to the
Rojos in exchange for their son.

Ramón leaves town on another "business" trip, after throwing a raucous banquet in which he debates with No Name the virtues of a Winchester over a pistol. No Name feigns drunkenness at the party but, after being taken to his room
in an apparent stupor, slips away and again rescues Marisol from the Rojos. Re-
uniting her with her husband and son, he sends the little family on its way, offering as explanation only the comment "I knew someone like you once, and there
was no one there to help." Returning to his room, No Name finds the Rojos
waiting for him. They beat him brutally in an effort to find out where Marisol is.

No Name's silence buys time for the family. Eventually, resigning themselves to learning nothing, the Rojos entertain themselves by torturing No Name.

While his guards are inattentive, the badly beaten No Name manages to engineer his escape. He distracts the Rojos by setting fire to their storehouse. During the ensuing confusion, he hides in a coffin and tells the undertaker to get him out of town to a hiding place. Thinking that the Baxters are responsible for the escape of No Name and the destruction of the storehouse, the Rojos burn the Baxters' house and slaughter the entire Baxter clan, as No Name and Silvanito look on.

When the Rojos find Silvanito sneaking food to No Name, they beat him to learn No Name's whereabouts. Meanwhile the coffin maker continues to bring provisions to the recovering No Name as, in hiding. he tries to regain his health and marksmanship. Returning to town, No Name faces Ramón and unnerves him by refusing to be killed. Knowing Ramón always shoots for the heart, No Name has fashioned a bulletproof vest from an old piece of iron. In a climactic confrontation, No Name kills Ramón and frees Silvanito. It is Silvanito who shoots Estéban, the last surviving Rojo. As the few survivors of the holocaust of San Miguel go about rebuilding their businesses and town, the Man with No Name rides away, unwilling to involve himself in the confrontation over the missing gold that will take place between the Mexican army and the U.S. Cavalry.

FOR A FEW DOLLARS MORE (*Per qualche dollaro in più*)

A Co-production of Produzioni Europee Associates (Rome), Constantin Film (Munich), and Arturo Gonzales (Madrid). American release: United Artists. 1965.

Direction: **Sergio Leone**. *Screenplay*: Luciano Vincenzoni and **Sergio Leone**, after a story by Fulvio Morsella and **Sergio Leone**. *Production Design*: Carlo Simi. *Cinematography*: Massimo Dallamano. *Editing*: Giorgio Ferralonga and Eugenio Alabiso. *Music*: Ennio Morricone. *Assistant Director*: Tonino Valerii. *Production*: Alberto Grimaldi.
Technicolor, Techniscope. Running time: 131 minutes.

Players

The Man with No Name ("Manco")	Clint Eastwood
Colonel Mortimer	Lee Van Cleef
"El Indio"	Gian Maria Volontè
Wild (Wild One, Hunchback)	Klaus Kinski
"Prophet"	Josef Egger
Woman in flashbacks	Rosemarie Dexter
Mary, the hotel landlady	Mara Krup
Niño, Indio's henchman	Mario Brega

Groggy, Indio's henchman	Luigi Pistilli
Sancho Perez	Panos Papadopoulos
Yuri	Benito Stefanelli
Station clerk	Roberto Camardiel
Cucillo	Aldo Sambrell
Guy Calloway	Luis Rodriguez
Indio's cell mate	Dante Maggio
Tucumcari bank manager	Sergio Mendizabal
Man in flashbacks	Peter Lee Lawrence

The Story

To Tucumcari comes a mysterious bounty killer in black who quickly kills a wanted criminal and collects a reward. The bounty killer asks about another outlaw and learns that this new prey is already being pursued by a rival bounty killer (identified in some prints by the name "Manco"). The rival bounty killer appears in a nearby town and guns down another wanted man. In a desolate Mexican prison, a convict is freed by outlaws who raid the facility. Before he leaves his cell, the outlaw kills his cell mate and takes with him a tiny model of a cabinet. The outlaw and his men shoot their way out of the prison, leaving only one guard alive.

The face of the escaped convict appears on a "Wanted" poster captioned "El Indio." Both bounty killers see the poster. The man in black asks in a bank where the strongest repository in the territory might be, and he is referred to the Bank of El Paso. Indio and his gang ride to an abandoned church where they make their hideout. There, Indio kills the wife and child of a former henchman who he believes betrayed him, then forces the man into a gunfight, timing the draw of the pistols with the winding down of a musical locket-watch he carries. The second bounty killer enters El Paso and pays a boy to find out if there are any strangers in town. The boy tells him another stranger has already come to town and is staying in the hotel above the saloon. In the abandoned church, Indio gives his men a "sermon" during which he tells them about his cell mate, who was an ex-carpenter. The cell mate, Indio tells his men, had told Indio that the safe in that bank is only a decoy, and that the real money is hidden in an ingenious cabinet that the cell mate had designed for the Bank of El Paso and that houses the real safe within its innocent-looking frame.

The bounty killer called "Manco" goes to the saloon and observes an encounter between the man in black and Wild, a hunchbacked member of Indio's gang. The man in black repeatedly insults the hunchback, who is restrained from drawing his gun by fellow members of Indio's gang. The two bounty killers watch Indio's men—and each other—as Indio's henchmen case the bank. The man in black learns from an old newspaper that his rival is a successful bounty killer with a good reputation. "Manco" learns from an old man called "Prophet" that the man in black is Colonel Douglas Mortimer, a dignified Carolinian turned bounty killer.

Manco tries to persuade Mortimer to leave town. The two engage in a confrontation that ends with each man acknowledging the other's skill. Mortimer suggests they form a partnership and that Manco infiltrate Indio's gang. As a gesture of good faith, Mortimer promises to split the bounty with Manco. Mortimer fingers a musical locket-watch like the one Indio carries. At the abandoned church, Indio does likewise and drifts into a reverie. He remembers (in flashback) an incident during which he came upon a young man and woman in bed together, with two lockets. In the flashback, Indio kills the young man and begins to rape the woman.

Manco proceeds with the plan to infiltrate Indio's gang. He springs Sancho Perez—a member of Indio's gang—from Alamogordo Jail, and brings Sancho with him as a peace offering. Indio is suspicious. He welcomes Manco into the gang but assigns him and three others to carry out a decoy bank robbery the next day—an operation he hopes will draw the law away from El Paso where the gang will pull off the big strike. Instead of carrying out the decoy job, Manco kills the men he is riding with and sends a wire saying that the bank in Santa Cruz has been robbed. The lawmen ride out of El Paso as Manco rides back into town. From different vantage points, he and Mortimer watch as Indio's gang blows open the bank's rear wall and makes off with the cabinet. Manco tries to dissolve his partnership with Mortimer. Mortimer shoots Manco—a grazing wound in the neck—so that Indio won't be suspicious that Manco alone survived the raid on Santa Cruz. He suggests that Manco tell Indio to ride north.

Manco catches up with Indio's men as they blow away the cabinet, revealing the safe within. Manco tells a story about the supposed Santa Cruz job, then advises Indio—against Mortimer's orders—to ride south. Indio considers this suggestion but decides to ride west to a town called Agua Caliente. Arriving at this desolate hellhole, Indio decides to test Manco by having him ride into town alone. Manco is greeted menacingly by some armed men; instead of shooting it out with them, he demonstrates his pistol skill by shooting apples off a tree for a small boy. His pistol is joined by Mortimer's rifle: the man in black fires from a veranda just above. The town gunmen are frightened by the demonstration of firepower and rush off.

Mortimer explains that, in advising Manco to tell Indio to go north, he was safe in assuming that Manco would do the opposite, and that the cagey Indio would opt for the third alternative. In the dingy cantina, Mortimer again encounters Wild, the hunchback, who seeks redress of old wounds. In a face-off, Wild is killed. Indio asks Mortimer who he is; Mortimer answers that he is the man who can open the safe for them. Using acid and explosive chemicals, Mortimer opens the safe. The men enjoy the money, until Indio orders that the shares will not be divided up until they have lain low a month in Agua Caliente. Manco and Mortimer slip away by night and rendezvous in the storehouse where Indio has stashed the money. Mortimer moves the money from the trunk into a pair of saddlebags, and he and Manco escape through the roof. As he lowers himself from the roof, Manco is seized by Indio and a henchman, Niño, but not before he throws the saddlebags full of money into a nearby tree. Indio says he has been aware all along that Manco is a bounty killer. As his men savagely beat

Manco and Mortimer, Indio toys with the idea of killing them both and framing them for the bank robbery. He has another reverie, recalling his violation of the woman of the locket. He then develops a better plan: he will allow Manco and Mortimer to escape and then send his whole gang after them in the hope they will all be killed during the ensuing gunfight; that way, he will have the money for himself. Indio's lieutenant, Groggy, having overheard Indio tell this to Niño, stays behind, kills Niño, and demands the money from Indio. When they open the trunk, however, the loot is gone; a copy of Indio's "Wanted" poster grins out at them.

As Groggy and Indio, with no knowledge of the whereabouts of the money and nothing better to do, sit down to await the outcome of the battle, Manco and Mortimer move through the streets of Agua Caliente, killing off Indio's men. Indio has a final recollection about the woman of the locket: while he raped her, she took his pistol from its holster and shot herself. Indio now broods over the locket and the haunting memory of the dead girl.

Indio's gang wiped out, Mortimer calls Indio out of the house; Groggy comes out first. When Mortimer shoots Groggy, Indio shoots Mortimer's gun away from him and sets up a final gundown. He opens the locket, saying, "When the chimes stop, pick up your gun." As the chimes wind down, Manco steps in with a second locket, which he has taken from Mortimer's vest. Manco rearms Mortimer—thus evening the odds—and acts as "referee" for the final gundown, in which Indio is killed. Mortimer reveals to Manco that the woman in the locket was his sister, then rides off, leaving Manco to collect all the bounty. Groggy, not yet dead, makes a last effort to shoot Manco, but the bounty killer guns him down. Manco drives a cart out of town, loaded with the bodies of Indio and his men, for which he will collect handsome rewards. He stops briefly to get the bank loot out of the tree, then drives on.

THE GOOD, THE BAD AND THE UGLY
(*Il buono, il bruto, il cattivo*)

A Production of Produzione Europee Associates (PEA). American release: United Artists. 1966.

Direction: **Sergio Leone**. *Screenplay*: Luciano Vincenzoni, **Sergio Leone**, and "Age-Scarpelli" (Agenore Incrocci and Furio Scarpelli); English Version, Mickey Knox. *Production Design*: Carlo Simi. *Cinematography*: Tonino Delli Colli. *Editing*: Nino Baragli and Eugenio Alabiso. *Music*: Ennio Morricone. *Assistant Director*: Giancarlo Santi. *Production*: Alberto Grimaldi. Technicolor, Techniscope. Running time: Original American release, 161 minutes; 2004 restored version, 179 minutes.

Players

"Blondie"	Clint Eastwood
"Angeleyes" (Setenza)	Lee Van Cleef
Tuco	Eli Wallach
Northern officer	Aldo Giuffrè
Corporal Wallace	Mario Brega
Captain Harper	Antonio Molino Rojo
Padre Ramirez	Luigi Pistilli
Tuco's nemesis	"Al Mulloch" (Al Mulock)
Maria	Rada Rassimov
Storekeeper	Enzo Petito
Baker	Livio Lorenzon
Stevens	Antonio Casas
Jackson/"Bill Carson"	Antonio Casale
Angeleyes' henchmen	Benito Stefanelli
	Aldo Sambrell

The Story

In a ghost-town hideaway, three gunmen attempt to kill a wiry Mexican bandit, but the bandit escapes after killing two of the gunmen and wounding the third. To a small farm comes a sinister, lanky gunman. Before killing the farmer and one of his sons, this gunman learns of a stolen Union gold shipment worth two hundred thousand dollars. The shipment's whereabouts is known by a man named Jackson, who is now hiding under the name Bill Carson. After returning to and killing the man who hired him to kill the farmer, the lanky gunman sets out to track down "Carson" and find the gold.

The Mexican bandit is set upon by three bounty killers who want to take him in for the reward, but an interloper shoots the three men dead. The bandit's thanks turn to ashes in his mouth when the new bounty killer turns him in at the nearest town and collects the reward. But just as the bandit (whose name is revealed as Tuco when the charges against him are read) is about to be hanged, the interloper shoots through the rope, freeing him, and he and Tuco flee the town together. In the hills, they divide up the money, though Tuco, since he is taking the more serious risk, expresses his dissatisfaction with the fifty-fifty arrangement.

In the next town, Tuco is again about to be hanged. The lanky gunman buys information from a legless Confederate soldier, who calls him "Angeleyes" and tells him the whereabouts of Bill Carson's girlfriend. Angeleyes gets into a coach and leaves town, just before the bounty killer—whom Tuco calls "Blondie"—shoots the rope, again freeing the bandit. Once more they split up the money, but Blondie tells Tuco he's tired of the arrangement and abandons Tuco in the desert.

Angeleyes brutalizes Carson's mistress into revealing the name and location of the regiment Carson has signed up with; he then goes in search of Carson. Tuco survives the desert and holds up a store with a pistol he has assembled using parts of guns taken from the display case. He then hires three killers to ambush Blondie, who has rented a room in the hotel. Blondie hears the bushwhackers in the hall and kills all three, but Tuco comes in by the window and disarms him. He makes Blondie stand on a stool with his head in a noose; but just as Tuco is about to shoot the legs off the stool, a Union cannonade begins and there is a direct hit on the hotel. When the smoke clears, Blondie is gone.

Tuco tracks Blondie, coming upon him just as Blondie is about to shoot the rope that is being used to hang his new partner, Shorty. Tuco disarms Blondie and, leaving Shorty to die at the end of the rope, forces his former partner into the desert. Tuco rides in comfort, beneath a parasol, with plenty of water, while Blondie walks in the scorching sun with nothing to drink. Just as Tuco is about to finish Blondie off with a mercy bullet, a carriage comes on the scene, filled with dead Confederate soldiers. One soldier is not quite dead, however: he is Bill Carson, and he promises Tuco two hundred thousand in gold in exchange for a drink. Carson tells Tuco that the gold is buried in a graveyard called Sad Hill, but he begins to fail before he can tell the bandit which grave holds the treasure. Tuco goes to get the dying man a drink and returns to find Carson dead and Blondie in possession of the name on the grave where the gold is buried.

In an effort to save Blondie's life, Tuco takes him to the nearby Mission San Antonio, where Tuco's brother, Padre Ramirez, is the prior. Blondie recovers his health; and, after a bitter argument with his brother over his desertion of their parents, Tuco is ready to leave. He and Blondie drive off in the carriage, Tuco dressed in the uniform of the dead Bill Carson. A cavalry detachment they take to be Confederates turns out to be Union soldiers with dust on their coats; Tuco and Blondie are taken prisoner. At the prison camp, the supervising noncommissioned officer is none other than Angeleyes, disguised as a Union sergeant. Angeleyes has his sadistic henchman, Corporal Wallace, torture Tuco into revealing the whereabouts of the gold (he knows better than to try to get the name of the grave from Blondie). Sending Tuco off with Wallace to an unspecified fate, Angeleyes forms a partnership with Blondie.

Handcuffed to Wallace, Tuco leaps from the train and kills Wallace, then frees himself by having a passing train cut his shackles. He travels into town and treats himself to a bath in a hotel room. He is interrupted by the surviving gunman from the ghost-town encounter in the first scene of the film—now minus an arm. Tuco kills the man with a pistol he has secreted under the suds in his bath. Across town, Blondie, camped out with Angeleyes and his hired men, hears the gunshot and recognizes Tuco's style. He slips away and links up with Tuco. Together they methodically shoot down Angeleyes' henchmen, but, when they reach Angeleyes' camp, they find only a cryptic note; Angeleyes has gone.

Traveling onward in quest of the gold, Tuco and Blondie come to a river. On one side is a Union army; on the other, Confederate forces. From a drunken Union officer, Tuco and Blondie learn that, each day, the two armies fight over the flimsy bridge that crosses the river. The two men take dynamite from the Union stores and resolve to destroy the bridge, so they can get across the river. While they are planting demolition charges, Tuco suggests that each tell the other his half of the secret, in case one of them doesn't survive. Tuco tells Blondie that the name of the cemetery is Sad Hill. Blondie tells Tuco that the name on the grave is Arch Stanton. As the wounded Union officer lies dying, he hears the explosion, and smiles, knowing that many lives will be saved now that the "strategic" bridge is no longer there. The two armies withdraw, and Tuco and Blondie cross the river.

As Blondie tends to a dying Confederate soldier on the other side, Tuco steals a horse and rides for Sad Hill. Blondie fires a cannon at Tuco, knocking the bandit off the horse, but Tuco is already at the entrance to the cemetery. Feverishly, he seeks for—and locates—the grave marked "Arch Stanton," and begins to dig with a board. Blondie arrives and gives Tuco a shovel. Angeleyes arrives with a second shovel, but Blondie refuses to dig. Tuco opens the coffin and finds that it contains only the remains of a corpse.

Blondie says he will write the name of the real grave on the bottom of a rock. He places the rock in the center of an open circle amid the graves. In the ensuing three-way face-off, Blondie draws and kills Angeleyes. Tuco draws and finds his gun empty. Blondie explains that he unloaded Tuco's gun the night before, while Tuco slept. He reveals that the gold is in a grave marked "Unknown," located next to the one marked "Arch Stanton." After Tuco digs up and breaks open the cashbox, he finds that Blondie has prepared a noose for him, strung over the limb of a nearby tree. Blondie forces Tuco to stand on the rickety arms of a cross—one of the grave markers—and place his head in the noose. Blondie takes his share of the gold and rides away, leaving Tuco's share, which the bandit can't reach without hanging himself. From a safe distance, Blondie fires a shot that splits the rope, then rides off into the landscape.

ONCE UPON A TIME IN THE WEST
(*C'era una volta il West*)

A Co-production of Rafran Cinematografica and San Marco Films, American release: Paramount Pictures. 1968.

Direction: **Sergio Leone**. *Screenplay*: **Sergio Leone** and Sergio Donati, after a story by Dario Argento, Bernardo Bertolucci, and **Sergio Leone**; English Version, Mickey Knox. *Art Direction and Costumes*: Carlo Simi. *Set Decoration*: Carlo Leva. *Cinematography*: Tonino Delli Colli. *Editing*: Nino Baragli. *Music*: Ennio Morricone. *Assistant Director*: Giancarlo Santi. *Production*: Fulvio Morsella. Technicolor, Techniscope. Running time (restored original uncut version): 165 minutes.

Players

The Man with the Harmonica	Charles Bronson
Frank	Henry Fonda
Cheyenne	Jason Robards
Jill	Claudia Cardinale
Morton	Gabriele Ferzetti
Brett McBain	Frank Wolff
Sheriff	Keenan Wynn
Sam	Paolo Stoppa
Wobbles	Marco Zuanelli
Bartender	Lionel Stander
Three gunmen in dusters	Jack Elam
	Woody Strode
	Al Mulock
Members of Frank's gang	John Frederick
	Aldo Berti
	Spartaco Conversi
	Benito Stefanelli
	Fabio Testi
One of Cheyenne's men	Mario Brega
Timmy McBain	Enzio Santianello
Maureen McBain	Marilù Carteny
Harmonica as a boy	Dino Mele

The Story

At a desolate railway station, three men wearing long "duster" coats wait for a train. The train arrives, then pulls away, leaving a lone man playing a harmonica. Shots are exchanged and all four men fall, but the Man with the Harmonica opens his eyes.

At a ranch in the desert, Brett McBain tells his daughter and two sons to get ready to meet his new wife, who is arriving that day. As they set the table for a picnic lunch, however, shots ring out: McBain's daughter, then McBain, then his older son are shot dead. As the younger boy, Timmy, dashes out of the stable, several men in dusters come out of the brush, led by a man whom one of them calls Frank. Frank smiles at Timmy and shoots him dead.

A train pulls into the town of Flagstone, and a well-dressed, fancy lady gets off. Surprised that no one is there to meet her, she hires a buckboard and heads toward a place called Sweetwater. On the way, she and the driver, Sam, stop at a tavern. The bartender tells her a story but is interrupted by the sound of horses' hooves and gunfire. Into the tavern comes Cheyenne, a raunchy bandit, who is still wearing the handcuffs that he had on him when he escaped from a posse just outside. A harmonica is heard, and Cheyenne discovers the Man with the Harmonica seated in a dark corner of the tavern. Recognizing the Man as a gunman, Cheyenne borrows his pistol and has one of the tavern's customers shoot the handcuffs off him. Cheyenne and the Man test each other with artful conversation, but maintain mutual respect. Several of Cheyenne's henchmen arrive, apologizing for being late. They wear dusters. The Man says he was ambushed at the railroad station by three men wearing dusters. Cheyenne says that only his men dress like that and that his men don't get themselves killed. Troubled by the implication that someone is deliberately impersonating his gang and committing murders, Cheyenne leaves. The bartender finishes telling the woman his story.

Sam and the woman arrive at Sweetwater in time to see the McBain family laid out for burial. The woman, Jill, travels on to the McBain farm, after acknowledging that she is McBain's wife (having married the man in New Orleans some time before). Suddenly a widow, and stunned, Jill moves lifelessly around the McBain house where she discovers, among other things, a trunk full of miniature buildings.

The Man with the Harmonica vents his anger at a man called Wobbles for having arranged the ill-fated meeting at the railway station. Harmonica tells Wobbles he wants to see Frank and no one else.

Cheyenne comes into the McBain house and questions Jill, hoping to learn what motivated the McBain murders. Jill, believing that Cheyenne's men did the killings, distrusts him. She considers assaulting him, then thinks better of it.

Frank and his boss, a railroad magnate named Morton, discuss the respective values of money and guns. They are troubled by the fact that Jill has appeared, seeing her as a new obstacle to their acquiring McBain's land for the railroad.

Back at the McBain house, Cheyenne mentions the Man with the Harmonica to Jill, implying that Harmonica, not he, might just as easily be responsible for the killings. He warns Jill that whoever committed the murders is likely to be

gunning for her as well: "When you've killed four, it's easy to make it five."
After Cheyenne leaves, the Man with the Harmonica shows up in Jill's barn and
asks her to bring him water from the well. As she does this, two more of Frank's
assassins appear. They are killed by the Man, as Cheyenne watches, approv-
ingly, from a different vantage.

Jill tells Wobbles she wants to meet with Frank. In the meantime, Frank
meets with Morton on his train, in order to discuss the situation. The Man with
the Harmonica appears and refuses to reveal his identity to Frank, instead nam-
ing some of the many men Frank has killed. During a brief flashback, the Man
envisions a younger Frank walking toward him out of the desert. Frank has the
Man with the Harmonica tied up in the train car. Wobbles arrives to tell Frank
that Jill wants a meeting. Frank kills Wobbles for having led the Man to him,
then leaves for the McBain house. Cheyenne arrives and rescues the Man from
the train.

A load of lumber arrives at Sweetwater, and Harmonica and Cheyenne realize that Brett McBain had been intending to build a railway station there. At the
McBain house, Jill looks at the miniature buildings stored in the trunk. Frank
appears, holding the one marked "Station." He asks, "Lookin' for this?"

Frank and Morton argue over Frank's handling of Jill, and Frank becomes
abusive, explicit in his disrespect for Morton. Meanwhile, Cheyenne and Harmonica set men building the railroad station, admonishing them that it has to be
ready by the time the railroad construction crew reaches Sweetwater. Frank beds
Jill, believing that she has given herself to him in order to save herself; he will
not abandon his mission of acquiring her land for the railroad.

Jill decides to sell the land at public auction, but Frank's men discourage all
prospective bidders, and the only bid made is two hundred dollars. In the meantime, Morton buys off Frank's henchmen with money, suggesting that they kill
Frank. Back at the auction, one of Morton's representatives raises the bid to five
hundred dollars, and no one else bids, all having been intimidated by Frank's
strongmen. Suddenly Harmonica appears and raises the bid to five thousand
dollars, offering—as collateral—Cheyenne, upon whose head is a reward of five
thousand dollars. Cheyenne is taken into custody by the sheriff and put on the
train for the "modern jail" at Yuma; Cheyenne's men follow, buying one-way
tickets. In the saloon, Harmonica talks with Jill. Frank enters, and offers to buy
Jill's land from Harmonica for five thousand and one dollars. In a second
flashback, Harmonica's memory of the young Frank becomes more distinct. He
rejects the offer, and accuses Frank of being a businessman and therefore betraying himself. Outside, Frank is ambushed by his own men, who have been bought
by Morton; but with Harmonica's help, he kills them all and survives.

Frank returns to the train to find it stopped in the aftermath of a massacre.
Morton dies in the mud; most of the other men are dead; Cheyenne has escaped.
Back at the McBain house, Cheyenne shows up again and gives encouragement
to Jill. At the same time, Frank returns to Sweetwater to confront Harmonica. As
the railroad construction draws near, Cheyenne tells Jill to bring water to the
men who are working to build the station. Outside, Frank and Harmonica face
each other. In a final flashback, Harmonica recalls the young Frank putting a

noose around the head of his older brother, standing him on the shoulders of Harmonica as a boy, and thrusting a harmonica into the boy's mouth, making him play until, exhausted, he falls, hanging his own brother. In the showdown, the Man shoots Frank. As Frank lies dying, the Man thrusts the harmonica into Frank's mouth.

Cheyenne and Harmonica bid farewell to Jill. Just beyond Sweetwater, Cheyenne falls off his horse. He tells Harmonica he was gut-shot by Morton in the battle at the train. Cheyenne dies, the Man with the Harmonica rides on, and Jill brings water to the workers as the railroad reaches Sweetwater.

DUCK, YOU SUCKER! (*Giu' la testa*)

Alternate titles: *A Fistful of Dynamite* (U.S.A.); *Once Upon a Time the Revolution* (*C'era una volta la rivoluzione*) (Europe).

A Co-production of Rafran Cinematografica, San Marco Films, and Miura Films. American release: United Artists. 1971.

Direction: **Sergio Leone**. *Screenplay*: Luciano Vincenzoni, Sergio Donati, **Sergio Leone** after a story by Dario Argento, Bernardo Bertolucci, and **Sergio Leone**. *Art Direction*: Andrea Crisanti. *Cinematography*: Giuseppe Ruzzolini. *Second Unit Cinematography*: Franco Delli Colli. *Editing*: Nino Baragli. *Music*: Ennio Morricone. *Assistant Director*: Giancarlo Santi. *Production*: Fulvio Morsella, Claudio Mancini, Ugo Tucci. Technicolor, Techniscope. Running time: varies from 137 minutes to 150 minutes. Best available version: 150 minutes.

Players

Juan Miranda	Rod Steiger
Sean Mallory	James Coburn
Dr. Villega	Romolo Valli
Adelita	Maria Monti
Santerna	Rik Battaglia
Don Jaime	Franco Graziosi
Colonel Günther Reza	"Jean-Michel Antoine" (Antoine Saint-John)
Niño	Goffredo Pistoni
Landowner	Roy Bosier
American	John Frederick
Solicitor	Nino Casale
Priest	Jean Rougeul
Pancho	Vincenzo Norvese
Sebastian	Corrada Solari
Benito	Biacco La Rocca
Pepe	Renate Pontecchi

Napoleon   Franco Collace
Yankee   Michael Harvey
Guttierez   Antoine Domingo
Peon   Amelio Perlini

The Story

A grubby Mexican named Juan Miranda hitches a ride on a large, luxurious stage and is alienated by the behavior of its aristocratic passengers. The stage is held up by a band of youths who, it turns out, are Juan's "boys." The passengers are stripped and robbed, and Juan rapes an aristocratic woman. A clergyman is killed when he tries to use a pistol on Miranda's gang. The surviving passengers are sent off in a rickety wagon. An explosion is heard, then several more; a lone figure on a motorcycle appears. This man, Sean Mallory, demonstrates for Juan the power of explosives. Juan sees Sean as his ticket to robbing the bank of his dreams in nearby Mesa Verde. Looking at newspapers from Sean's satchel, Juan discovers that Sean is an Irish revolutionary wanted in his native land. As Juan explains to Sean about the bank he wants to rob, Sean drifts into a reverie and remembers a time when he and another man were motoring with a girlfriend in Ireland. Juan criticizes the revolution that is under way in Mexico (it is 1913), saying that it turned a great bandit (Pancho Villa) into a revolutionary general; he asks Sean if he has come to join the revolution. Sean denies this. He gets on his motorcycle to ride away but is stopped when Juan shoots out his rear tire. Without a word, Sean walks into the wagon that serves as a base of operations for Juan's family, kneels as if in prayer before a shrine to Juan's beloved bank, then leaves the wagon saying, "Duck, you sucker." The wagon blows up. Riding down the tracks toward Mesa Verde, Juan feels he has persuaded Sean to join in his plan to rob the bank. But when a train passes between them, Sean disappears.

Juan and some of his boys are on a train illegally. The conductor questions Juan, who is almost found out but escapes trouble with the help of another passenger, Dr. Villega—one of Villa's revolutionary leaders. In Mesa Verde, Juan is alarmed to see how the city of his dreams has changed. At a café he earlier told Sean about, he finds Sean, who tells him that the confusion of revolution is exactly the atmosphere during which their goals can be achieved. In a brief flashback, Sean recalls handing out leaflets with his friend in Ireland. In a back room of the café, Dr. Villega and other revolutionaries are meeting. Sean brings Juan to them, and a plan is hatched for the robbery of the Mesa Verde bank.

One of Juan's boys plays with a toy train in front of the main entrance to the bank. Sean detonates the explosive concealed in the train, and Juan and his gang storm into the bank, only to discover that the vaults are filled with people, not money: the bank has become a political prison and, in liberating the prisoners, Juan has become a hero of the revolution. A young federal officer leads an army against Mesa Verde while Juan and Sean debate the politics of revolution, Juan arguing that revolution makes no difference to the peasants; inevitably, they are killed in the resulting wars. The revolutionary army advances as far as a crucial bridge, then receives orders to fall back as the federal army approaches. Sean determines to stay and either hold the bridge or blow it up; he deceives Juan into staying with him. They kill many people with their machine gun, then blow up the bridge.

Juan returns with Sean to a mountain hideaway and discovers that his "boys" have all been murdered. Embittered, Juan, despite Sean's protests, rushes off. In rainy Mesa Verde, the federal army is rounding up revolutionaries. Behind the windshield wipers of a federal jeep, Sean sees the captured Dr. Villega informing on his comrades. In a third flashback, Sean remembers drinking in an Irish pub; British soldiers enter, holding his friend prisoner. The friend points out to the British the IRA men at the bar; Sean is among them.

Captured and identified by Villega, Juan is led before a federal firing squad; Sean rescues him. As the executions continue, Sean and Juan hide in a railroad car, determined to leave the revolution and go to America to rob banks. The federal governor, Don Jaime, boards the train. When rebels attack, he seeks safety in the freight car where Sean and Juan are hiding. Sean holds the governor at gunpoint, then gives the gun to Juan, who accepts the "fortune" the governor offers Juan to spare his life; Juan kills the governor anyway.

The revolution is now on its way to being successful, and Juan is a bigger hero than ever. In a train car conference attended by Dr. Villega, Sean proposes to destroy a trainload of federal soldiers and supplies headed toward them. He says he needs one man to accompany him. Juan assumes he is chosen, but Sean picks Villega.

Aboard an engine loaded with explosives, Sean confronts Villega with his treachery. Villega says the federal army tortured him into collaborating and asks Sean how Sean knows what he would have done in a similar situation. Sean slips into another flashback and remembers how, in the pub, he killed the British soldiers and his friend. As the engine approaches the oncoming federal train, Sean jumps free and calls to Villega to save himself, but Villega stays aboard and is killed in the explosion.

During a night battle at the site of the train wreck, Sean and Juan are together again, fighting the federal army. The young federal officer shoots Sean and is then killed by Juan. Juan goes to get help for Sean, who, dying, lights a cigar and drifts into a happy memory of Ireland before the revolution when he was motoring with his friend and their girlfriend. Suddenly there is a cataclysmic explosion—Sean has set off the arsenal of explosives he carries under his coat. Juan is left alone, wondering what he is to do next.

MY NAME IS NOBODY (*Il mio nome è Nessuno*)

A Co-production of Rafran Cinematografica, Les Films Jacques Leittienne, and Rialto Film Preben-Philipsen. American release: Universal Pictures. 1973.

Direction: Tonino Valerii. *Screenplay*: Ernesto Gastaldi, after a story by Ernesto Gastaldi and Fulvio Morsella, from an idea by **Sergio Leone**. *Art Direction*:

Gianni Polidori. *Cinematography*: Giuseppe Ruzzolini (America), Armando Nannuzzi (Italy/Spain). *Editing*: Nino Baragli. *Music*: Ennio Morricone. *Production Executive*: Fulvio Morsella (Rafran). *Production Supervision*: **Sergio Leon** (Rafran). *Producer*: Claudio Mancini. Technicolor, Panavision. Running time: 115 minutes.

Players

Nobody	Terence Hill (Mario Girotti)
Jack Beauregard	Henry Fonda
Sullivan	Jean Martin
Red	Leo Gordon
Honest John	R G Armstrong
Sheriff	Piero Lulli
"Big Gun"	Remus Peets
"Squirrel"	Neil Summers
Fake Barber	Steve Kanaly
Leader of Wild Bunch	Geoffrey Lewis
Pedro	Mario Brega
Scape	Antoine Saint-John
Porteley	Benito Stefanelli
Don John	Mark Mazza
Treno	France Angrisano
Rex	Alexander Allerson
Bartender	Angelo Novi
Juan	Tommy Polgár
Mother	Carlo Mancini
Official	Antonio Luigi Guerra

With: Emile Feist, Antonio Palombi, Humbert Mittendorf, Ulrich Müller, Claus Schmidt.

The Story

Three gunmen ride into a small town to ambush Jack Beauregard, a gunfighter who has become a legend in his own time. Beauregard is trying to book passage to Europe on a ship leaving New Orleans in ten days, but first, he must make a five hundred dollar deposit. Beauregard walks into a barber shop that has been taken over by the gunmen. One of the men poses as barber, having locked the real barber and his son in a closet. The fake barber applies a razor to Beauregard's throat; Beauregard cocks his pistol and aims it at the man's crotch. The gunman carefully gives Beauregard a proper shave. Afterward, in a fast shootout, Beauregard kills all three gunmen. He releases the barber and his son from the closet, and the boy, having heard only one shot, is amazed that three men have been killed. The barber tells his son that nobody is faster than Beauregard.

A country boy who calls himself "Nobody" catches a fish with his bare hands as Beauregard looks on, en route to the cabin of a former partner named Red. Finding Red shot and dying, Beauregard tries to find out why and learns that it has something to do with an old gold mine that Red had operated with Beauregard's brother.

At the gold mine, an outlaw tells a respectable businessman named Sullivan that the gold from the mine must be refined legally and that Sullivan must find a way of buying off Jack Beauregard or of having him killed, since Jack is getting close to discovering what really happened.

Nobody is discovered sleeping in a pile of junk at a way station. He says he wants a horse, and some questionable characters promise to give him one if he will deliver a basket to Jack Beauregard, who is eating in the nearby cafe. Nobody agrees and delivers the basket to Beauregard, but cautions him that it probably contains a bomb, and throws it back outside. Telling Beauregard of his admiration for him, Nobody reveals a dream: that Beauregard would one day stand alone to face "the Wild Bunch," a gang of a hundred and fifty ruthless outlaws. Beauregard tells Nobody he is aiming to retire, but Nobody insists that Jack must "go out in style." Back outside, Nobody claims the horse; when the men try to stop him, he demonstrates without shooting anyone how fast he can draw, and the men let him have the horse.

At a remote cemetery in Navajo country, Beauregard, searching for his brother, finds Nobody waiting for him. One of the graves is marked "the Nevada Kid," and Jack realizes his brother is dead. Uncertain of Nobody's motives, Beauregard draws on him and shoots his hat off. When Nobody holds his hat on, Jack shoots through it four times. Nobody tells Beauregard of his admiration for the "good old days" of gunfighting. Beauregard denies that there ever were any "good old days" and grows impatient with Nobody's insistence that he should face the Wild Bunch.

The circus has come to the town where Sullivan is headquartered. Nobody encounters a number of Sullivan's gunmen enjoying the carnival atmosphere. Nobody humiliates several tough gunslingers in a barroom game of pistol skill, and is invited into Sullivan's office. Sullivan offers Nobody money to kill Beauregard. As Beauregard rides into town, Nobody, seated in a chair in the street, returns his hat-shooting; but before the two can confront each other, the Wild Bunch rides into town.

While Nobody is otherwise occupied, Beauregard learns from a knowledgeable, but spooked, old man that Red killed Nevada and that both men disappeared about the time the mine started "producing" again. Beauregard then calls on Sullivan and learns of the Wild Bunch's connection with the mine. Sullivan, in an effort to buy out Nevada's claim on the mine, offers Beauregard his dead brother's share. Beauregard takes five hundred dollars to make the deposit that will reserve his place on the Europe-bound ship, and walks away.

Nobody humiliates a few more of Sullivan's men in the town and tells Beauregard that he may run into his destiny even as he tries to escape it. Beauregard sets out to catch a train to New Orleans.

At a small water station, a train full of gold suddenly starts pulling away without its engineer. The guards give chase, but the train gets away from them and heads into the desert. Waiting in the desert to flag down the train, Beauregard sees the Wild Bunch approaching and gets his weapons ready to face them. The train comes down the tracks and stops, but backs away when he attempts to board it. Nobody is driving the train, and Beauregard's ride to New Orleans will be his reward for fulfilling Nobody's dream of destiny and facing the Wild Bunch. In a frozen moment of history, Beauregard kills off large numbers of the outlaw horsemen as they ride down on him. Nobody picks Beauregard up, and the train whisks them away as the last of the Bunch scatter in confusion.

In New Orleans, Nobody stages a gunfight to be fought by him and Beauregard. Photographs and witnesses bear evidence that Nobody has killed Beauregard. In reality, Beauregard is on the ship bound for Europe, having "gone out in style" while allowing Nobody to make a reputation for himself. In a long letter to Nobody, Beauregard reflects on the passing of the old West and the coming of the new-style gunfighter. He cautions Nobody to be on guard against those who will now want him dead. Nobody goes into a barber shop. As the "barber" applies the razor to this throat, Nobody places a stiff finger against the man's backside. The man proceeds to shave Nobody.

ONCE UPON A TIME IN AMERICA

A Ladd Company Release, through Warner Brothers. 1984.

Direction: **Sergio Leone**. *Screenplay*: Leonardo Benvenuti, Piero de Bernardo, Enrico Medioli, Franco Arcalli, Franco Ferrini, and **Sergio Leone**, based on the novel *The Hoods* by Harry Grey (Harold Goldberg). *Additional Dialogue*: Stuart Kaminsky. *Art Direction*: Carlo Simi. *Cinematography*: Tonino Delli Colli. *Editing*: Nino Baragli. *Music*: Ennio Morricone. *Costume Design*: Gabriella Pescucci. *Executive Producer*: Claudio Mancini. *Producer*: Arnon Milchan. Technicolor. Running times: Full European version: 238 minutes. Longest American-release version (and Warner Brothers DVD version): 229 minutes. American general theatrical release version: 144 minutes.

Players

David "Noodles" Aaronson	Robert De Niro
Max Bercovicz/Bailey	James Woods
Deborah	Elizabeth McGovern
Carol	Tuesday Weld
Fat Moe	Larry Rapp
Philip "Cockeye" Stein	William Forsythe
Patrick "Patsy" Goldberg	James Hayden
Jimmy Conway O'Donnell	Treat Williams
Frankie Minaldi	Joe Pesci

Detroit Joe	Burt Young
Chief Aiello	Danny Aiello
Eve	Darlanne Fluegel
Young Noodles	Scott Tiler
Young Max/David Bailey	Rusty Jacobs
Young Patsy	Brian Bloom
Young Cockeye	Adrian Curran
Dominic	Noah Moazezi
Young Deborah	Jennifer Connelly
Young Moe	Mike Monetti
Bugsy	James Russo
Monkey	Paul Herman
Peggy	Amy Ryder
Whitey ("Fartface")	Richard Foronjy
Van Linden	Dutch Miller
Sharkey	Robert Harper
Crowning	Gerard Murphy
Chicken Joe	Richard Bright
Willie the Ape	Angelo Florio
Girl in coffin	Ann Neville
Chauffeur	Arnon Milchan
Sgt. Halloran	Bruce Bahrenburg
The Capuano brothers:	
Al	Clem Caserta
Fred	Frank Sisto
Johnny	Jerry Strivelli
Syndicate thugs:	
Mandy	Mario Brega
Trigger	Ray Dittrich
Beefy	Frank Gio
Cemetery caretaker	Marty Licata
Cemetery director	Louise Fletcher*

*This role survives in only the 238-minute European version.

The Story

"God Bless America" is heard, then fades, as a young woman (Eve) enters her apartment. She is brutalized and killed by thugs wanting her to reveal a man's whereabouts. Elsewhere, a fat man is badly beaten before he reveals the man's hideaway—a Chinese theatre that fronts for an opium den. In an opium crib, a man (David Aaronson, known as "Noodles") is haunted by the sound of a ringing telephone and images of dead bodies in the rain and a fateful telephone call. He is alerted as gunmen enter the theatre searching for him, and escapes by another exit. Using an empty elevator as decoy, Noodles kills the gunman waiting for him at the fat man's place and learns from the badly beaten man (Fat Moe) that the thugs have already killed Eve. Noodles takes a key from Moe and goes to the station. He opens a locker and removes a suitcase; the suitcase is empty. Noodles buys a ticket for Buffalo, which is as far as the money in his pocket will take him.

The decor and music change. Noodles, thirty-five years older, arrives at the station. He goes to Fat Moe's and returns the clock key. He tells Moe he has been living for thirty-five years in Buffalo, but was called back by a mysterious letter from a rabbi asking about relocating the graves of three men—those who were seen dead in the rain during Noodles's pipe dream. Noodles is curious about who is calling him back to New York after so long. He is also nostalgic about the past. He goes into the toilet cabinet in Moe's delicatessen. There he finds a peephole and looks through it. A girl (Deborah) plays "Amapola" on a gramophone and performs eurhythmic dancing as Noodles—nearly fifty years younger—watches her.

On the street, Deborah rejects Noodles, calling him a "cockroach." The boy goes to join his friends Patsy, Cockeye, and Dominic, and they all set fire to a newsstand whose proprietor has failed to pay protection money to Bugsy, a local thug. Then they go to Monkey, Bugsy's payoff man, who gives them the option of taking one dollar in pay or being allowed to roll the drunk of their choice from Monkey's saloon. The friends choose a drunk who has a handsome pocket watch. But before they can roll him, they are detained briefly by the local cop, "Fartface." A boy on a wagon, meanwhile, offers the drunk a ride and spirits him away.

Noodles goes into a hallway toilet to read. When a local girl (Peg) comes in, Noodles tries to have sex with her, but she refuses him, saying he will first have to bring her a pastry. Outside, Noodles sees the boy on the wagon, who now has a camera and the drunk's pocket watch. Noodles tries to take the watch from the boy (Max), but Fartface comes and takes the watch from both of them. Meanwhile, Patsy has purchased a Charlotte Russe and brought it to Peg's in hopes of putting an end to his virginity. When Peg is delayed, Patsy eats the pastry himself. He sees Peg go up to the roof, then catches sight of Fartface as well. He tells his friends, and Max and Noodles photograph Fartface *in flagrante* with Peg. They use the photo to blackmail Fartface into giving them a foothold in Bugsy's territory. They also each try out Peg, but each encounters sexual failure. Noodles goes to peep at Deborah again, and she catches him. Deborah admits she is attracted to him, but knows he will "always be a two-bit punk" and never her beloved. Noodles wants to stay with her, but is drawn away by Max calling from outside. In the alley, Noodles and Max are savagely beaten by Bugsy and his gang. When Noodles knocks on the door of the delicatessen to get Deborah to let him back in, she won't.

Noodles and his friends sell a new invention for smuggling liquor to a bootleg operation run by the Capuano brothers. When they make their first run, Max and Noodles fall into the water. Max pretends to be drowned, scaring Noodles briefly. The boys go to the station and, in a suitcase stashed in a locker, set up a cache for their criminal earnings. They agree to give the key to Moe for safekeeping, but on their way home they are set upon by Bugsy; Dominic, the youngest of the gang, is killed. Noodles stabs Bugsy to death and is apprehended by mounted policemen who take him to prison as Max, Patsy, Cockeye, and Moe wave farewell.

In an elaborate mausoleum, Noodles, in 1968, looks at the crypts of Max, Patsy, and Cockeye, all killed, according to the plaques on the wall, in 1933. Another plate declares the mausoleum to have been erected by Noodles; hanging from the plate is a key.

At the station, Noodles tries the key in the locker. He finds a new suitcase filled with money and the note "Advance payment for your next job." After a nervous walk through dark streets with the suitcase, Noodles is suddenly whisked back to the day he got out of prison. Max picks up Noodles in a hearse owned by one of the gang's front businesses and Noodles is treated to a sexual episode with a woman who emerges from a coffin. Then Max takes Noodles to a speakeasy around the corner from Fat Moe's delicatessen where he finds that little has changed: the gang is prospering more than ever from criminal activities, Deborah is dancing professionally and still yearns to make it big, Peg has become a prostitute and operates a class establishment. Moe has the orchestra play "Amapola," and Noodles and Deborah enjoy a brief talk. Once again Max intervenes, and Noodles goes off to join his friends.

They have been offered a job by Frankie Minaldi. A guy from Detroit named Joe tells them of the location of a certain shipment of diamonds he wants to intercept. He also tells them about his inside source, a woman he asks them to be easy on. During the heist, the woman, Carol, tells Noodles to hit her to "make it look real." Noodles rapes her savagely instead. When the gang delivers the jewels to Joe, Noodles finds something he hasn't bargained for: Patsy shoots Joe and one of his bodyguards. The gang has been paid by Frankie to double-cross Joe and eliminate him. One of the bodyguards escapes, and Noodles has to track him down and kill him. Afterward, he argues with Max about the wisdom of joining up with Frankie. When they fail to agree, Noodles suggests they "go for a swim" and drives the car into the harbor.

On a television newscast watched by Noodles and Moe in 1968, a damaged car being hosed off turns out to be a burned automobile. Mysterious slayings appear to be tied to a congressional committee's investigation of crime syndicate activities. One of the interviewees is a union leader, identified as James Conway O'Donnell. Noodles remembers Conway. In 1933, in a factory, Chicken Joe and Willie the Ape douse Conway with gasoline and threaten to burn him if he doesn't sign a proposed agreement between management and the union. Conway rejects the agreement; Max and Noodles show up with their friends and Crowning—Joe and Willie's boss. They extort Crowning into calling off his thugs. Conway expresses his distaste that the union has affiliated itself with criminals as despicable as those in Max's gang.

Police Chief Aiello falls under criticism for having used police force to protect scab-labor and break a strike by the union at a major factory. Nothing can perturb Aiello, however, because he is, after fathering four girls, at last the father of a son. At the hospital, Max, Noodles, Patsy, and Cockeye switch all the babies in the nursery around so that Aiello gets a girl. They force Aiello to call off police protection of the strikebreakers, if he wants his son back.

At Peg's bordello, the gang again encounters Carol, who is a weekend regular. After a sexual flirtation with the four, Carol takes up with Max. Noodles, meanwhile, leaves for a date with Deborah. At a seaside resort, Noodles tries to rekindle his flame for Deborah, but she tells him she is leaving the next day—she's had an offer in Hollywood. On the way home in the limousine, Noodles rapes Deborah. Later he goes to the train station but catches sight of Deborah only as her train pulls away. Deborah lowers the shade on her window, and the train—and Noodles—are lost in a cloud of steam.

Max has assumed leadership of the gang and is perturbed at Noodles's long absence—he has spent several days in the opium den after losing Deborah. Max demonstrates his loyalty to Noodles and the gang by abusing Carol and ordering her out. The gang gets a call from Conway, in the course of which the union leader is shot down. In revenge, the gang sets up a hit on Crowning's goons, shooting Chicken Joe and Willie the Ape dead in the street, but leaving Crowning alive. In the hospital, Conway goes into surgery. A political party boss, Sharkey, offers Max and Noodles the chance to go legitimate, with party and union support. Noodles proclaims his distrust of politicians. As Noodles leaves, Max catches up with him and the two agree to "go swimming."

On the beach in Florida, they wonder what to do now that Prohibition is coming to an end. Max reveals to Noodles his dream of robbing the federal reserve bank of fifty million dollars. When Noodles tells Max he's crazy, Max becomes angry and goes off alone.

Outside the federal reserve bank, Carol tells Noodles that Max is serious—that he will not give up the crazy idea of hitting the bank. She tells Noodles he has to get Max arrested on some petty charge so he can cool off in jail and stay out of trouble. At a party at Fat Moe's celebrating the end of Prohibition, Noodles tells his girlfriend, Eve, that he won't be home that night, or for many nights, because he'll be going to jail. Intending to set up the gang, Noodles goes to the office; he telephones the police, and reports the bootleggers' plans to bring in their last shipment. When Max finds him, Noodles again calls Max crazy, and Max knocks Noodles out.

A much older Carol, at an establishment called the Bailey Foundation, tells Noodles that Max is always afraid of ending up like his father, who died in a mental institution. The night of the last shipment, Max started shooting first, desiring his own death, she says. Still seeking the source of the mysterious letter and the money, Noodles looks for Deborah and finds her in the dressing room of the theatre where she is performing. Though it is thirty-five years since he has seen her, she has aged very little. She acknowledges that she has been the lover of the enigmatic Secretary Bailey, and she urges Noodles not to attend Bailey's party, to which he has been invited. Noodles cannot disappear again, as Deborah wants him to. Deborah introduces Noodles to a young man who is a dead ringer for the young Max: "This in Secretary Bailey's son. His name is David—just like yours."

Noodles goes to the party. In Secretary Bailey's private office he discovers that Bailey is Max. Max explains how he had set up the police raid in which Patsy and Cockeye were killed: "That was a syndicate job, Noodles. ... Your eyes were too full of tears to see that that wasn't me lying there dead, it was someone else. I took away your whole life ... I took your money, I took your girl, and left you with nothing but guilt for having killed me." What Max wants now is for Noodles to kill him for real. He is apprehensive about the upcoming congressional investigation and wants to end it all but hasn't the nerve to do it himself; he can accept death only from Noodles. Noodles refuses to do the job and clings to his version of the truth—that Max died in 1933.

Outside Secretary Bailey's house, a large garbage truck starts its engine. Max comes out and walks toward Noodles; when the truck passes between them, Max is gone. Tears fill Noodles's eyes as he sees the rotating blades in the rear of the truck. Then he hears and sees a carload of revelers celebrating the end of Prohibition. "God Bless America" is heard again. Shadow puppets play on the screen of the Chinese theatre as Noodles, in 1933, enters the opium den, draws deeply on the pipe, and relaxes into a broad smile.

Recommended Discography

Motion Picture DVDs (Region 1)

The Colossus of Rhodes. Warner Home Video DVD.
A Fistful of Dollars. MGM 2-Disc Collector's Edition.
For a Few Dollars More. MGM 2-Disc Collector's Edition.
The Good, the Bad and the Ugly. MGM Special Edition, 2-Disc DVD Collector's Set.
Once Upon a Time in the West. Paramount DVD 2-Disc Set.
Duck, You Sucker! (aka *A Fistful of Dynamite*). MGM 2-Disc Collector's Edition.
My Name Is Nobody. Image Entertainment.
Once Upon a Time in America. Warner Home Video DVD 2-Disc Special Edition.
The Sergio Leone Anthology. MGM 8-Disc Boxed Set. (*A Fistful of Dollars, For a Few Dollars More, The Good, the Bad and the Ugly*, and *Duck, You Sucker!*).

Music CDs

Per un pugno di dollari. GDM 2066.
For a Few Dollars More. RCA / BMG 828765 89972. No full score edition of the soundtrack to this film exists. This recording remains the best, though it contains only eight cuts.
Il Buono, il brutto, il cattivo. The Complete Original Motion Picture Soundtrack. GDM CD Club 7001.
C'era una volta il West. GDM 2062.
Giu' la testa. Cinevox CD MDF 312.
Il mio nome è Nessuno. Original Motion Picture Soundtrack—Definitive Edition. Screen Trax CD ST 330.
Once Upon a Time in America. Special Edition. Restless/Rykodisc 73767.
Ennio Morricone: The Legendary Italian Westerns. The Film Composers Series, Volume II. RCA / BMG 9974-2-R. This sampler of Morricone's Western scores is an ideal starter's collection.

Bibliography

Books and Book Excerpts

Bondanella, Peter. *Italian Cinema: From Neorealism to the Present.* New York: Ungar, 1983.

Bruschini, Antonio and Tentori, Antonio. *Western all'Italiana: The Specialists.* Florence: Glittering Images edizioni d'essai, 1998.

Bruschini, Antonio and de Zigno, Federico. *Western all'Italiana: The Wild, the Sadist and the Outsiders.* Florence: Glittering Images edizioni d'essai, 2001.

Carlson, Michael. *Sergio Leone.* Harpenden, Herts: Pocket Essentials, 2001.

De Fornari, Oreste. *Sergio Leone: The Great Italian Dream of Legendary America.* Rome: Gremese International, 1997.

Di Claudio, Gianni. *Directed by Sergio Leone.* Chieti: Libreria Universitaria Editrice, 1990.

Downing, David and Herman, Gary. *Clint Eastwood: All-American Anti-Hero.* New York, London, and Tokyo: Quick Fox Press, 1977.

Fawell, John. *The Art of Sergio Leone's* Once Upon a Time in the West: *An Appreciation.* Jefferson, No. Carolina: McFarland & Company, 2005.

Frayling, Christopher. *Spaghetti Westerns: Cowboys and Europeans from Karl May to Sergio Leone.* London: Routledge & Kegan Paul. 1980.

———. *Once Upon a Time in Italy: The Westerns of Sergio Leone.* New York: Harry N. Abrams, 2005.

———. *Sergio Leone: Something to Do with Death.* New York and London: Faber and Faber, 2000.

French, Philip. *Westerns.* New York: Oxford University Press, 1977.

Fridlund, Bert. *The Spaghetti Western: A Thematic Analysis.* Jefferson, North Carolina: McFarland & Company, 2006.

Hays, Lee. *Once Upon a Time in America.* (Novelization from the film.) New York: Signet New American Library, 1984.

Hughes, Howard. *Once Upon a Time in the Italian West: The Filmgoers' Guide to Spaghetti Westerns.* London and New York: I. B. Tauris, 2004.

———. *Spaghetti Westerns.* Harpenden, Herts: Pocket Essentials, 2001.

Johnstone, Iain. *The Man with No Name: The Biography of Clint Eastwood.* New York: Morrow, 1981.

Kitses, Jim. *Horizons West.* New Edition: *Directing the Western from John Ford to Clint Eastwood.* London: BFI Publishing, 2004.

Kitses, Jim and Rickman, Gregg, eds. *The Western Reader.* New York: Limelight Editions, 1998.

Knox, Mickey. *The Good, the Bad, and the Dolce Vita.* New York: Nation Books, 2004.

Lambert, Gavin. *Les Bons, les sales, les mechants et los propres de Sergio Leone*. Paris: Solar, 1978.

Leinberger, Charles. *Ennio Morricone's* The Good, the Bad and the Ugly: *A Film Score Guide*. Lanham, Maryland: The Scarecrow Press, 2004.

Martin, Adrian. *Once Upon a Time in America*. London: BFI Publishing, Modern Classics Series, 1998

Millard, Joe. *For a Few Dollars More*. (Novelization from the film.) New York: Universal Publishing, 1965.

Mitchell, Lee Clark. *Westerns: Making the Man in Fiction and Film*. Chicago and London: University of Chicago Press, 1996.

Peary, Danny, ed. *Closeups*. New York: Workman, 1978. Articles: "New Western Hero" (on Clint Eastwood) by Danny Peary; and "Sergio Leone Remembers" (on Henry Fonda) by Sergio Leone.

Peary, Danny. *Cult Movies*. New York: Dell Delta, 1981. Article: "*Once Upon a Time in the West*."

Pugliese, Robert, ed. *Sergio Leone*. Venice: Circuitocinema, 1989.

Richie, Donald. *The Films of Akira Kurosawa*. Berkeley: University of California Press, Revised Edition, 1984.

Rood, Richard. *Cinema: A Critical Dictionary: The Major Film-makers*. New York: The Viking Press, 1980. Volume 2. Article: "Sergio Leone" by Richard Corliss.

Sarris, Andrew. *The John Ford Movie Mystery*. Bloomington and London: Indiana University Press, 1975.

Schickel, Richard. *Clint Eastwood: A Biography*. New York: Vintage, 1997.

Smith, Paul. *Clint Eastwood: A Cultural Production*. Minneapolis and London: University of Minnesota Press, 1993.

Staig, Lawrence and Tony Williams. *Italian Western: The Opera of Violence*. London: Futura Publications, Ltd., 1975.

Wallach, Eli. *The Good, the Bad, and Me in My Anecdotage*. New York: Harcourt, 2005.

Weisser, Tom. *Spaghetti Westerns—the Good, the Bad and the Violent: 558 Eurowesterns and Their Personnel, 1961-1977*. Jefferson, North Carolina: McFarland & Company, 1992

Witcombe, R.T. *The New Italian Cinema*. London: Oxford, 1982.

Wollen, Peter. *Signs and Meaning in the Cinema*. Bloomington and London: Indiana University Press, 1969, 1972.

Wright, Will. *Sixguns and Society: A Structural Study of the Western*. Berkeley: University of California Press, 1975.

Critical and Journalistic Articles in English

Beale, Lewis. "Leone: From Out of the Westerns." *Los Angeles Times*, April 11, 1982, Calendar, 21ff.

Bogdanovich, Peter. "Two Beeg Green Eyes." *New York* 6:78-9, November 26, 1973.

Corliss, Mary. "Once Upon a Time." *Film Comment*, August 1984, 18-21.

Grenier, Cynthia. "Pastalong Cassidy Always Wears Black." *Oui* 2:74-6+, April 1973.

Hamill, Pete. "*Once Upon a Time in America*." *American Film*, June 1984, 20-29, 54.

Jameson, Richard T. "Something to Do with Death: A Fistful of Sergio Leone." *Film Comment* 9:8-16, March/April 1973.

———. "Update: Sergio Leone." *Film Comment* 10:32-3, March/April 1974.

Kaminsky, Stuart. "The Grotesque West of Sergio Leone." *Take One* 3:9: 26-32, Jan/Feb 1972.

———. "Once Upon a Time in Italy: The Italian Western Beyond Leone." *Velvet Light Trap* 12, Spring 1974.

Lomanzo, Elaine. "A Fable for Adults." *Film Comment*, August 1984, 21-23.

Nicholls, David. "Once Upon a Time in Italy." *Sight & Sound* 50:1:46-9, Winter 80/81.

Sarris, Andrew. "Spaghetti and Sagebrush." *Village Voice* 13:49:53 and 13:50:51-2, September 19 and 26, 1968.

Simsolo, Noel. "Sergio Leone Talks." (trans. P. Lebensold, from an interview originally published in *Zoom*). *Take One* 3:26-32. Jan/Feb 1972.

Witonski, Peter. "Meanwhile ... Back at Cinecittà." *Film Society Review* 4:1:37-40, September 1968.

Index

About the Author

Robert **C. Cumbow** is a lawyer, teacher, and writer. He lives and works in the Seattle area, where he practices and teaches intellectual property law and writes and lectures on film, language, and law. He is the author of *Order in the Universe: The Films of John Carpenter*, also published by Scarecrow Press.